"Utilizing a unique combination of cutting-edge research into the brain and human consciousness and the possibility that ancient civilizations possessed knowledge of resonance and vibratory patterns, Jones and Flaxman have produced an engaging and highly readable work which dares to explore nothing less than the nature of reality itself. The Resonance Key is not only a valiant attempt by its authors to bridge the ever widening gap between science and the supernatural, but an entertaining read as well."

—Brian Haughton, author of *Hidden History* and *Haunted Spaces, Sacred Places*

"A stimulating and spirited look into both our inner and outer worlds, into the unique harmonic relationship existing between human consciousness and the greater reality, this is a timely read."

—Michael Hayes, author of *The Hermetic Code in DNA*

"The authors explore methodically and with clarity the phenomena of resonance in a variety of contexts and its implications on paranormal phenomena. The authors have undertaken a profound quest that may ultimately dramatically change our views of our place in this universe and open up pathways to new and hitherto unexplored worlds. The book is written in an interactive and personal style that will make any reader feel that he or she is undertaking this exciting quest together with the authors."

—Jay Alfred, author of *Brains and Realities* and *Dark Plasma Theory*

THE RESONANCE KEY

THE RESONANCE KEY

EXPLORING THE LINKS BETWEEN VIBRATION, CONSCIOUSNESS, AND THE ZERO POINT GRID

BY MARIE D. JONES AND LARRY FLAXMAN

New Page Books
A Division of The Career Press, Inc.
Franklin Lakes, N.J.

The Resonance Key
Edited and Typeset by Gina Talucci
Cover design by Lu Rossman/Digi Dog Design
Printed in the U.S.A.

To order this title, please call toll-free 1-800-CAREER-1 (NJ and Canada: 201-848-0310) to order using VISA or MasterCard, or for further information on books from Career Press.

The Career Press, Inc., 3 Tice Road, PO Box 687, Franklin Lakes, NJ 07417
www.careerpress.com
www.newpagebooks.com

Library of Congress Cataloging-in-Publication Data

Jones, Marie D., 1961–
     The resonance key : exploring the links between vibration, consciousness, and the zero point grid / by Marie D. Jones and Larry Flaxman.
          p. cm.
     Includes bibliographical references and index.
     ISBN 978-1-60163-056-8
     1. Parapsychology and science. 2. Resonance—Miscellanea. I. Flaxman, Larry.
          II. Title.
BF1045.S33.J665 2009
130--dc22

                                                                    2009007685

DEDICATIONS

For Max and Mary Essa

ACKNOWLEDGMENTS

Marie and Larry would like to thank Lisa Hagan, agent extraordinaire, friend, and ally, for her unwavering belief in our work. Also, to Michael Pye, Laurie Kelly-Pye, and the entire staff at New Page Books—you are the best and we thank you for this opportunity to continue our work and get it out to the world. Thanks also to the wonderful staff at Warwick Associates for their fantastic publicity and promotion of our books. And of course, to the mighty Suzanne Weaver for her amazing Website design.

Marie would like to thank:

My mom, Milly, and my dad, John, for never laughing at my dreams and always believing in my crazy ideas, even when they led to huge holes in the backyard or embarrassing moments climbing Bear Mountain in New York with my tiny hammer in hand. Thanks always to my sis, Angella, my bro, John, and my extended family: Winnie, Efren and kin, Alana, Aaron, the Avakians, The LaContes, and to all of my dear friends and colleagues who never fail to support me and believe in my goals. Thanks to those of you who have read my books, listened to me on the radio, and come to hear me speak. I appreciate it more than you know. Without readers, a writer is just a person who puts words on a page. You make it happen for me. Thanks most of all to my number-one guy, Max, who makes my heart resonate...

You are absolutely frikkin' nuts, and Lord knows what planet you came from, but every day you crack me up, make me think, and remind me why God is good. You are the wisest person I know, despite being only 8. And to my dear, dear friend and partner Larry Flaxman for sticking by my side through this chaotic up-and-down elevator known as writing. We have only known each other a short time, but look at what we have accomplished so far! May our partnership flourish and grow in the coming years. May all our goals reach fruition, especially the one about global domination! Never thought I could enjoy working with a partner... You have proven me wrong.

Larry would like to thank:

Another book, more acknowledgements! There are so many people I am indebted to for my successes that it might require a book itself! I would like to thank my parents, Drs. Norman and Sheila Flaxman, for believing in me, motivating me to be the best person I can, and being not only my heroes, but also my best friends. My brother Jon for providing that boundless energy, drive, and comedic relief that only a younger brother can offer. Thank you to my wife, Emily, for being supportive and understanding of my often extremely hectic schedule—especially writing days and nights, which seemed to increase exponentially as time went on! To all of the friends, fans, and especially critics I have gained in this field—thank you! You folks keep me grounded, vigilant, and on my toes. The biggest thank-you goes to my "little buddy"—my daughter, Mary Essa. Every single second I spend with you not only teaches me more about how precious life is, but also about myself. I never imagined that anything could permeate through my soul on so many levels. Whether we are watching *Caillou*, *Dragon Tales*, or *Berenstain Bears*; playing at the park; reading Fancy Nancy or Dora the Explorer; or just hanging out and petting Do Do or Kitty, I have found a new appreciation for life and its incredible shortness. I love you!

"Neither a lofty degree of intelligence nor imagination nor both together go to the making of genius. Love, love, love, that is the soul of genius."

—Wolfgang Amadeus Mozart

And last, but, certainly not least, thank you to my dear friend and partner Marie Jones. It seems so long ago that I read your book and contacted you. Who would have guessed that we would have hit it off so well, and would ultimately unite in an effort to bring our common platform to the masses? And your kid... Where can I even start? Max has provided boundless humor and inspiration to the both of us. Some of his questions ("Do ghosts poop?") certainly have incited us in creative ways. He's a keeper for sure. Your understanding, motivation, and assistance have been incredibly valuable, and I hope that we continue on a long and prosperous journey together.

CONTENTS

FOREWORD

Some months ago, I was asked to pen an endorsement for *11:11—The Time Prompt Phenomenon: The Meaning Behind Mysterious Signs, Sequences, and Synchronicities* by Marie D. Jones and Larry Flaxman. Because Larry was a friend of mine, I felt an obligation to attempt to wade through what I assumed would be a manuscript filled with charts, graphs, and numbers. I further assumed that Larry had collaborated with a mathematical whiz who would explore the "time prompt phenomenon" in lofty, rather obscure terms.

What a delight to find that the collaborative effort between Jones and Flaxman was a fascinating read with complicated theories explained in an easy-to-comprehend—but thorough—manner. Later, when I met Marie via a talk show interview, I found that she was not a mathematician, but a fellow humanities major. The success of their book lay in the fact that Jones and Flaxman are simply darn good writers and extremely adept at making exceedingly complicated matters understandable to lay readers. All in all, reading their book gave me "good vibrations."

Isn't it interesting how often we use that expression? "I got kind of bad vibrations from that guy." "Man, she gave off good vibes!"

In *The Resonance Key: Exploring the Links Between Vibration, Consciousness, and the Zero Point Grid,* Jones and Flaxman explain the profound and often complex insights that we are expressing when we assess someone's or something's "vibrations." To speak of our universe sending us "vibrations" was not simply a lyric we picked up from the Beach Boys or from trying to sound cool in our younger days.

Vibration is resonance, a synched frequency, and the coming together of attracting forces, "to allow or to manifest that which did not exist before."

Vibration, Jones and Flaxman inform us, is the very resonant frequency of creative power. Consciousness is the modus operandi by which our inner power creates, and the Zero Point Grid is the "pool of potentiality" from which all is created.

We each broadcast energy that will determine its own consequences. We thus become the generators of our own destiny. Quoting author Sandra Ann Taylor, "The links between vibration, our own, and our consciousness create exactly what we need to manifest.... Beliefs. Ideas. Actual physical objects. What we send out is what comes back to us in return."

Our reality, then, is a holographic grid program created by our thought consciousness that cycles, repeats itself, and can be best understood by studying sacred geometry. These grids are a matrix of sound, light, and color through which we virtually experience time and emotion. Reality is a never-ending process of change, growth, and expansion. There is no fixed truth.

The Zero Point Grid, Jones and Flaxman maintain, is the repository of all matter, form, thought, and action—where we must go to find the place where ideas become objects, where inspirations become inventions. Anything physical, they remind us, begins with a thought.

I have always found great primal meaning in the fact that Native or Aboriginal cultures have a song for everything they do—for creating, for living, for dying. Many ancient cultures believe that the Old Ones literally sang the world into existence.

This recognition of the power of the human voice has often made me think of the beginning scripture passage in St. John that tells us "in the beginning was the Word," the sound, the vibration. Rupert Sheldrake has commented that this passage, in his opinion, means that "in the beginning was the cosmic creative process with consciousness, meaning, and a vibratory nature."

Reality *is* Mind, state Jones and Flaxman, "and it all happens because we, in our consciousness, vibrate in resonance with that which we hope to create."

Marie and Larry, you have done it to me again. Your new book has filled me with "good vibrations" and made me sing my song to the world.

—Brad Steiger
author/coauthor of 170 books on paranormal and metaphysical subjects

INTRODUCTION

The new physics will have to account for a "field of consciousness," and it may have to deal with the idea that intelligence and awareness does not require a physical body in the sense we are used to.
—Claude Swanson, *The Synchronized Universe*

A coherent space-time structure theoretically enables instantaneous communications to occur over a range of time scales and spatial extents. What this implies in practice is a vast, unexplored area, as the notion of non-linear structured time this entails is alien to the conventional, Western scientific framework.
—Dr. Mae Wan Ho, *The Rainbow and the Worm*

Have you ever lay upon your back looking at the starry sky, contemplating and pondering your place in the universe? As part and parcel of this timeless question, it is likely that not only did you consider your station in life, but also the very nature of reality itself.

But this begs the question—what exactly is reality? According to Dictionary.com, the concept of reality is defined as "The state or quality of being real; actual being or existence of anything, in distinction from mere appearance; fact."

Is reality simply what we experience through our eyes, and within our three-dimensional world? Is it simply composed of the five traditional senses—seeing, hearing, feeling, smelling, and tasting? Do our physical senses define the nature of reality itself, or is there something more? Maybe the answer lies somewhere in between…and perhaps it is much more meaningful and significant than we could ever imagine.

For a moment, rather than looking outside the box, let us turn our focus inward. What if the true nature of reality was a lot like an onion, made up of layers upon layers of different levels of reality that, when peeled back, exposed a creative, self-regenerating, web-like core? An infrastructure that contains the whole of all that is, was, and ever will be. A source from which everything is interconnected within a grid-type framework.

As modern theoretical physicists search for a unified "Theory of Everything" that will condense the four fundamental forces of nature into one mathematically sound truth, those who dare to explore the paranormal have also begun to search for a cohesive theory that may assist in explaining the vast unknown, such as UFOs, ghosts, poltergeists, cryptids, mysterious energy vortices, remote viewing, psi abilities, clairvoyance, mind over matter, and teleportation. How do these things happen? Where do they come from? What is the mechanism that triggers their manifestation in our simple, three-dimensional reality? Although their motives, methodologies, and reasoning may seem different, scientists and paranormal investigators alike ultimately strive to know the same thing, and to answer the same questions.

What is the nature of reality? What role do we play in perceiving and experiencing it?

With new discoveries in the cutting-edge sciences of quantum theory, brain research, and consciousness studies, that paranormal Theory of Everything may be much closer than we think. And more excitingly, that same theory may also be the veritable Holy Grail sought by physicists and scientists in their attempts to understand how the universe works, not to mention how we as human beings work. Behind all the excitement is what the authors of this book call "The R Word."

Resonance.

As we will explore in more detail, resonance is an "object or force getting in tune with another object or force." That may sound simple, and in some ways it is. Think about how one can shatter a wine glass by hitting a musical note on the same frequency as the natural frequency of the glass. We may not see it, but everything in the world is in a state of motion, which, in solid objects, manifests as vibration. When the vibrations produced by one object align with those of another, this is called resonance. Resonance is behind many familiar events, such as the feedback produced by an electric guitar to the cooking of our food in a microwave oven.

More and more scientists, as well as paranormal researchers, are looking at resonance as one possible explanatory hypothesis of the Big One, the potential Theory of Everything (TOE). This comprehensive model may bridge the gaps between science and the supernatural, the normal and the paranormal, and go one step further to explain every facet of reality in between. This theory may indeed center on the vibratory nature of matter as it relates to both the natural and "unnatural" worlds, as well as on harmonics and sound. In fact, as we intend to show you, there are specific links between resonance and nearly every manner of mysterious phenomena reported.

But if resonance is the basis for the Theory of Everything, or at least the best theory we have to explain much of what we consider to be "anomalous" or "paranormal," then how does it work? And what is the relationship between reality, perception, and consciousness? Is consciousness a doorway through which resonance allows the paranormal to manifest? Could it also be the doorway through which every aspect of our reality manifests, from the most mundane things we experience to the most miraculous?

Do we, as conscious, sentient beings, have a say in whether we experience the paranormal or not? Are we creating these events entirely within our minds, or, as the authors believe, does our individual consciousness link to some grander, greater state of reality from which all matter and form emerges? Can mass consciousness produce waves of paranormal activity in a type of "contagion" of shared experience? Is reality and consciousness inextricably linked?

Questions. We all have questions. We are reminded of the famous French philosopher François-Marie Arouet, more commonly known as Voltaire, who said "Judge others by their questions rather than by their answers."

Research conducted throughout the last decade has shown irrefutable evidence that the nature of consciousness is associated with the degree of consciousness present and the number of neurons in the brain actively assembled in a synchronized state. This state generally lasts only for a few milliseconds, and then the neurons reassemble, allowing for a continuously variable state of consciousness. Is it then possible that paranormal phenomena is observed when the brain is experiencing a specific momentary assembly of large numbers of neurons at just the right time to create an altered state of perception?

First, we must understand the conditions that determine to what extent a system has consciousness. This raises the question as to why consciousness is generated by certain parts of our brain, such as the thalamocortical system, but not by other parts, such as the cerebellum. We must also come to understand why consciousness is so different during wakefulness, the dreaming state, and dreamless sleep, when there appears to be no awareness at all.

But is consciousness the only connection to the manifestation of reality? Socrates once argued that consciousness was created by the cerebrum in the brain, whereas Thales, Plotinus, and other panpsychists saw consciousness and conscious experience as a fundamental feature of reality.

Normally we think of all matter coming down to the action of particles, and that causation occurs from the bottom up. But there is another worldview that asks: Is it true that everything starts with consciousness, as many in the more metaphysical community suggest? That is, is consciousness the ground of all being? In this view, our free will is real, and when we act in the world we really are acting with causal power. We are causing things to happen because of our conscious will. Matter can still be causal in principle from elementary particles upward, so there is upward causation, but there is also downward causation from our own consciousness that allows for creativity, free will, and free thought.

Reality is all-encompassing, and yet remains veiled—seemingly always out of grasp of our full comprehension. However, one thing remains constant: the connection between resonance and "everything." The authors are big fans of the *Matrix* movie trilogy. Perhaps there was some truth in the fictional account of Neo's adventures. As Morpheus said, "This is your last chance. After this, there is no turning back. You take the blue pill—the story ends, you wake up in your bed and believe whatever you want to believe. You take the red pill—you stay in Wonderland and I show you how deep the rabbit-hole goes."

Which pill will you take?

AUTHORS' NOTE

Scattered throughout various points in this book, you will see sections of text set off from the rest of the book. This denotes select, true experiences of the authors that involve the concepts presented in the book. Although we cannot offer them as undeniable proof of the links between vibration, consciousness, and the Zero Point Grid, we do provide them as experiential evidence that there truly is more to the whole of reality than anything even the most skeptical and zealous scientist among us can prove or imagine. Those of you who have likewise experienced such things will certainly understand.

1

WHAT'S THE FREQUENCY?

I count all the time on resonance. I call on this, you see.

—Josef Albers

Remember those cheesy coin-operated vibrating beds that were all the rage in nearly every motel back in the 1970s? How about alphanumeric pagers that would vibrate when someone paged you? Has some heartless idiot ever driven through your neighborhood in the middle of the night "bumping" the latest rap hit? It seems as though everything vibrates. From the invisible photons that collectively make up the light you are using to read this book, to the cells that form our bodies, everything has a vibration, a frequency, and a resonance. What we perceive as solid form is anything but, for beneath it all lies a field of vibrating waves and particles...even down to the subatomic level, popping in and out of existence from a sea of virtual foam.

According to physics, resonance is described as the tendency of a system to oscillate at maximum amplitude at certain frequencies. Although this is a vastly oversimplified definition, resonance can and does mean so much more.

It is the science of vibratory frequencies that synch up and create amplification, whether it is of sound, energy, or force. Human behavior tells us that resonance is the synchronization of beliefs, goals, and commonalities that occur between people. We "resonate" with this. We "feel good vibrations" about him or her. Hopefully we are "on the same frequency" or "riding the same wavelength" as our spouse or partner.

Yet behind this seemingly simple concept of the vibratory reality of, well, reality, there is a stunning suggestion that resonance may be what truly makes reality real. A mouthful to be sure, but if everything has its own frequency, and matching frequencies produce specific changes and effects in the environment, we cannot help but wonder if what we see, feel, hear, and experience is all about the patterns that emerge when resonance occurs.

So, if resonance is so important, what exactly is it, and who discovered it? Italian physicist, astronomer, and philosopher Galileo Galilei first experimented the concept of resonance in 1602. Using a pendulum, Galileo determined that the swing rate of the pendulum—the push of the pendulum in time with the natural interval of the swing from one direction to another—was its resonant frequency. Unfortunately, his theory that a pendulum's swings always take the same amount of time was later proven incorrect.

This same phenomenon is seen on modern playground swing sets. If you push a person on a swing in time with the natural interval of the swing, the person will swing higher. Push harder or softer and you mess up the resonant frequency. This is due to the amount of energy absorbed by the swing being maximized when the push is "in phase" with the swing's natural oscillation rate. The opposing force of the pushes lessens the swing's energy when they are not "in phase." And it doesn't do any good to push the swing when it is away from you, because no energy gets transferred into the motion of the swing's original oscillation. The key is to push the swing at just the right time during each repetition of the swing motion to get the maximum impact (and hopefully not send your kid flying over the top bar and into the sand).

To simplify this concept, when things synch up, they flow. When they don't, they are forced and expend more energy, thus preventing resonance from occurring. Interestingly, Galileo was also one of the first scientists to work with sound frequency. He scraped a chisel at different speeds and linked the pitches of the various sounds to the spacing of the chisel's skips, thereby determining their frequency. He wrote about his findings in his 1632 book *Dialogue Concerning the Two Chief World Systems*. Galileo's work was instrumental in the later development of cymatics, which is the study of wave phenomena associated with physical patterns produced through the interaction of sound waves in a particular medium.

The concept of cymatics is an important one, and forms the basis of several theories that we shall expand upon later. In 1967, the late Swiss doctor and researcher Hans Jenny published the bilingual book *Cymatics: The Structure and Dynamics of Waves and Vibrations*. In this book, Jenny, similar to Chladni 200 years earlier, showed what happens when one takes various materials such as sand, spores, iron filings, water, and viscous substances, and places them on vibrating metal plates and membranes. After a short amount of time, shapes, motions, and patterns appear, from the nearly perfectly ordered and stationary to those that are turbulent, organic, and constantly in motion.

Jenny called this new area of research "cymatics," which comes from the Greek word *kyma*, meaning "wave." Cymatics could be defined as the study of how vibrations, in the broad sense, generate and influence patterns, shapes, and moving processes.

This phenomenon has a three-part unity. The fundamental and generative power is in the vibration that, with its periodicity, sustains phenomena with its two poles. At one pole we have form, the figurative pattern. At the other is motion, the dynamic process.

These three fields—with vibration and periodicity as the ground field, and form and motion as the two poles—constitute an indivisible whole, even though one can dominate sometimes. Does this trinity have something within science that corresponds? Yes, says American polarity and music therapist John Bealieu. In his book *Music and Sound in the Healing Arts*, he draws a comparison between his own three-part structure, which in many respects resembles Jenny's, and the conclusions researchers working with subatomic particles have reached. "There is a similarity between cymatic pictures and quantum particles. In both cases that which appears to be a solid form is also a wave. They are both created and simultaneously organized by the principle of pulse [read: principle of vibration]. This is the great mystery with sound: there is no solidity! A form that appears solid is actually created by a underlying vibration."

This unity or underlying vibration between wave and form, in which the quantum field, or the vibration, is understood as reality, then posits that the particle or form, and the wave or motion, are two polar manifestations of that one reality: vibration.

As we further our understanding of resonance, we must take a moment to clarify the concept of standing waves. Standing waves occur when a steady wave runs into a "reflecting barrier" or wave. The incoming wave and the reflective wave travel at the same rate, but because they are going in the opposite directions, the peaks and valleys of one create interference with those of the other wave. These peaks and valleys create a pattern called "nodes" and "anti-nodes," which are still points and the points of alternating crests and troughs (or peaks and valleys).

The strongest standing waves occur when waves are reflected back again, and fit perfectly inside a space the right size and shape to allow the incoming waves to be "in phase" with their own reflections and re-reflections. The frequencies at which these occur are the "resonant frequencies" of the object the waves are within. This bouncing back, or reflection and re-reflection, of waves within a whole number of wavelengths is responsible for creating the sound we hear when a tuning fork is struck. The tuning fork rings at a particular pitch, which is the number of times the sound wave travels from one end of the object to the other and back again within a second. Synched or in-phase sounds with matching resonant frequencies actually create larger waves or vibrations, until "damping" occurs, which stops the entire process. (Think of the opera singer shattering the vibrating glass with her high note. She damped that sucker!)

■ ■ ■ ■ ■ ■ ■ ■ ■ ■ ■

Natural Resonance

Resonance occurs throughout nature, as well as in many man-made devices. Some of the examples of natural and man-made resonance include:

1. Acoustic resonances of musical instruments and human vocal cords.
2. The timekeeping mechanisms of all modern clocks and watches; the balance wheel in a mechanical watch and the quartz crystal in a quartz watch.

3. The tidal resonance of the Bay of Fundy.
4. Orbital resonance as exemplified by some moons of the solar system's gas giants.
5. The resonance of the basilar membrane in the cochlea of the ear, which enables people to distinguish different frequencies or tones in the sounds they hear.
6. AM radios that use resonant coil pickups on ferrite rods as compact aerials (much smaller than the wavelength).
7. Electrical resonance of tuned circuits in radios and TVs that allow individual stations to be picked up.
8. Creation of coherent light by optical resonance in a "laser" cavity.
9. The shattering of a crystal wine glass when exposed to a musical tone of the right pitch (its resonance frequency).

Courtesy of Wikipedia

■ ■ ■ ■ ■ ■ ■ ■ ■ ■ ■

If all this science has made you hungry, fear not! You will be delighted to know that resonance can even be linked to the cooking of your food. For instance, did you know that the great bastion of convenience—the microwave oven—operates by cooking without the use of external heat? Would you believe that resonance is responsible? Hungry for a nice, thick, juicy steak? Put a steak in a microwave oven, and the microwave radiation created within the oven interior assumes the same resonant frequency as the water molecules in the steak, thus heating it and cooking it from within. How is that possible? Although the delicious steak may appear to us as a solid object, it is in fact an oscillating mass of molecules that contain water. When energy (and thus, amplitude—the extent of a vibratory movement measured from the mean position to an extreme, or the maximum departure of the value of an alternating current or wave from the average value) is added courtesy of the microwaves, it heats up and turns the raw mass of meat and water into a juicy, mouthwatering porterhouse.

Of all the different types of resonance, "mechanical resonance" is one of the more intriguing. Mechanical resonance describes how a mechanical system can absorb more energy when the frequency of its oscillations, or vibrations, match those of the system's own natural frequency more so than it

Figure 1-1. Tacoma Narrows. The Tacoma Narrows Bridge collapses in November of 1940 allegedly due to mechanical resonance. Image courtesy of Wikipedia.

would the frequencies of other resonances. Some objects do have more than one natural resonant frequency, especially harmonics, which are made up of multiple frequencies.

An interesting example of mechanical resonance can be found in the anecdotal tale of soldiers marching across a bridge. Because marching in lockstep could create a resonant frequency equal to that of the bridge, and thus cause it to possibly collapse, there is a longstanding myth that soldiers are ordered not to march in lockstep and to occasionally break step to avoid mechanical resonant failure. Whether or not they could actually collapse a bridge by marching in unison, we do know that there has been some precedent set.

Back in November of 1940, the Tacoma Narrows Bridge in Washington was determined to have collapsed due in part to the complicated match of oscillation between the bridge's own resonant frequency and that of the strong winds passing through it. The bridge collapse actually had lasting effects in the field of engineering. In some undergraduate physics texts the bridge collapse is still presented as an example of elementary-forced resonance, with the wind providing an external periodic frequency that matched the natural structural frequency. Since then, the real cause of the bridge failure was determined to be aeroelastic flutter. Nevertheless, that collapse fueled additional important research in bridge aerodynamics/aeroelastics and influenced the designs of all great long-span bridges since.

London's Millennium Bridge, a steel suspension bridge crossing the River Thames, was also closed after only a few days due to a wobble when more than 80,000 people walked across the bridge on opening day in June of 2000. Structural engineers stated that the lateral vibration (resonant structural response) caused the bridge to be closed for modifications. Londoners nicknamed the bridge "Wobbly Bridge."

Even buildings can fall prey to mechanical resonance. One of our favorite science luminaries, Nikola Tesla, is considered by many to be one of the pioneers in resonance experimentation. Tesla was a Serbian mechanical and electrical engineer who has often been described as the most important scientist and inventor of the modern era. Tesla created his own mechanical oscillators in his New York lab, which resulted in some rather annoying shaking of local buildings. The NYPD became intimately familiar with Mr. Teslas's exploits! In Chapter 2, we will look more deeply into Tesla's contributions to the field of resonance.

Tesla stated before he died that he had created such an "earthquake machine," and today's retrofitted buildings in earthquake zones do indeed include systems of dampers that can absorb the incoming waves from major quakes. The buildings that suffer the most extensive damage in quake zones are actually those with matching resonant frequencies to the quake's waves, a time when resonance is surely not such a "good vibration."

Just as buildings, bridges, and earthquakes have their own resonant frequencies, so too does the planet Earth. Known as the Schumann Resonance, this frequency measures approximately 7.83 hertz, or just a little more than seven and one half beats per second. Scientists suggest the origin of this frequency is located in the area between the surface of the Earth and the ionosphere. The set of spectrum peaks in this extremely low frequency (ELF) portion of the Earth's electromagnetic field was named after physicist Winfried Otto Schumann, who discovered it in 1952. This Earth's dimensions act as a "resonant cavity" for these electromagnetic waves in the ELF band. Lightning and major storm activity excites energy in the cavity, which is also linked to the North American power grid.

Actually, there are several Schumann Resonances. The 7.83 Hz Schumann Resonance was made popular by researcher Robert Beck whose work on ELF signals, Earth resonances, and their affect on Alpha brainwave frequencies was presented at a U.S. psychotronic conference and published in late 1970s. In theory, 7.83 Hz is a brainwave frequency often associated with intuitive and psychic abilities. But it is wrong to say that the Earth only resonates at 7.83 Hz. There are several frequencies between 7 and 50 hertz that compose the Schumann Resonances, starting at 7.8 Hz and progressing by approximately 5.9 Hz (7.8, 13.7, 19.6, 25.5, 31.4, 37.3, and 43.2 Hz). These resonances are not considered fixed frequencies, and all of these frequencies fluctuate around their nominal values. Changes in these frequencies are quite normal. For example, the fundamental Schumann Frequency fluctuates between 7.0 Hz and 8.5 Hz. These frequencies also vary from specific geological location to geological location, and often have naturally occurring interruptions.

The Schumann Resonances of 7.83 Hz result from cosmic energy buildup within the cavity between Earth's highly conductive surface and the conducting layer in the ionosphere, creating broadband electromagnetic impulses that fill the entire cavity and cause the cavity to resonate. These frequencies create the Earth's "harmonic signature."

The Schumann Resonance, as we will see in future chapters, is linked with the pyramids in Egypt, sacred geometry, ley lines, and other sacred locations and paranormal hot zones. It might even have an effect on our own bodies.

Electromagnetic radiation itself is classified into types according to the frequency of the wave. In order of increasing frequency, these include:

▶ Radio waves.
▶ Microwaves.

▶ Terahertz radiation.

▶ Infrared radiation.

▶ Visible light.

▶ Ultraviolet radiation.

▶ X-rays.

▶ Gamma rays.

Radio waves have the longest wavelengths—the size of buildings—with gamma rays having the shortest length—smaller than the nucleus of an atom.

The distance between two adjacent crests and troughs is the actual wavelength. Electromagnetic radiation does actually consist of both wave-like and particle properties, with the wave properties more common when the electromagnetic radiation is measured throughout larger time frames and distances, and the particle properties more common at smaller time frames and distances.

Visible light makes up only a small window of these frequencies, most of which are invisible to the eyes of living organisms. Light has a spectrum of frequencies, which together form a light wave with different frequencies having different angles of refraction. White light, when passed through a prism, is separated into different frequency waves. This occurs because of the wavelength dependant refractive index of the prism material.

Radiation with a frequency in this visible spectrum reflects off of an object and strikes the eye of the observer, resulting in visual perception and imagery. The human brain then processes the reflected frequencies into various shades, hues, and colors, resulting in most humans perceiving the same object in the same way. In other words, a red rose usually looks like a red rose, unless one is colorblind.

Perhaps the most fascinating type of resonance occurs within the realm of sound. Acoustics is the science of sound, ultrasound, and infrasound, which includes all mechanical waves in gases, liquids, and solids. The word *acoustic* is derived from an ancient Greek term meaning "to be heard." The study of acoustics began in the ancient Greek and Roman cultures between the sixth century BCE and first century BCE, and, naturally, began with the study of music. Pythagoras took a deep interest in the science and nature of musical intervals, and helped to propel the field of study forward, with further research done by the likes of Aristotle and Galileo.

■ ■ ■ ■ ■ ■ ■ ■ ■ ■

Infrasound

▶ Avalanches: location, depth, duration.

▶ Meteors: altitude, direction, type, size, location.

▶ Ocean waves: storms at sea, magnitude, spectra.

▶ Severe weather: location, intensity.

▶ Tornadoes: detection, location, warning, core radius, funnel shape, precursors.

▶ Turbulence: aircraft avoidance, altitude, strength, extent.

▶ Earthquakes: precursors, seismic-acoustic coupling.

▶ Volcanoes: location, intensity.

▶ Elephants, whales, hippos, rhinoceros, giraffes, okapi, and alligators are just a few examples of animals that create infrasound.

▶ Some migratory birds are able to hear the infrasonic sounds produced when ocean waves break. This allows them to orient themselves with coastlines.

▶ An elephant is capable of hearing sound waves well below the human hearing limitation (approximately 30 hertz). Typically, an elephant's numerous different rumbles will span between 14 and 35 hertz. The far-reaching use of high-pressure infrasound opens the elephant's spatial experience far beyond our limited capabilities.

Ultrasound

▶ Animal echolocation.

▶ *Microchiropterans,* or microbats: carnivorous bats (*not* fruit bats or flying foxes).

▶ *Cetaceans*: dolphins, porpoises, orcas, and whales.

▶ Two bird species: swiftlets and oilbirds.

▶ Some visually impared humans have learned this technique.

▶ Sonar (an acronym for *sound navigation and ranging*) .

▶ Bathymetry.

▶ Echo sounding.

▶ Fish finders.

Adapted from *www.hyptertextbook.com.*

■ ■ ■ ■ ■ ■ ■ ■ ■ ■ ■

The idea that sound and sonic vibration was such a fundamental part of the construct of reality was nothing new, and persists even to this day. Similar to visual perception, the realm of sound seems to cross the lines between the seen and unseen.

In nature, animals use sound to locate objects. Echolocation is the act of emitting sound waves and detecting the echo to locate an object or for navigational purposes. Fishing bats have developed such sophisticated echolocation abilities that they can detect the fins of a minnow, which have the consistency of a human hair, protruding only two millimeters above a pond surface. Dolphins and whales also echolocate, also referred to as *biosonar*, emitting calls into their environment and using the return echo as a way of finding everything from food to danger to a potential mate. Birds and shrews also have the skill of biosonar, although perhaps not as sophisticated as the bat.

Echoes can help in navigation as well, and, as in the case of bats, to forage for food. Calls are measured based upon intensity, frequency modulation (FM), constant frequency (CF), harmonic composition (one frequency or multiple frequencies that make a harmonic series), and note duration (a single bat echolocation note can last up to 100 milliseconds). The ability to echolocate involves the auditory system (which is adapted specifically for this purpose), and specialized primary sensory neurons in the brain that can sense and interpret the calls. Various parts of the animal's brain play roles, including a structure in the middle brain of bats called the inferior collicus. The auditory cortex is much larger in echolocating creatures than in mammals that do not use the skill.

There have been cases of human echolocation, allegedly used by blind people to navigate their environment. Tapping canes or clicking noises can help the blind find their way in a world void of visual cues. With heightened auditory ability, they can use the sound waves reflected by nearby objects to determine how close they are, or the size of the object as they move along.

Because humans are not able to make the sounds at the higher frequencies of bats and other animals, to which the skill comes naturally, human echolocation is crude by comparison.

Acoustic location is the use of sound in general to locate objects, and also encompasses sonar and echo sounding, which measures the distance to the bottom of the ocean using the echo of sound pulses. Ultrasounds are used in the medical field to view the insides of the body. Radar detects the echo of radio waves to locate or pinpoint the position of an object.

Some critters, such as the *Aeds aegypti*, the species of mosquito that serves as a vector for dengue and yellow fevers in humans, use sound to attract the opposite sex. Talk about resonating with another! This mosquito literally sings its own special "love song," using the resonation of its beating wings in the thoracic box. The frequency of a female's "song" falls between 300 to 600 Hz and easily attracts the male, who gives off his own matching "song" in the 600 frequency range, creating a lovely harmonic of "come and get me baby." Together, but only if they are a true tonal match, they make beautiful music and breed a ton of new fever-carrying mosquitoes.

For years scientists thought mosquitoes could not even hear in this frequency range, but now realize that this use of harmonics might actually be used to one day get rid of these nasty disease-carriers for good. But for now, they engage in "harmonic convergence," something no other creature has yet been proven to do.

Sound has played a vital role in our lives throughout time, and even Egyptologists who study the meaning behind the Great Pyramid at Giza suggest that sound and resonance were of the utmost importance to highly advanced ancient civilizations.

■ ■ ■ ■ ■ ■ ■ ■ ■ ■

Sounding Off on Sound

▶ Sound is a mechanical, longitudinal wave.

▶ Sound is produced by small and rapid pressure changes.

▶ The speed of sound depends upon the medium and its state.

▶ The amplitude of a sound wave corresponds to its intensity or loudness.

▶ The frequency of a sound wave corresponds to its pitch.

▶ The upper frequency limit for human hearing is around 18,000 to 20,000 Hz.

▶ Frequencies above the range of human hearing are ultrasonic.

▶ The lower frequency limit for human hearing is around 18 to 20 Hz.

▶ Frequencies below the range of human hearing are infrasonic.

▶ The frequency of a sound wave does not change as the sound wave propagates.

▶ Large objects generally produce long-wavelength, low-frequency sounds.

▶ Small objects generally produce short-wavelength, high-frequency sounds.

▶ The ability of an animal or electronic sensor to identify the location or direction of the origin of a sound is known as sound localization.

▶ A reflected sound wave is known as an echo.

Adapted from *www.hypertextbook.com.*

■ ■ ■ ■ ■ ■ ■ ■ ■ ■ ■

Acoustic resonance works just as mechanical resonance does, but the system is one based upon harmonics and musical instruments. String instruments, such as harps, guitars, violins, and pianos, have resonant frequencies that relate directly to the mass, length, and tension of each string. Even tube instruments, such as flutes, clarinets, and horns, measure their own resonance in accordance with the length and shape of the tube, as well as whether or not it is open or closed at the ends. A modern flute is an open pipe, whereas a clarinet is considered closed. Vibrating air columns create similar resonances to the harmonics created by strings.

Sound vibrations, when matched in resonance, create lovely harmonics, but unwanted resonance can also result in a "wolf note," or a particular resonant note that causes the instrument to resonate a bit too loudly. Single notes of sound create music, but even a single note can result in ear-splitting feedback when a microphone is in the range of a speaker or amplifier, reproducing the sound waves picked up from the opposite side of a room, but one or more wavelengths behind. Any musician or fan of live music has had to deal with the perils of feedback.

One very amusing example of acoustic resonance at work exists in the town of Lancaster, California. Known as the "musical highway," there is a stretch of road about a mile outside of the city that, when driven over, plays the theme from the *Lone Ranger*. This oddity has drawn thousands of curiosity seekers to the area who delight in driving over the otherwise unimpressive stretch of road again and again (you can experience it on YouTube!). The musical effect comes from grooves cut into the road surface, an idea of the auto manufacturer, Honda, as a way to promote their Honda Civic, which they claim gets the best musical results when driven at 55mph on the road. The car's weight and combined speed are optimal for hearing the asphalt overture. Similar musical highways now appear in the Netherlands, Japan, and South Korea.

Nature has its own "boom boxes" too, most notably the Singing Sand Dunes of the Atlantic Sahara in Morocco, one of 35 known locations around the globe that make their own brand of mysterious music. In a recent LiveScience article, "Singing Sand Dunes: The Mystery of Desert Music," staff writer Michael Schirber reports on the mysterious sounds that emanate from the dunes in a loud, low-pitched rumble that can last as long as 15 minutes. Bruno Andreotti, a scientist at the University of Paris, took some high-tech equipment to study the barchans, or large crescent-shaped dunes, which are said to "sing" two or three times a day if the winds are just right. Andreotti and his team also found they could induce the sounds by creating little avalanches, but were still not able to pinpoint the actual mechanism behind the music.

Using measurements of the vibrations in the sand and air, Andreotti was able to detect surface waves on the sand that emanated from the avalanche at the relatively slow speed of about 130 feet per second. The face of the dune acted like a huge loudspeaker—with the waves on the surface producing the sound in the air. Andreotti believes the sound comes from the collision of the grains of sand that create a "feedback loop," which then causes the sound waves to synchronize the collisions of sand grains so that they end up being all on the same beat.

The sound the sand dunes makes is low-pitched, between 95 and 105 Hz, described as something akin to a low-flying propeller aircraft.

Again, this is music created purely by the resonance of sand grains against each other, the wind, and the air to create just the right mix for making sweet song…if you are into music that sounds like propeller aircraft, that is.

Many people who study consciousness and the human body suggest that acoustic resonance can influence the body's organs and cells, even the functioning of the brain. In future chapters, we will explore the links between vibration, sound, and altered states of consciousness, as well as the manifestation of paranormal phenomena. A simple example of how music can affect the body, though, can be seen in the lovely Tibetan Singing Bowls. Also known as Himalayan Bowls, these "standing bells" are made of Panchaloha, or five specific metals comprising a bronze alloy of copper, tin, zinc, iron, and other small traces of metals. These bowls produce multiphonic and polyharmonic overtones, unique to the bowls alone, and are believed to induce a highly meditative state, trance induction, and altered states of consciousness.

The bowls vibrate to produce sound when their sides or rims are struck in a certain way, or exposed to the friction of a wooden, plastic, or leather mallet that "rubs" the rim of the bowl to create the singing sound. The bowls are known to produce rather complex chords of harmonic overtones, as well as soft bell-like tones, many of which are used in specific rituals to mark the passing of time, or certain events and holy times. Some scholars suggest that singing bowls have been in use in the Himalayan region as far back as the eighth century BCE as an enhancement to meditative practices, as well as trance induction and prayer. Author's note: I (Larry) own an antique Tibetan singing bowl, and although it sounds really cool and "new agey," I've yet to find myself rocketing into some transcendental state of Zen while playing it.

But just as the Singing Bowls produce sounds that supposedly transform one to a higher level of consciousness, rumor suggests that sound can also do some rotten things to the human body. One particularly nasty legend of the infamous Brown Note persists. As it's name implies, the Brown Note is reportedly the specific infrasound frequency that causes humans to lose control of their bowels. Though there is absolutely no scientific evidence of the reality of the Brown Note, and shows such as *Mythbusters* and *Brainiac:*

Science Abuse have tested the note to no avail, the rumor persists that high-power sound waves below 20 Hz are felt by the body as a vibration, rather than heard by the ear as a noise. The Brown Note frequency range is said to be between 5 and 9 Hz, and the authors of this book challenge any reader to prove it is a real note and not just another urban legend!

According to her thesis paper entitled "Mark Twain and Nikola Tesla: Thunder and Lightning," Katherine Krumme tells the story of Tesla receiving a very special visitor to his laboratory—Mark Twain. While Twain was at the lab, Tesla had been experimenting with the interesting effects of a mechanical oscillator, which produced alternating current of a high frequency. Tesla was especially interesting in the significant low frequency vibrations the machine produces and wondered if the vibrations might have therapeutic or health benefits.

Twain then asked to experience the vibrations and stood on a platform of the machine while Tesla set the oscillator into operation. Twain was enjoying himself greatly and exclaimed: "This gives you vigour and vitality." Tesla warned Twain not to stay on the platform too long, but Twain remained, stating he was having too much fun. Tesla again insisted, but Twain stayed on the machine for several minutes more, until, suddenly, he exclaimed: "Quick, Tesla. Where is it?"

Without hesitation, Tesla pointed to the restroom. Twain had experienced firsthand what the laboratory workers had known for some time: the laxative effect of the machine's low frequency vibrations. Although we have no way of corroborating the facts surrounding that incident, perhaps this may have been the genesis of the Brown Note legend!

Many acoustics experts insist that there is no real evidence that infrasound can cause vomiting or defecation; however, some conspiracy theorists point to the military's ongoing interest in developing ultrasonic weapons as evidence to the contrary. There is some evidence that loud concert music, especially when coming from subwoofer arrays of speakers, is responsible for the lung collapse of people standing too close to the arrays (*Wired* magazine, September 2004). Author's Note: Marie can attest to this after attending a Judas Priest concert in the 1980s. She still can't breathe!

For the purposes of this book, infrasound is perhaps the most important sound frequency range that we shall discuss. Infrasound is simply sound with a frequency that is too low for the human ear to audibly discern. The range of what is considered infrasonic covers sounds below the lowest limits of the human ear, from 20 hertz down to 0.001 hertz. Interestingly enough, this is the range of sound utilized by seismographic instruments for detecting earthquake activity. The volcanic eruption of Krakatoa in Indonesia in 1883 first introduced the observations of naturally occurring infrasonic waves. During the eruption, the acoustic waves circled the Earth several times, and were recorded on barometers at various locations around the globe.

The man considered the pioneer of infrasound research is French scientist Vladimir Gavreau, who experienced everything from inner ear pain to shaking lab equipment while experimenting with infrasonic waves in the 1960s. From his research, he went on to invent an infrasonic whistle.

Infrasound occurs naturally during times of severe weather, avalanches, and seismic activity such as earthquakes and volcanoes, iceberg cavings, lightning, tornadoes, and other natural phenomena, as well as man-made sonic booms and chemical and nuclear explosions. Even diesel machinery and wind turbines can create infrasonic waves, as well as those subwoofer speakers responsible for lung collapses at loud concerts.

Animals are able to perceive sound in the infrasonic range. As a matter of fact, animals have been known to evacuate an area during earthquakes and other natural disasters. They are able to utilize the naturally emitted sounds created by the events as a type of early warning system, as was seen during the 2004 Indian Ocean tsunami, when thousands of animals reportedly fled the general area. In addition to the use as an "emergency notification system," whales, elephants, giraffes, rhinos, and even alligators use infrasound as a form of communication, and migrating birds might also utilize infrasound as a navigational tool.

In *Nature* magazine's "Can Animals Predict Disaster?" studies have indeed shown that even zoo animals respond to infrasound, although in a more muted reaction due to their constant exposure to such sounds in their usual urban settings. Alligators specifically use infrasound to signal to a mate and can produce a number of infrasonic sounds by "vibrating air inside special sound-producing sacs in their chins."

Human beings also appear to have an intrinsic response to infrasound. In fact, during World War II, it is believed that Nazi propaganda engineers used infrasonic sound as a means to rouse anger among the sizeable crowds that would gather to hear Hitler. Infrasound may have been one factor in creating an entire nation filled with hatred and anger. In addition, and as we will see in a future chapter, infrasonic sound has been associated with the perception of "paranormal" phenomena. Sounds spooky! But studies have been conducted at musical concerts involving human response to differing types of music, and according to the *Nature* report, more than one quarter of the listeners reported "ghostly" feelings of anxiety, sorrow, fear, and even chills down the spine while listening to infrasonic melodies.

These kinds of studies have put infrasound front and center in the field of paranormal research. But before we tune in to that ghostly frequency, let's look at some of the brains behind the science of resonance.

2

BEHIND THE RESONANCE RENAISSANCE

An invasion of armies can be resisted, but not an idea whose time has come.
—Victor Hugo

Galileo Galilei (1564–1642) was the son of a man who believed in the Pythagorean tradition that numbers were behind musical theory. Vincenzio Galilei was a talented musician in his own right, and it was his interest in music, as well as the underlying numerical ratios of musical notes, that eventually led his son, Galileo, to experiment with "sonorous numbers" involving the vibration of strings and the uniformity of the vibrations of a weight hanging on a string. These early pendulum experiments may have been inspired by Galileo's observations of a swinging lamp in a Pisa cathedral in 1583.

In Galileo's final year of life, he designed an escapement mechanism for a pendulum clock based upon his father's theories. Christiaan Huygens later perfected this device in the 1650s into a much smaller working clock. But it was Galileo's work involving physics of the swings of a pendulum, as well as his extensive studies of the frequency of sound and pitch that set the stage for future experiments into resonance. Incidentally, he also presented the basic principle of relativity, providing the framework for later work by Newton into the laws of motion and, of course, Einstein's Special Theory of Relativity. No wonder he has been called the Father of Physics, the Father of Modern Science, and the Father of Modern Observational Astronomy.

But as with any great theory, much of Galileo's first work with resonance and vibrational frequency was the foundational basis that others would add to and perfect throughout the years. Though Galileo cannot be said to have discovered resonance, he certainly pioneered the scientific research behind it. Heinrich Hertz (1857–1894) was a German physicist and electronic engineer who pioneered and expanded research into the electromagnetic theory of light, becoming the first scientist to demonstrate the existence of electromagnetic waves. His interest began in the field of meteorology; however, he became widely known for his contributions to electrodynamics and contact mechanics, eventually leading to his research into the photoelectric effect that Einstein later perfected.

Hertz's study and observations into the photoelectric effect and the production and reception of electromagnetic waves was published in 1887 in the *Annalen der Physik*. Later, his experiments with electromagnetic wave detection led to his development of the Hertz Receiver in 1886, which was an antenna receiver that consisted of a set of ungrounded terminals. Hertz also developed a type of transmitting dipole antenna, and his experiments with radio waves led to his altering the work of his predecesor James Clerk Maxwell. Maxwell, along with Michael Faraday, had proposed that traverse free-space electromagnetic waves could travel over certain distances. Hertz measured and recorded these traverse waves and recorded their component directions, as well as demonstrated that the velocity of radio waves equaled the velocity of light.

Hertz had no idea when he died at the young age of 36 that his work would have major implications for the future. In actuality, he thought his work was quite pointless at the time. But today, we measure frequencies, or the number of cycles occurring per second, by hertz units. 1 Hz is equal to one cycle per second, and so on, and this measurement system was established by the International Electrotechnical Commission in 1930, and adopted by the International System of Units, now used globally for general and scientific means. The term *cycles per second* has officially been replaced by *hertz* since the 1970s.

SI multiples for hertz (Hz)

Submultiples			Multiples		
Value	*Symbol*	*Name*	*Value*	*Symbol*	*Name*
10^{-1} Hz	dHz	decihertz	10^{1} Hz	Hzda	decahertz
10^{-2} Hz	cHz	centihertz	10^{2} Hz	Hzh	hectohertz
10^{-3} Hz	**mHz**	**millihertz**	10^{3} Hz	**kHz**	**kilohertz**
10^{-6} Hz	**µHz**	**microhertz**	10^{6} Hz	**MHz**	**megahertz**
10^{-9} Hz	nHz	nanohertz	10^{9} Hz	**GHz**	**gigahertz**
10^{-12} Hz	pHz	picohertz	10^{12} Hz	**THz**	**terahertz**
10^{-15} Hz	fHz	femtohertz	10^{15} Hz	PHz	petahertz
10^{-18} Hz	aHz	attohertz	10^{18} Hz	EHz	exahertz
10^{-21} Hz	zHz	zeptohertz	10^{21} Hz	ZHz	zettahertz
10^{-24} Hz	yHz	yoctohertz	10^{24} Hz	YHz	yottahertz

Common prefixed units are in bold face.

Both sound and electromagnetic radiation are described utilizing hertz units. Sound waves are perceived as pitch by the human ear, with each note corresponding to a particular frequency that ranges between 20 Hz and 16,000 Hz. The range of human hearing is generally considered to be from 20 Hz to 20 kHz; however, it is far more sensitive to sounds between 1 kHz and 4 kHz.

Beyond the human range of the audible spectrum are the ultrasound and infrasound frequencies, along with physical vibratory frequencies that venture well into the megahertz range and beyond.

Radio frequencies are measured and labeled as kilohertz, megahertz, and gigahertz. Light is a higher frequency, ranging from infrared (IR) levels to the terahertz (THz) range of ultraviolet light. Gamma rays are measured in exahertz (EHz).

If it seems like nothing can escape resonance and frequency, you are correct! Even the CPUs that drive our computers are labeled according to clock speed in megahertz or gigahertz.

Many of these frequency ranges have obvious practical implications, but as we shall explore in future chapters, some of these frequencies have a more "paranormal" bent, and might possibly be linked to the many unexplainable experiences of those exposed to their vibratory rates.

The real Renaissance man of resonance was undoubtedly Nikola Tesla. Many people continue to credit Thomas Edison as the father of electricity as we know and use it today, but engineers and historians know that the real credit goes to Tesla. Tesla's greatest contribution to science may have been the understanding that AC electricity was superior to Edison's DC. The Discovery Channel named the Serbian-born Tesla one of the 100 greatest Americans of all time.

Figure 2-1. Tesla Oscillator. Nikola Tesla's mechanical oscillator, shown at the World's Columbian Exposition. Image courtesy of Wikipedia.

Though he did not pioneer the discovery of resonance, his seemingly obsessive research into it has led to some of the most intriguing demonstrations of how it works. This enigmatic genius, who was also obsessed with germs and the number 3, began his interest in resonance with an experiment in 1898 at his New York City laboratory. By placing a vibrating apparatus driven by compressed air next to an iron column in his lab, he noticed that other objects in the lab would move and shudder when the device vibrated at certain frequencies. Unfortunately, he was so distracted by his findings that he failed to realize that the iron column ran the height of the building down into the foundation, and the subsequent shaking led to a visit by the local police when tenants reported the floors and walls shaking violently! Apparently, even a building several blocks down the street was shaking on its foundation, as Tesla had unknowingly found the resonant frequency of the deep layer of sandy subsoil beneath the building.

An article titled "Tesla's Controlled Earthquakes" in the July 1935 issue of the *New York American,* Tesla was quoted as stating, "The rhythmical vibrations pass through the Earth with almost no loss of energy. It becomes possible to convey mechanical effects to the greatest terrestrial distances and produce all kinds of unique effects. The invention could be used with destructive effect in war...." Additional newspaper reports labeled it the "Tesla Effect," stating that electromagnetic frequencies could be transmitted through the earth, which would then form standing waves.

In the April 2005 issue of *New Dawn Magazine*, the article titled "Suppressed Research: Tesla Technologies" quotes leading Tesla researcher and nuclear engineer, Lt. Col. Thomas Bearden, from a lecture he gave in 1981: "Tesla found he could set up standing waves...in the Earth, the molten core, or, just set it up through the rocks—the telluric activity in the rocks would furnish activity into these waves and one would get more potential energy in those waves than he put in." This idea was crucial to the concept that through this technique, much more energy is present in the standing wave than the original amount fed in from the surface of the Earth.

Bearden went on to claim that the standing wave created a "triode" that changed the frequency of the Earth itself, ionized the air, and could potentially change weather flow patterns such as jet streams. "You can change all that—if you dump it gradually, real gradually—you influence the heck out of the weather. It's a great weather machine." In Chapter 5 we will take a deeper look at the use of resonance to manipulate the weather.

Tesla stopped his quake-creating experiments immediately upon learning of the damage they caused, but not his research into the principles of resonance and its use in transmitting and receiving radio waves. This was well before Marconi developed his own work into radio waves, and scholars now confirm Tesla as the original inventor of the radio, not Marconi. In fact, a

1943 Supreme Court ruling backs up the claim that determined Tesla's radio patents had indeed been submitted before Marconi's.

Tesla's work was not motivated by a desire for wealth. Many considered him a bit of a mad scientist, neurotic, and obsessed. Of course, those are not necessarily unanticipated or surprising traits for a genius!

His obsession led to research and development of AC power distribution systems, as well as his drive to one day produce wireless energy transmission. Tesla is also credited with inventing the first radio-controlled robotic vehicles.

Though Tesla made statements throughout his life that he had invented a Death Ray, no one has ever been able to physically locate one. The Death Ray was supposedly capable of destroying up to 10,000 enemy aircraft at a distance of 250 miles! Tesla's Death Ray was even featured in the July 23, 1934 issue of *Time* magazine, which stated that Tesla had announced a combination of four weapons that would make war "unthinkable." The article went on to describe the Death Ray as submicroscopic particles flying at velocities approaching the speed of light.

In 1931, Tesla purportedly fitted a Pierce-Arrow with an 1,800 rpm AC electric motor and got the sedan up to 70 mph speeds. He did this by powering the motor with two rods inserted by hand. These rods may have been able to generate electricity on a similar scale to his larger experiments with wireless electrical transmission via transmission towers.

Around the turn of the 20th century, Tesla set about developing his own lightning-producing machine at his lab near Colorado Springs, Colorado. This device utilized special induction Tesla Coils to send out a series of pulses into a large standing wave that would encircle the planet. He was successful in transmitting more than 10,000 watts 26 miles without wires. Supposedly, the device was built utilizing his understanding of the Earth's Schumann Resonant Frequency to assist in producing waves of lightning pulses. These high-frequency electromagnetic pulses succeeded in ionizing the air and acting as antennae.

The Colorado Springs experiments helped Tesla to understand the electromagnetic waves surrounding the planet, and eventually provided him with the information that he needed to construct a large tower near Shoreham, New York. The intended purpose of this new tower was to provide free electrical energy to the world. Unfortunately, the tower was demolished, some say by order of J.P. Morgan, who had conflicting interests with Tesla in the energy industry. Other rumors suggest that before the tower was destroyed, Tesla had an opportunity to fire it off one time, causing a massive disturbance to the Schumann Resonance of the Earth, and destroying miles and miles of wilderness, inextricably linking the event to the "nuclear" explosion in Tunguska, Siberia.

The tower, which Tesla so eloquently named Wardenclyffe Tower, has produced a resurgence of interest in past years from physicists anxious to retest Tesla's theories of free energy. They pulsed a broadband Tesla Coil at a rate of 8 Hz to closely match the Earth's Schumann Resonance of 7.83 Hz, to affect the cavity that surrounds the Earth, acting as a huge atmospheric storage battery. This cavity filled with terawatts of free energy sparked studies to further the work Tesla began in his Manhattan lab, shaking up his neighbors and further aggravating the police.

Many believe Tesla's wireless energy system has the potential to meet our future global energy needs, if more money and research is put into the theory. But now, four years later, little advancement has been seen in the field of free energy studies, and the world still waits to see if Tesla's brilliance can power the world grid without wires.

Tesla's work and discoveries proved to be just as critical to science as Edison, Einstein, or any other contemporaries or followers. To Tesla, the manipulation of the Earth's resonant electromagnetic field, the Schumann Resonance, could cause any number of interesting occurrences that had similar properties to nuclear or atomic explosions. Although Tesla was not the first scientist to experiment with resonance, or even electromagnetic fields (EMF), he was most certainly the boldest, and to this day his many "followers" claim he was the most brilliant genius ever to walk the planet.

On an interesting side note, in their quest to understand the manifestation of ghosts and other energy-based apparitions, some of today's top paranormal investigators have begun experimenting with high-voltage devices, such as the Tesla Coil, in an effort to increase the EMF levels in a particular location. One of the most compelling theories regarding the manifestation of paranormal activity is that "spirits" or "entities" are somehow able to utilize the available energy in a given location in an effort to form an observable

Figure 2-2. ARPAST members John and Aimee Mimms watch the Tesla Coil discharge at an allegedly haunted private residence. Image courtesy of Larry Flaxman.

Figure 2-3. ARPAST leader Larry Flaxman utilizes a modern, custom-made Tesla Coil in paranormal research. Image courtesy of Larry Flaxman.

representation (either visual or auditory). If energy cannot be created nor destroyed, is it possible that a form of energy transference or covalent bonding may be the explanatory agent for all manner of ghostly encounters? Perhaps this may help to explain such phenomenon as "cold spots" (where the ambient environmental temperature is lowered by the "removal" of the heat energy, thus leaving cold), or batteries being rapidly drained during a paranormal investigation.

In an attempt to validate this claim, ARPAST, The Arkansas Paranormal and Anomalous Studies Team, of which coauthor Larry Flaxman is founder and senior researcher, has conducted several controlled experiments utilizing a custom-developed 500kV SSTC (Solid State Tesla Coil) to great effect. The coil shape is perfect for the allowance of the highest voltage energy to be produced at the top, away from the base of the coil. This focused electrical field creates a sort of ionized beam that can act as both a transmitting antenna and as a directed discharge to alter or manipulate the local EM field. After following a standardized coil ionization/deionization procedure, a variety of anomalous effects have been noted, to include visual, auditory, and individually perceived experiential data. ARPAST continues to study the interaction and correlation between high EMF/voltage fields and alleged paranormal phenomena.

The research of Tesla, who made the cover of the 1931 edition of *Time* magazine to celebrate his 75th birthday, and those who followed in his footsteps, would eventually influence resonant studies into the Great Pyramid at Giza, as detailed in Chapter 3. His work would also influence the work of another pioneer, Vic Tandy, who would take the quest into a much more shadowy realm—seeking the "ghost frequency."

But first, we have seen that resonance can create earthquakes, possibly power the world for free, and even make lightning arcs where none existed before. The next question is, could it also build the pyramids?

3

DID RESONANCE BUILD THE PYRAMIDS?

2560 BCE—Giza Plateau, Egypt

About 200 men stood in a circle around a huge flat piece of rock, its polished surface reflecting the unrelenting desert sun. In a round cavity in the center of the rock was a bowl-like depression with a diameter of 1 meter and depth of 15 centimeters. A slab of limestone weighing at least 50 tons had been maneuvered into this cavity.

The Pharaoh Cheops (Khufu) watched in the background as his vizier and royal seal-bearer Hemiunu entered the circle, surrounded by a cadre of guards and high priests, and stood before the stone. Hemiunu looked upon the stone proudly. In his hands, he held a papyrus drawing of the architectural masterpiece he had designed for his uncle, the Pharaoh, laid out in a grid format that was now duplicated with lines drawn into the sand just beyond the circle. He closed his eyes, as if in prayer, and then raised his arms to the skies.

The priests circling the stone sat down, except for 19 men situated at equal spaces around the circle. Thirteen of these men held in their hands a trumpet-like instrument, which they pointed in the direction of the stone slab and rose to their lips. The other six men, also situated around the circumference of the circle in equal distances, held large drums fixed on mounts positioned toward the stone slabs. One of the priests signaled with his arm, and the men slowly began to play in unison—creating a rising monotone of sound, a pulsing harmonic that literally began to shake the very earth beneath their feet.

The other priests, still seated, began to chant out loud in unison, their voices rising and joining the horns and drums, increasing their tempo. They continued to chant and sound the horns and beat the drums, which were synched in a haunting and powerful sonic phase. After a few moments, the limestone slab that Hemiunu and his guards stood before began to vibrate, at first almost imperceptibly, then greater and greater still, swaying and rocking side to side. As the speed of the drumming and the intensity of the horns increased and resonated through the air, the slab shook against the cavity it lay upon, as if trying to break free from its earthbound anchor.

Hemiunu's guards backed away in awe from the shuddering stone, leaving the architect standing alone, his eyes closed, arms outstretched toward the sun. The men watched in wonder as the limestone slab slowly began to levitate, rising off the ground. A loud and deep resonant sound came from the rock itself, as if joining in the choir of the instruments.

Several of the men stepped forward and, with very little physical effort, used nothing but a simple block and tackle to lever and guide the stone slab to the place upon the grid to which Hemiunu had directed them. Suddenly the horns and drums became quieter, the chanting died to a murmur, the resonant tones softened, and the stone came down with a thunderous report that shook the very ground beneath their feet.

In five days, they created the Great Pyramid at Giza.

This fictional account is just one possible scenario for the building of the Great Pyramid, as well as other ancient sites and huge stone megaliths. Although the concepts of sonic levitation and acoustic resonance continue to intrigue researchers anxious to explain how such massively weighted objects might have been moved and placed so intricately into position, to date there have been no substantiated or confirmed theories that adequately explain the precision engineering of these accomplishments. Throughout the ages, there have been many failed attempts at providing answers, but the mystery has endured, as none have been able to recreate these achievements with comparable precision.

Many of the theories focus on the use of various construction techniques, including hydraulic lifts, the use of ramps and counterweights, and of course, good old-fashioned labor-driven blood, sweat, and tears (usually facilitated by slave labor).

But none of the aforementioned techniques adequately answer how massive stone slabs could be cut, moved, and transported up mountainsides, such as the 100-ton sandstone blocks of Puma Punkhu, situated at approximately 13,000 feet above sea level in the mountains of Bolivia, or the 120-ton red sandstone blocks that make up the base wall of Peru's Sacsayhuaman, blocks that had to have been transported miles upon miles over mountains and valleys before reaching their destination. Even with today's technology, such a feat would be extremely difficult to achieve.

Perhaps it was not blood, sweat, and tears, nor some manner of clever ramp or leverage system that created the pyramids and megalithic structures of ancient civilizations. Perhaps it was much simpler. Perhaps sound itself was responsible for the movement of these colossal stones.

The concepts of sonic levitation and acoustic resonance are not new, nor are they the stuff of ancient legend, myth, or fiction. In fact, the use of sound vibrations to lift objects is taken quite seriously by such agencies as NASA. NASA is allegedly testing an Acoustic Levitation and Positioning Device that was created by the private company Intersonics in the early 1990s. The actual patent brief can be viewed at: *www.freepatentsonline.com/EP0484734.html.*

NASA's *Tech Briefs* May 1, 2005 report on machinery and automation confirms the agency is also taking part in the development of a "sonic jackhammer," which is a device that combines ultrasonic and sonic vibrations to cut through various materials in the same manner in which a drill would cut through cement.

A small-scale prototype of this sonic jackhammer has actually been publically demonstrated and could lead to a larger-scale version that may be able to cut through concrete, rock, asphalt, and other hard materials. Perhaps way back in 2560 BCE, a device similar to this had already been envisioned and implemented for use in the cutting of the stone slabs used to build the pyramids—as well as many other megalithic stone structures throughout history.

The modern use of sonic levitation and acoustic levitation mainly involves the technique known as "containerless processing." This method involves the melting and solidification of a sample—all without contact within its container. Using sonic technology, this technique was actually put into practice on board two space shuttle flights using ceramic samples.

Quite simply, an acoustic levitator is nothing more than a resonance machine of sorts—a way of introducing two opposing sound frequencies with interfering sound waves, thus creating a resonant zone that allows the levitation to occur. Theoretically, to move a levitating object, simply change or alter the two sound waves and tweak accordingly.

The concept of acoustic levitation closely parallels the theorem of Sympathetic Vibratory Physics explored in detail by the late John Ernst Worrel Keely (1827–1898). Keely spent most of his life examining the ability of sound to propel and move materials, as well as altering the physical properties of objects. He is known for inventing a cadre of strange machines to demonstrate his theories, including a device that allegedly disintegrated rock, a vibratory cannon of interest to the U.S. Navy, and a technique for disintegrating quartz and other hard rocks.

Keely, an orphan raised by his grandparents, discovered a principle for power production in 1872 that was based upon the vibrations of tuning forks. Keely posited that, via resonance, musical vibrations could match frequencies of atoms in the "luminiferous aether," a fluid that permeated all of space, and he built a number of machines he claimed demonstrated his vibratory generation techniques. But years of legal problems, financial issues, and even accusations of fraud led Keely to hoard his own research, refusing to share his findings with the likes of Thomas Edison and Nikola Tesla.

The range of Keely's research was vast, including experiments into negative attractive force, or implosive force, and the "Law of Assimilation" involving the neutral balance of both light and dark radiating forces. He also believed that all force manifested as a vortex and that vibratory energy manifested in three vectors: rotational, longitudinal, and transverse. Some of his claims were a bit out there for his time, especially his claim that he could operate his machines with his own brainwaves when tuned into specific frequencies, and that the body was like a radio that picked up on "etheric currents."

Sadly, after his death, most of his instrumentation and equipment was either confiscated or proven not to work as Keely had stated. Even today, many scientists consider him to be an enigma, quite like Tesla. But Keely did succeed in starting the branch of science/philosophy now known as "vibratory physics" or "sympathetic vibratory physics," a field of study that many researchers hope will one day be taken more seriously.

Shattering a piece of quartz may sound a lot easier than levitating a 70-ton slab of granite or limestone (not to mention moving it onto a precisely positioned mark). However, there are eyewitness accounts who have witnessed this type of phenomenon occurring with incredible ease.

Henry Kjelson, a Swedish civil engineer, includes one such account in his book *The Lost Techniques*, involving a friend of his, Dr. Jarl, who journeyed to Tibet to treat a high Lama at the request of a young Tibetan student. While there, Dr. Jarl was made privy to areas no tourists were ever allowed to enter, including a sloping meadow near a monastery where he first saw sonic levitation at work.

Dr. Jarl was taken into the field and shown a large slab of stone with a hollowed-out central cavity, which was quite similar to the one described in the fictional scenario that opened this chapter. While he stood and watched in utter shock, several Tibetan monks stood and beat drums while others played a type of trumpet called a Ragdon. These instruments were situated in an arc of 90 degrees and precisely 63 meters from the slab.

Next, a smaller stone was placed upon the cavity, and Dr. Jarl witnessed the monks play the instruments for about four minutes.

Nothing seemed to happen at first, but the tempo of the terrible noise increased and the stone block in the center cavity began to rock and sway, and then hurled itself into the air toward a platform outside a cave entrance, where it landed in the exact position that the monks had intended it to! Dr. Jarl stated that the monks repeated this same process over and over, moving five to six blocks per hour in the hurling method he had often heard others speak of, but none had ever witnessed before.

In the 1930s, an Austrian filmmaker named Linauer is alleged to have also witnessed a similar demonstration in a remote area of Northern Tibet, this time involving a large, gong-type instrument composed of various metal alloys with a soft gold center, and a second metal stringed instrument that was not touched by humans, but rather "played itself" in conjunction with the resonant thud made by the gong. The instruments were played toward two large screens, which were apparently designed to direct the sonic waves, thus rendering large stone blocks weightless, as if gravity had ceased to exist.

Whether these reports are true or not, various theories exist regarding the science behind levitation. One theory purports that acoustic resonance does not cancel gravity, but rather opposes it, producing a sort of magnetic levitation induced by the right combination of harmonic frequencies. Mastering this form of levitation would simply require taking the time to play a certain sonic frequency before a slab of stone until some effect was felt—perhaps a tiny vibration or "jiggle," then finding a matching frequency that amplifies the physical influence upon the stone. Once the proper two or more harmonics were aligned, the stone would seemingly defy gravity and lift off the ground, or, as in some eyewitness accounts, hurl itself toward its specified destination.

Imagine how easy it would be to load up a moving truck the next time you relocate by simply gathering up some friends and playing a snappy tune!

Interestingly, drums and sounding boards are able to resonate in two dimensions and allow for more resonant frequencies to be achieved. This could certainly explain why drumming by the Tibetans reportedly helped to achieve the levitation of the stone slabs. The sonic waves act like those of tuning forks, which are fixed at one end and will only resonate with a wave at odd multiples of their lengths (see Chapter 1).

Ideally, one would stumble upon the exact sound combination that affects a particular property quickly, but doing so would most likely require a significant amount of time and effort, as well as an understanding of rock and crystal properties. Additionally, one would require solid knowledge of harmonics and sound. In other words, find the resonant frequency of a big chunk of stone and you could very well raise your own Easter Island right in your own backyard. But first, you might also need to construct a stabilized magnetic field upon which the levitation could take place and move around.

Doing so would require control of outside EMF influences, which would be more conducive to a controlled laboratory setting—and quite difficult in the hot Egyptian desert. However, if a strong geomagnetic grid could be generated, one could possibly manipulate stones in much the same way that a paper clip can be manipulated between two weaker dime-store magnets.

Some researchers have also theorized that the type of stone used would also make a huge difference. Granite is a composite stone, and might prove harder to find a resonant match than a simpler stone such as limestone. By identifying the type of stone the famous megaliths, pyramids, and rock formations consist of, one can then better determine their mineral and chemical makeup, and thus, their resonant signature.

Perhaps the Earth's own Schumann Resonance itself plays a role in the building of such amazing and mysterious structures. As we saw in Chapter 2, Nikola Tesla utilized these earth frequencies in much of his groundbreaking research into both electromagnetic energy and the wireless transmission of electricity.

In terms of the Great Pyramid at Giza, the advanced scientific knowledge of the Egyptian priests and Pharaohs may have included techniques for manipulating and harnessing this Schumann Resonance. Combined with their knowledge of sacred geometry and the power of vibration and frequencies, especially when in phase with one another, it would have been relatively easy for them to locate the exact longitude and latitude points of intersection to create an amplified harmonic state upon which to build. Perhaps, as some suggest, the intention of doing so was to stabilize the Earth's energy field, by locating monoliths, megaliths, and holy sites equidistant to each other.

The Great Pyramid also boasts interior chamber walls constructed of rose granite, which is well known for its resonant qualities. Acoustical engineer J. Reid conducted acoustic experiments in the upper chamber that revealed its resonant frequency at 121 Hz, and 117 Hz inside the upper chamber's granite box. These two frequencies slightly offset each other, and the strongest interactions were recorded within the chamber box, creating a beat frequency closely matching that of a human heart. Was this merely a coincidence? One theorist, Alexander Putney, proposed on his Website (*www.humanrsonance.org/pyramid.htm.*), that the upper chamber and chamber box were not tombs at all, but infancy centers to "stabilize the biorhythms of mother and child during separation at birth."

Many researchers and visitors report that chanting and meditating in the King's Chamber produces powerful emotional and physiological results—likely due to the amazing resonant properties of the prism-like structure of the leaning walls and the intricate placement of various walls and openings. Indeed, those who have dared to take a turn lying in the huge, lidless granite "sarcophagus" inside the King's Chamber often report having incredibly spiritual transformational experiences!

One of the most notable and widely respected pyramid researchers is geologist Robert Schoch, a full-time faculty member at the College of General Studies at Boston University since 1984, with a PhD in geology and geophysics at Yale University. Schoch is world-renowned for his pioneering research recasting the date of the Great Sphinx of Egypt, and is also known for his work on ancient cultures and monuments in such diverse countries as Peru, Bosnia, Egypt, and Japan. The author of many books, including *Pyramid Quest: Secrets of the Great Pyramid and the Dawn of Civilization*, and *Voyages of the Pyramid Builders*, Schoch wrote about once such encounter with the resonance of the King's Chamber on his Website (*www.robertschoch.com*). He referred to the narrow passages and two chambers, one located off the top of the Grand Gallery, the other off the bottom of the Grand Gallery. Known as the King's and Queen's Chambers, these were lined with granite from Aswan down the Nile, contributing to both their visual and acoustic resonant qualities. Schoch found these qualities, and the entire pyramid, striking. "To chant and meditate in the King's Chamber is a powerful emotional experience, one that I shared vicariously with Napoleon." Schoch goes on to describe how the dictator sent his aides away, desiring to be left alone in the King's Chamber for the night. "The next morning he emerged pale and shaken, refusing until his dying days to talk about what he had experienced there," Schoch writes.

It seems the King's Chamber resonates to an F# chord, and the King's Chamber Coffer to an A, which is the minor third of F#. An engineer and former NASA consultant named Tom Danley conducted some intriguing sonic experiments in the King's Chamber, which involved measuring the dimensions of the five rooms located above the Chamber, then installing amplifiers and speakers within the Chamber to create sounds. He then measured the standing frequencies of the five rooms and found them to be

16 Hz below the range of human hearing. Danley theorized that the dimensions of the pyramid combined with the materials it is constructed with serve to amplify the sounds made within the King's Chamber, and that the pattern of the frequencies matched the tonal structure of the F chord.

Some ancient texts state that the Egyptians believed the Earth resonated to the F chord, and that this was the harmonic frequency of the planet. This theory is also backed up by the works of Chris Dunn, author of *The Giza Power Plant*, and Boris Said, a member of Tom Danley's research team, who is quoted on his Website (*www.lauralee/com/said.htm*) as stating that Danley's experiments in the King's Chamber "suggest the pyramid was constructed with a sonic purpose."

But some propose that matching the Earth's own frequencies, perhaps for purposes of creating healing waves of energy, or energy for much more mundane uses as well, may not have been the only "sonic purpose" of the pyramid. There may even be a connection between the harmonics associated with the resonant frequencies in the Great Pyramid and our own DNA.

Susan Alexjander, a widely known musician, and Dr. David W. Deamer, a professor of chemistry and biochemistry at U.C. Santa Cruz, describe such connections in their 1999 article "The Infrared Frequencies of DNA Bases, as Science and Art," in *Engineering in Medicine and Biology* magazine. The paper describes actual experiments conducted by Deamer in 1988 with the musician, who authored the paper, measuring the "vibrational frequencies of the four DNA base molecules, translating them into sound, programming them into a Yamaha synthesizer, and using this tuning system as the basis for original compositions entitled 'Sequencia'...." The paper goes on to suggest that DNA has a harmonic "fabric," and that our bodies may have techniques for "recognizing their own electromagnetic patterns through the resonance of tone."

This raises many questions of how to properly translate "light into sound," as the bases of DNA and RNA resonance frequencies related to the absorption of infrared light. By looking at the patterns the sound made when translated into the light spectrum, the resulting "patterns of ratios in light" are then translated back into a sound medium, thus revealing what information they contain. All of this is highly speculative, but some pyramid researchers often refer to the structure as possibly using sonic resonance as a way to affect the human body, maybe even on the level of stimulating DNA itself.

If the builders of the pyramids and other spiritually important megalithic structures knew about the affects of resonance on human physiology, could that explain why many people report altered states of consciousness within the King's Chamber when certain tones or utterances reverberate from wall to wall? This suggests that the pyramid may have acted as a sort of "power generator" that used resonance as a means of amplifying the resonance of the Earth, while also working in conjunction with other pyramids around the planet. This energy might operate at the same harmonic of the Earth and have healing properties. If not properly aligned, the two harmonics could instead create detrimental conditions, something that we will explore in more detail in Chapter 5 when we discuss the U.S. military's interest in infrasonics and harmonic resonance for defensive purposes, such as crowd control, warfare, and disabling the enemy.

Perhaps this energy might even continue to affect living things long after the actual "power generator" was turned off. Could it be possible that the pyramids are still influencing all organisms that possess DNA even today, thousands of years later? Is it possible for resonance to influence the environment in an ongoing sense, like a pebble that causes a ripple in a pond, which creates a tidal wave thousands of miles away, resulting in catastrophic destruction? All because of one simple vibration or waveform? This might suggest that all living (and perhaps even inanimate) things are in some way still experiencing the greatest moment of dynamic resonance of all—the Big Bang—on a cellular level in our DNA.

We do know that resonance can destroy objects in the more immediate sense, just as it may also be instrumental in creating them. Earthquakes most often damage buildings, which have the unfortunate similar resonant frequency as the quake (remember Tesla?). Recall that one of the ways geophysicists and seismologists work with architects and designers is to fit tall buildings, such as skyscrapers, with systems of built-in "dampers" that help offset the vibrations of the earthquakes' waves. Wind can also create a similar frequency resonance with tall buildings, usually causing them to sway rather than crumble. And we have all felt the vibrations in dance clubs and at sports events when large numbers of people stomp in unison, causing the floor beneath our feet to feel as though it might actually drop out from under us!

Figure 3-1. Inside the Coral Castle in Homestead, Florida. Image courtesy of Christina Rutz.

Whether used for destruction or creation, the matching of resonant frequencies is critical to architectural design, especially when it comes to sacred spaces and holy places. Modern concerns involve building safety and structural integrity, but for ancient civilizations, and even more recent designers utilizing sacred geometry for the placement of temples and churches, resonance is the key to creating a location of greatest impact in a more metaphysical sense. Sometimes that impact is just as mysterious as the structure itself. Two notable structures that fit that bill come to mind: Florida's enigmatic Coral Castle and the hauntingly beautiful Rosslyn Chapel of *Da Vinci Code* fame.

About 30 miles south of Miami, Florida, sits a strange structure that many people claim should have been impossible to build. The Coral Castle was considered the life's work of a Latvian immigrant named Edward Leedskanin. A small and uneducated man, Leedskanin managed to somehow construct a huge "castle" made of coral throughout 30 years, and rumors continue to fly as to just how he did it.

Allegedly, Leedskanin began building the Coral Castle in 1920 after being dumped by his 16-year-old fiancé on the day of their nuptials. The small-statured immigrant cut, quarried, and constructed more than 1,020 tons of coral, continually shaping it into furniture and walls until his death in 1951. Although the main theory behind the Coral Castle construction involves nothing more than an advanced type of weight and leverage system, some reports claim that Leedskanin would levitate the coral by "singing" to it, reminiscent of the harmonic resonance reportedly used to lift the limestone slabs of the Great Pyramid. Unfortunately, the only photographic evidence of his feats show actual pulleys, weights, and tripods, which were used during the construction of the castle, although rumors persist that there was more to the story than simple human ingenuity.

Leedskanin said, "I have discovered the secrets of the pyramids. I have found out how the Egyptians and the ancient builders in Peru, the Yucatan, and Asia, with only primitive tools, raised and set in place blocks of stone weighing many tons." Some authors, such as Mark Lehner, in his 1997 book *The Complete Pyramids*, back up this claim of the use of weights and leverage. Regardless of the lack of physical proof, the whole levitation rumor persists, especially in terms of the use of "earth energies" and magnetism, two subjects in which Leedskanin supposedly had great interest. Just looking at the impossibly huge walls and towers does give one pause:

- One obelisk weighs 28 tons.
- The wall surrounding the Coral Castle is 8 feet tall and consists of blocks weighing several tons a piece.
- There is a 9-ton swinging gate that can be moved with a simple touch of a finger.
- Some of the stones weigh twice the weight of the largest blocks used at the Great Pyramid.
- Large stone crescents are perched upon 20-foot-high walls.

Could one small immigrant with scant education really do all this by himself, or did he somehow unlock the secrets of the ancients? Unfortunately, there are no actual eyewitnesses who watched Leedskanin build the structures. And according to the information booth at Coral Castle, no scientist or engineer has ever visited the location to conduct a scientific investigation. Though there are reports of his neighbors in Homestead, Florida, seeing Leedskanin transport the coral blocks by truck, none actually saw him "put them up" and create the castle. Beyond the physical structure, we have very little substantiated facts. What we do have are the theories and rumors of several young teenagers, as reported in a *FATE* magazine article, which detailed their late-night experience of seeing Leedskanin float the blocks through the air "like hydrogen balloons." We also have the alternative science concepts of a secret world grid of energy lines that Leedskanin was somehow able to manipulate in order to move and place the blocks. A National Airways Corp. captain named J. Cathie suggests that this grid may also be responsible for many UFO sightings, because it creates the right "geometric harmonics" necessary for manipulating gravity.

Regardless of the lack of definitive evidence for accomplishing his feats, however, Leedskanin was definitely intrigued by magnets and hinted at their role in accomplishing his amazing feats of engineering. Perhaps he used magnetic forces to manipulate gravity? Maybe he was able to alter the entire landscape in order to enable him to move mountains—well, coral blocks, that is. Leedskanin even wrote several booklets, one of which was called "Magnetic Current," and in it he cryptically revealed his "levitation secrets" when he stated, "The real magnet is the substance that is circulating in the metal. Each particle in the substance is an individual magnet by itself...they are so small that they can pass through anything. In fact they can pass through metal easier than through air. They are in concentrated points of telluric power where they intersect...."

Incredibly enough, his idea resembles sacred geometry. Perhaps the intersection points of this earth energy is precisely how Leedskanin, and conceivably the ancient Egyptians as well, were able to move large and heavy blocks using the planet's own "unseen power."

One theorist, Jon DePew, even claims the existence of a "Coral Castle Code," which he reveals on his Website, *www.coralcastlecode.com*. Using physical experiments involving magnetic currents and properties, DePew states that he has discovered this code, and that two individual magnetic forces or currents are responsible for "all of our weather cycles, earthquakes, volcanoes, hurricanes, tornadoes, water movements, and every single change that takes place on Earth and beyond at the Micro and Macro levels."

Whether Coral Castle was built with a lot of blood, sweat, and tears, and some good old bait and tackle ingenuity, or by aligning with the resonant frequencies of the Earth to create a grid of power, or even by using magnetics to create a region void of gravitational pull, the tourist spot remains a mystery, not just because it is a huge undertaking by a small man, but because he alone was able to keep it such a mystery to begin with.

Another enigmatic structure associated with harmonic resonance is the Rosslyn Chapel, a 15th-century Scottish chapel. The chapel was designed by William Sinclair of the St. Clair family, who were descendents from the Norman knights, and, some claim, linked to the Knights Templar. Rosslyn Chapel sits approximately five miles away from the village of Temple, believed to have been an ancient Templar headquarters site. Originally known as the Collegiate Chapel of St. Matthew, Rosslyn Chapel won a newfound claim to fame courtesy of the best-selling book and movie *The Da Vinci Code* by Dan Brown, which linked the chapel to the Holy Grail, and the bloodline of Christ and Mary Magdalene.

The chapel's construction began in 1440 and lasted 40 years. Throughout its history, Rosslyn Chapel has been associated with mystery, intrigue, the occult, and hidden knowledge. There are some scholars who suggest that the design of Rosslyn mimics that of Solomon's Temple in Jerusalem.

Collegiate chapels such as Rosslyn were intended to be both spiritual and educational in purpose, but Rosslyn held, and continues to hold, even deeper mysteries, many of which are suggested in a three-volume study by Father Richard Augustine Hay, the principal authority on the chapel and the St. Clair Family, who called Rosslyn Chapel a "most curious work, which it might be done with greater glory and splendour." Sir William hired the very best masons and workmen available, and thus created the association with the Knights Templar and Freemasons that continues to haunt Rosslyn to this day.

Rosslyn researchers suggest that the west wall of the chapel is a model of Jerusalem's Wailing Wall and were intended by design to be so. Most fascinating to visitors and researchers alike, though, are the mystical symbols carved into the stone ceiling, which were reportedly discovered in 2005 to be a musical cipher. Scottish composer Stuart Mitchell located mysterious codes hidden in 213 cubes in the ceiling. The cubes, when combined, formed a series of patterns that resulted in a one-hour musical accompaniment for 13 medieval prayers!

When the composer also discovered that the stones at the foot of 12 pillars formed a classic 15th-century cadence, or three chords at the end of a musical piece, he suggested that the music sounded like a nursery rhyme, a childlike tune that would have been more fitting of a man such as William Sinclair, who may have been a great architect, but a lousy musician. Mitchell is the son of Thomas Mitchell, who spent more than two decades trying to unravel the musical code on the chapel ceiling. Stuart's recording of the mysterious musical notes is called "The Rosslyn Motet," and it is his hope that when played on medieval instruments it creates a resonant frequency throughout the chapel similar to a Cymatics or Chladni pattern, which form when a sustained note vibrates a sheet of metal covered in a powder. The frequency creates a pattern in the powder, and different musical notes produce different patterns, such as rhombuses, flowers, diamonds, hexagons, and other shapes...all found on the Rosslyn ceiling cubes.

Mitchell suggests that these musical tones and corresponding ceiling cubes are far more than just coincidence, and that one day someone may unlock a medieval secret by playing the repeated frequencies over and over. That secret could be the Holy Grail, or evidence of its existence. Or it could point to the location of the alleged Templar Treasure, perhaps even somewhere within, or below, the chapel itself.

Perhaps William St. Clair was familiar with sacred geometry, resonance, and harmonics, and utilized them in the building of this magical, mystical chapel. These esoteric, yet science-based mysteries, combined with the many links of Rosslyn to the Masons, Knights Templar, and other secret societies keep Rosslyn a popular tourist spot and place of intrigue. Two of the chapel's pillars are believed to refer to the pillars of Boaz and Jachin, and there are pictorial references on wall carvings to the Key of Hiram, and to certain plant species found only in America, which would not be officially discovered for some 100 years or more.

In *Forbidden Religion: Suppressed Heresies of the West*, researcher Jeff Nisbit writes in "Cracks in the Da Vinci Code" about another intriguing mystery behind the design of Rosslyn. Nisbit points to a carving of St. Peter that differs in photographs from the real view, and suggests that some of the elements of Rosslyn Chapel could have been added on much later and were not a part of the original design and construction. He points to the potential influence on the sculptor of the Peter statue by photographic pioneer Louis Daguerre, inventor of the diorama. Could Daguerre's ability to take a two-dimensional painting and give it the illusion of three-dimensional reality with proper lighting create the differences Nisbit found in the photographs of the statue?

Perhaps sacred places that resonate with mysterious power are as old and magical as their originators claim to be, but we also must face the fact that there is a sucker born every minute, and not everything is at it appears to be. In 1954, Scotland's Ministry of Works coated the chapel interior with a type of cement layer to keep out moisture and prevent rot. These kinds of up-grades and changes, although intended to preserve a locale, might actually be whittling away more and more evidence of secrets and mysteries locked into the symbology of the architecture.

Tourists and researchers alike continue to flock to Rosslyn to attempt to hear it sing its song of ancient mysteries, and reveal its secrets to anticipating ears. Even if that never happens, we always have Dan Brown's book and movie.

Lest you think that Stonehenge is without its own resonant history, new research by a university professor named Rupert Till shows that the enig-matic standing stones might have been home to ancient trance dances! In a January 2009 article for the *UK Telegraph*, Till, an expert in acoustics and music technology at Huddersfield University in West Yorks, England, states that Stonehenge's massive stones had "the ideal acoustics to amplify a repeti-tive trance rhythm." Using a computer model to conduct his sound experi-ments, Till determined that the sound made by the original Stonehenge, before some of its stones partially collapsed, would have been "a very pleas-ant, almost concert-like acoustic." He and his colleague, Dr. Bruno Fazenda, visited a full-size replica of Stonehenge made of concrete, and were able to conduct some experiments using computer-based acoustic analysis software and some high-tech gadgets to create music and even the sound of someone speaking and clapping. The results showed that the replica resonated just like a wine glass when you run your fingertip around the rim, suggesting that something like a simple drumbeat or chant inside the structure could have taken on a very dramatic sound, and possibly put those in attendance in a trance. Till concluded, "The space had real character; it felt that we had gone somewhere special."

In the next chapter, we will delve into the links between resonance and the paranormal. Is it possible that ghosts and UFOs might have their own resonant vibration for manifestation? Is there a "psychic symphony" of harmonics that opens the portal to the unknown? Can low-frequency sounds create ghostly and poltergeist activity? Can our own DNA help to explain paranormal events such as clairvoyance, healing, remote viewing, and auras, as a Russian scientific study suggests?

Perhaps it's all about simply being in synch...

4

PARANORMAL FREQUENCY

I know this sounds crazy, but ever since yesterday on the road, I've been seeing this shape. Shaving cream, pillows.... Dammit! I know this. I know what this is! This means something. This is important.
—Roy Neary from *Close Encounters of the Third Kind*

As a kid growing up in the early 1980s, Steven Spielberg's *Close Encounters of the Third Kind* was undoubtedly one of my (Larry's) first introductions to the world of the unexplained. I remember thinking, "Was it real?" To this day, I still can't help but wonder if the whole premise of the movie might not have been an attempt by our beloved government to acclimate the public into accepting the possibility (nay, likelihood) of extraterrestrial life by utilizing Hollywood as the proverbial messenger. Regardless of the movie's original intention, I was hooked. From that point forward, UFOs, ghosts, Bigfoot, the Loch Ness Monster, and even ESP and PSI abilities enthralled me.

You might ask what possible connection there could be between a character who enjoyed creating mashed potato sculptures and frequency, sound, and resonance. Ahhh, that's easy. In the final climactic sequence at the Devils Tower National Monument, the alien mothership lands, and our intrepid scientists attempt to communicate with it via a series of five musical notes.

From ars-nova.com: "The five musical tones in *Close Encounters* are, in solfege, Re, Mi, Do, Do, So, as below. The second Do is an octave below the first. The five tones were chosen by composer John Williams after trying about 350 of the approximately 134,000 possible five-note combinations available in the 12-tone chromatic scale." The result is one of those snippets of song that no one can forget, and somehow makes its way into the annals of cultural history. Had cell phones been the rage during the release of *Close Encounters of the Third Kind*, we imagine everyone would have the same ringtone!

So, if modulated frequency in the form of sound can be used to communicate with extraterrestrials, what else might be possible? Can resonance be capable of more? It certainly is not outside of the realm of possibility to imagine that certain frequencies might be responsible for a multitude of other anomalous and unexplained phenomena.

Do you believe in ghosts? Have you ever had an experience that seemingly defies rational explanation? If you have, rest assured that you are not alone! According to a recent study conducted by Baylor University, 37 percent of Americans believe in ghosts and spirits. Nearly 20 percent believe it is possible to communicate with the dead. Surprisingly, 13 percent believe in the ability of psychics, astrologers, fortune-tellers, and palm readers. And one only has to look at both the network and cable television lineups on any given night to see how popular paranormal subjects have become as forms of entertainment and reality programming.

Due to this recent proliferation of television programming focused on paranormal and unexplained phenomena, "ghost hunting" is currently one of the hottest topics. From the corner barbershop to the school lunch line, people are talking about their favorite ghost hunters. Whatever your interest, there is likely a show for you. Nearly every major network has jumped on the bandwagon, and now offers its own intrepid paranormal investigators traipsing around in dark, supposedly haunted locations. Meanwhile, across the country, thousands of groups have sprung out of the woodwork, with spooky names and a stash of gear at the ready for a nighttime romp at the local haunted house.

Of course, the methodologies and often ridiculous drama-prone dynamics of many of the television ghost-hunting team members present a stark contrast to the serious research that is being conducted by legitimate, science-based organizations. Certainly these shows, and the groups they have spawned, have provided both positive and negative aspects to the field of paranormal research.

Although the breadth of paranormal-themed programming has unquestionably helped to expand the public's awareness of the field, the study and "hunting" of ghosts has been occurring for far longer than the current jump-on-the-bandwagon fad might lead you to believe. You may be surprised to know that cutting-edge scientific research is being conducted by leading luminaries in the field of physics, parapsychology, and other disciplines. Studies have shown specific links between sound, resonance, and unexplained phenomena. Before we delve into the research, it is important to get a little background about the history of ghost hunting itself.

Pliny the Younger recorded the first story of a ghost hunt in 100 AD. The story centers on a haunted house in ancient Athens that was investigated by a philosopher named Athenodoros Cananites.

The Ghost Club, founded in London in 1862, is believed to be the oldest paranormal research organization in the world. Famous members have included Charles Dickens, Sir William Crookes, Sir William Fletcher Barrett, and Harry Price. In the mid-1880s, William James, philosopher and founder of the American Psychological Association, suggested applying scientific method to paranormal anomalies such as ghosts or spirits. He found allies in Alfred Russel Wallace; Cambridge philosopher Henry Sidgwick and his wife, Eleanor; Edmund Gurney; and others, who all formed the core of the Society for Psychical Research. The society's goal was to collect evidence concerning apparitions, haunted houses, and similar phenomena.

The investigators gathered case studies, attended séances, designed tests of claimants' veracity, and ran the Census of Hallucinations, keeping track of persons said to have made spectral appearances on the day they died. Harry Price conducted similar investigations for the London's National Laboratory of Psychical Research during the 1920s, and later in the 1950s and 1960s, German and American independent researchers such as Hans Holzer and Ed and Lorraine Warren took up the cause. Others, such as Loyd Auerbach, Christopher Chacon, and William Roll were independently conducting field and laboratory investigations in the 1970s and 1980s, long before the advent of reality TV came into play and social networks such as MySpace spawned hundreds of paranormal groups running around singing the *Ghostbusters* theme song as they waved their EMF meters about.

Do a quick Google search using the keywords "ghost hunting group" and you will find that there are currently more than 900,000 hits! New groups are being formed daily, likely due to the scope of television programming and the abundance of books on the subject catering to this niche.

The nearly universal title of "Paranormal Investigator" has been increasingly adopted primarily by nonscientific hobbyist groups that engage solely in the pastime of ghost hunting, eschewing other aspects of the paranormal such as psychokinetic abilities, extra-sensory perception (ESP), cryptozoology, spontaneous human combustion, remote viewing, and extraterrestrials.

The field of paranormal research has come under scrutiny by skeptics and disbelievers due to the lack of standardized methodologies and practices in many of these organizations, as well as the utilization of low-tech equipment in their search for answers to the question we have all asked at some point in our lives: "What happens when we die?"

Of course, there are certainly legitimate researchers in this field who are conducting science-based inquiries utilizing a variety of technologies and methods.

One of the most fascinating and compelling areas of paranormal research these groups are undertaking is the study of EVP, or Electronic Voice Phenomena. EVP has garnered considerable attention, and a large, worldwide association was formed in response. The American Association of Electronic Voice Phenomena (AAEVP) is a nonprofit educational association that is dedicated to the support of people who are interested in or studying Electronic Voice Phenomena (EVP) and instrumental transcommunication (ITC).

EVP were originally referred to as Raudive Voices, named after the Latvian psychologist, Dr. Konstantin Raudive, who developed much of the process by which EVP are obtained using specific radio frequencies against a background of white noise.

AAEVP describes EVP as the term traditionally used for unexpected sounds or voices sometimes found on recording media. EVP recording initially involved audio-tape recorders, but later, virtually any recording medium became a vehicle for trying to find proof of the elusive phenomena. The term *instrumental transcommunication* describes these expanded modes of audio and video format communication. Other acronyms used include Electronic Disturbance Phenomena (EDP) and Trans-Dimensional Communication (TDC). The co-fonder and lead researcher into ITC is Mark Macy, an American who authored *Conversations Beyond the Light* in 1995 and publishes a newsletter on the use of radios, televisions, telephones, and personal computers to communicate with the dead, or as ITC refers to them, "transpartners." These are loved ones and colleagues who are now deceased, and ITC, which has been operational since the 1980s, continues to use modern electronics and technology to make contact with them.

The scientific study of EVP, and the newer term, ITC, can trace its lineage to leading scientists of the time. Thomas Edison was involved in the study of EVP! Considered to be one of the world's most respected scientists, Edison believed that it would be possible to build a machine that would enable humans to one day communicate with the dead. According to howstuffworks.com, he said, "If our personality survives, then it is strictly logical or scientific to assume that it retains memory, intellect, other faculties, and knowledge that we acquire on this Earth." All that would be needed is an instrument delicate enough to record these personality fluctuations.

Apparently, Edison was so enamored with the possibility of after-death communication that, during an interview for *Scientific American*, he said: "It is possible to construct an apparatus which will be so delicate that if there are personalities in another existence or sphere who wish to get in touch with us in this existence or sphere, this apparatus will at least give them a better opportunity to express themselves than the tilting tables and raps and Ouija boards and mediums and the other crude methods now purported to be the only means of communication."

Due to the relative low cost and ease, paranormal groups throughout the world have included the study of EVP in their work. Although their methodologies and analysis differ, many of those groups have posted their finest examples on their Websites, including *www.arpast.org*—many of which are truly spooky-sounding!

■ ■ ■ ■ ■ ■ ■ ■ ■ ■

If you are interested in conducting your own EVP work, here are some excellent tips for the beginner:

▶ **Recording Equipment**—Digital voice recorders are recommended for EVP. Less expensive models produce more internal noise that is useful for voice formation. High-quality units will probably require added background noise. A computer can also be used, but will probably require added noise.

▶ **Scheduling**—Entities will speak at any time of day or night. In the beginning, however, it is advisable to record at a regular time and place. By doing this, the entities learn when there will be an opportunity for contact, and expectation of the upcoming session helps focus attention on the process. Try to find a place that will be quiet and free of interruptions. Background sounds are okay, but it is important to be aware of these, so that they can be distinguished from the EVP.

▶ **Background Sound Source**—Research has shown that for transform EVP, the entities use sounds in the environment to help form the words. Most recording situations have some background sounds, but it may be necessary to add noise with something like a fan or running water. Some people use foreign language radio, crowd babble or audio tapes, but the AAEVP discourages the use of radio static or live voice of any form.

▶ **Preparation**—Begin with meditation and a short prayer to ask for only those intending the highest good and an invitation to friends on the other side to participate. It is best to record when personal energy is highest.

▶ **Recording**—Vocalize your comments during an EVP session. The entities will often come through as soon as the recorder is turned on. These beginning messages may be the loudest, so it is a good idea to turn on the recorder and wait a few seconds before speaking. Questions should be recorded, and a period of time between each comment should be left for the entities to respond—about 10 seconds. At the end, ask if the entity has something to say.

▶ It may help to make an "appointment" with the intended entity the day before during prayer or meditation. Some also provide feedback before the session, so that the entities will know what worked in the last experiment. It is not necessary to record in the dark.

People often try different devices and energy sources to help the entities communicate. Leaving written questions in the EVP experiment area the day before has worked for some.

▶ Keep recordings short. Recordings should be closely examined, at least until it is understood where to find the voices. A best practice for field recording is to use two recorders. As a rule, EVP will only occur on one recorder or sound track, making it possible to avoid mistaking local sounds for EVP (false positives).

▶ **Playback**—In transform EVP, the voice is usually not heard until playback. Experimenters report that the voices tend to become stronger and clearer as the entities gain in experience, but at first the voices may speak in whispers. Voices may not be recorded in every session, and it may take several sessions to discover the first voice. Hearing the voices is a learned ability. It might take 30 minutes to examine a three- or four-minute recording.

▶ The first few times that you attempt to capture your own EVP you may get frustrated—don't give up! Eventually, you will get something. Once your ears have become acclimated to listening to hours and hours of "nothing," eventually you will hear something, and it will blow you away!

■ ■ ■ ■ ■ ■ ■ ■ ■ ■ ■

So, is the phenomenon of EVP real? Is it possible to hear short snippets of audio that have somehow been passed from the ethereal plane? Certainly, many of the examples to be found on the Internet seem to be extremely compelling evidence…if they have not been tampered or altered.

Utilizing a combination of traditionally accepted methods (such as white noise and analog recording), as well as new techniques and tools, ARPAST (coauthor Larry's Arkansas Paranormal and Anomalous Studies Team) has conducted nearly two years of continuous scientific study of the EVP phenomenon. We have developed standardized procedures that strictly adhere to the scientific method. Utilizing the resources of our on-staff consultants and engineers, we have designed and built custom equipment, such as a Faraday cage, in our quest to determine whether EVP is truly the "holy grail" of evidence proving that life exists beyond the grave.

We are currently testing a potentially paradigm-shifting tool. Nicknamed "Frank's Box," as well as the "telephone to the dead," this supposed two-way

Figure 4-1. Larry leads ARPAST through experiments with a ghost box. Image courtesy of Larry Flaxman.

communication device is creating quite a buzz within the paranormal community. The device was developed in 2002 by Frank Sumption after supposedly being prompted to do so from the spirit world. The first boxes were made using spare radio, electric, and computer components. The system consists of a random voltage generator used to tune an AM receiver module rapidly. The audio from the tuner (raw audio) is amplified and fed to an echo chamber, where the spirits allegedly manipulate it to form words. Sumption has been able to make each successive box smaller in size and alleges that he himself has had success contacting "transdimensional beings."

Is it possible that a highly modified radio receiver truly can allow us to speak to those from beyond the grave? Does this device provide the "holy grail" that we are searching for? The jury is still out; however, we at ARPAST have utilized the device on several investigations, and have been able to validate many of the answers that were received during "conversations" with the box.

Throughout the course of our research, we have identified several unique characteristics common to EVP and these supposed "spirit voices." Until the data has received proper peer review, we are not yet ready to publicly comment on our hypothesis. With that being said, we definitely believe that there is "something" to the phenomenon; however, the "something" is what we are still actively engaged in researching. We will continue to collect data toward the goal of eventual public disclosure.

Another interesting phenomenon currently being studied within the field of paranormal research lies within the infrasonic range of the audio spectrum. Webster's Dictionary defines *infrasonic*, or *infrasound*, as "1: having or relating to a frequency below the audibility range of the human ear. 2: utilizing or produced by infrasonic waves or vibrations."

These sounds lie below the range of the human ear's ability to perceive sound. However, just because we can't hear it does not mean it does not affect us! Studies show that infrasound can produce some very unique (and quite frightening!) effects on the human body. The following frequencies are a few examples of the effects on human physiology that can be induced by infrasonic waves:

▶ **1–10 Cycles Per Second (Hz)**—Lethal infrasonic pitch lies in the 7 cycle range. Small amplitude increases affect human behavior, and intellectual activity is first inhibited, blocked, and then destroyed. As the amplitude increases, there begins a complete neurological interference. The action of the medulla is physiologically blocked, and its autonomic functions cease.

▶ **7 Cycles Per Second (Hz)**—The most profound effects at this infrasonic level occur here. Seven Hz (close to the Earth's Schumann Resonance of 7.83 Hz) corresponds with the median alpha-rhythm frequencies of the brain. It is alleged that this is the specific resonant frequency of the body's organs, causing organ rupture and death to occur at high-intensity exposures.

▶ **12 Cycles Per Second (Hz)**—Walt Disney and his artists accidentally experienced infrasound on one occasion when they slowed a cartoon sound effect at 60 cycles per second to 12 cycles per second via a tape-editing machine, then amplified it through the theater system. The resulting brief tone produced nausea for many attendees that lasted several days.

▶ **100 Cycles Per Second (Hz)**—A person experiences irritation, mild nausea, giddiness, skin flushing, and body tingling. Also, people may then experience everything from vertigo, anxiety, extreme fatigue, and throat pressure, to respiratory dysfunction.

▶ **0–73 Cycles Per Second (Hz)**—Here we see coughing, severe sternal pressure, choking, excessive salivation, swallowing difficulty, inability to breathe, headache, abdominal pain, and in the post-exposure phase, test subjects continued to cough, exhibit fatigue, and have skin flushing for up to four hours.

▶ **43–73 Cycles Per Second (Hz)**—This stage leads to lack of visual acuity, IQ scores fall to 77 percent of normal, distortion of spatial orientation, poor muscular coordination, loss of equilibrium, slurred speech, and even potential blackout.

The discovery and subsequent theory of infrasound as one possible explanatory agent linking sound and some paranormal experiences occurred completely by accident! Vic Tandy (founder of Radio Shack), whom coauthor Larry had the honor of corresponding with shortly before he passed away unexpectedly in late 2005, was working in his lab one evening designing medical equipment in the early 1980s when he had a startling experience. Although the staff wholeheartedly believed the lab to be haunted, Tandy maintained his skepticism and scoffed at the ghostly allegations. According to the October 16, 2003 edition of the *Guardian* newspaper, Tandy was working late one night in his lab when he began to feel uncomfortable, breaking into a cold sweat as the hairs on the back of his neck stood on end. He felt a sense of paranoia, and out of the corner of his eye, Tandy noticed an "ominous grey shape drifting slowly into view," but when he turned to face it, it was gone. Terrified, he went home. Aww shucks! Just when things were getting good!

The next day, Tandy, also a keen fencer, noticed that a foil blade clamped in a vice was vibrating up and down rather quickly. Upon further study, Tandy was able to determine that the vibrations were caused by a standing sound wave bouncing between the end walls of the laboratory, reaching peak intensity in the middle of the room. The frequency of the standing wave was calculated at approximately 19 Hz (cycles per second), and Tandy discovered that a newly installed extractor fan was the culprit. When the fan was turned off, the sound wave disappeared immediately.

The key here is frequency: 19 Hz is in the range known as infrasound, below the range of human hearing, which begins at 20 Hz. Tandy learned that low frequencies in this region can affect humans and animals in several ways, causing discomfort, dizziness, blurred vision (by vibrating your eyeballs), hyperventilation, and fear, possibly leading to panic attacks.

More recently, in an allegedly haunted 14th-century pub cellar in Coventry, people have reported terrifying experiences including seeing a spectral grey lady. Here Tandy also uncovered a 19 Hz standing wave, adding further evidential weight to his theory. Researchers have also recorded, prior to an attack, that a tiger's roar contains frequencies of close to 18 Hz, and suggest this frequency may be a sort of "frequency of fear" that paralyzes people under extreme duress into immobilization.

Did Tandy's surprising incident lay the foundation to unlock the answers to such unknown phenomena as "ghosts," "poltergeists," and "spirits"? Is the phenomenon of a haunting solely predicated on the physiological reaction of the human body to certain sound frequencies? In his paper "Something in the Cellar," published in the *Journal of the Society for Psychical Research*, Tandy describes his further investigations into sound frequencies and their effects on human behavior, as well as those done by other researchers in the field. J.E. Green, for the *Journal of the Acoustical Society of America*, conducted one of extreme interest. Green drew correlations between naturally occurring infrasound and selected human behavior, testing the effects of the natural infrasound found in a storm 1,500 miles away on the population of an area with normal weather. He found that there was an increase in auto accidents and higher absentee rates in schools when the storm infrasound was present, compared to when normal weather prevailed.

Tandy also recognized the use of infrasound for military applications, referring to experiments done with Pulsed Periodic Stimuli (PPS) to cause "perceptual disorientation in targeted individuals." Tandy noted that modulation of these pulses was the key to enhancing their effectiveness. Low-intensity, pulsed, acoustic energy was found to induce strong effects, including the sense of the presence of "apparitions," as well as physiological disease.

This research is backed up by Dr. Michael Persinger, professor of psychology and neuroscience at Laurentian University in Canada, who used strong electromagnetic fields to affect a human's brain. Persinger found that mild electromagnetic stimulation of the temporal lobe could evoke the feeling of a presence (also known as the sensed presence), disorientation, and other perceptual irregularities. It could activate images stored in the subject's memory, including nightmares and monsters that are normally suppressed. Persinger wrote more about this in his article, "On the Possibility of Directly Accessing Every Human Brain by Electromagnetic Induction of Fundamental Algorithms," pointing to the potential of a technical capability for inducing and influencing the "major portion of the approximately six billion brains of the human species, without mediation through classical modalities, by generating neural information with a physical medium within which all members of the species are immersed." Persinger identified the sub-harmonic frequency that might do this very thing at approximately 10 Hz.

Tandy's findings emphasize the importance of the 19 Hz infrasound band as being conducive to paranormal manifestations or sensations, and offered plenty of his own proof with his experiments. In an article he wrote titled "Ghost Story: Low Frequency Illusions—Standing Firm in the Presence of Standing Waves," Tandy even suggested that "Infrasound + Spookiness = Apparition." To Tandy, being in a spooky place and being exposed to infrasound was fertile ground for a ghostly sighting or two! From a physiological perspective, infrasound can cause hyperventilation, nausea, and even feelings of panic. At the same time, panic can cause hyperventilation, leading to a positive feedback loop with rather profound effects. Other similar works also suggest that the mechanism for physical manifestation could be the vibration of the eyeball, which has a resonant frequency around 20 Hz. Tandy's findings correspond to those of many modern paranormal investigators, who report a growing connection between the psychological states of their team members with increased reports of activity, often a product of mental suggestion. ARPAST is currently working with these concepts to see just how much of what we deem to be paranormal is or is not a product of the mind and consciousness.

Fear, or even anticipation, might be a nice piece of leverage when encouraging the appearance of a ghost, which may indicate why most allegedly haunted locations often feel that way! This is echoed in a statement made by Richard Wiseman, a psychologist at the University of Hertfordshire in England, after conducting controlled experiments with Dr. Richard Lord, an acoustic scientist. "Some scientists have suggested that this level of sound [infrasound] may be present at some allegedly haunted sites and so cause people to have odd sensations they attribute to a ghost. Our findings support these ideas."

Or you might say that infrasound is what puts the spook in spooky locations, leading one to wonder how many allegedly haunted places are really the products of some crafty, resourceful folks who are using infrasound to scare people and bring in more business. Some "haunted bed and breakfasts" come to mind.

Another theory exists that says it's the spirits themselves manipulating specific frequencies to leave EVP or make an appearance to a family member. Perhaps the answers to the mystery behind communication with the dead lie not in finding our own technological means to do so, but in determining what the ghosts are using on the other side! An intriguing take on this would be a haunting that occurs again and again in the same location, as if it was somehow imprinted upon the environment, or recorded as sound waves and light waves upon the environment. What ghost hunters pick up on EVP recording equipment or digital cameras are these auditory and visual imprinted waves and frequencies that originate on the other side of the veil, made manifest here on our side. In other words, each location may have its own combination of pre-recorded "sound and vision" just waiting to be discovered by those of a paranormal bent.

John Sabol, founder and principal investigator for the Center for the Anthropological Studies of the Paranormal for the Eastern Region proposed a very intriguing theory. Sabol authored two articles about historical haunted locations and resonance. In these articles, titled "Natural Selection and the Involution of the Gettysburg Ghosts" and "Ritual, Resonance, and Ghost Research: The Play in the Fields," he wrote for Ghostvillage.com about the idea of repetitive behavior creating a resonance at a particular location, then later associated with ghosts.

Using the rich historical site at Gettysburg, Sabol postulated that ghostly phenomena occurs due to the existence of activity and/or event fields, "including rhythmic behavioral movements (such as walking, reading, and gazing) that are repeated over and over again in a given area." The repetition would then form a pattern that, via resonance, would continue to manifest long after the initial pattern was created.

Some things Sabol feels might be behind this resonance are:

1. "Bleeding" from the past due to resonant activities, a bleeding of energy, so to speak.

2. Paranormal phenomena that have been reported and observed in the past at these locations.

3. Other activities are suppressed by the dominating resonance of the battlefield activity's more powerful resonance.

4. The location environment focused entirely on both the battles and ghost-related themes.

This mirrors the belief by many paranormal investigators that ghosts are simply energy imprints left behind, often repeating the same movements over and over again, without any sense of awareness or cognizance of the witnesses that are observing them. But one does have to wonder if the additional energy supplied by the repetition of ghost hunters visiting such sites over and over again adds to the initial activity. In other words, can ghost hunting actually assist in the manifestation of a ghost? Does the actual presence of paranormally inclined investigators assist in the ongoing activity at specific sites and locations?

Houses and buildings are believed to have a "feel" or "vibe." Have you ever entered a location and experienced an odd or unusual feeling that you were unable to explain? This might also explain why animals seem more sensitive to "haunted" locales, able to pick up on sound waves and light waves just out of the human range. They are merely identifying frequencies we cannot, and their strange actions often look as though they are hearing or seeing a ghost hovering in the air, barking and growling, even backing away from it in fear of something we cannot sense. Let's remember, humans can hear between 20 Hz and 20,000 Hz. Dogs hear in a range of 50 to 45,000 Hz, and cats hear in a range of 45 to 85,000 Hz. That's an awful lot of noise we have no access to.

Apparently, even Guglielmo Marconi, the alleged inventor of the wireless radio, had been interested in capturing the voices of the dead, and conducted his own research throughout his career until his death in 1937. With newfound interest and awareness of spiritual matters, the idea of communication with ghosts and speaking to the dead was quite popular throughout the early 1900s. Likely as a result of technological advances, radio became a natural means of doing so, attracting even the likes of Thomas Edison into the search for the perfect outlet through which spirits could make their presence known. Many scientists and inventors of Marconi's time were eager to fuse both technical innovation and mysticism.

Marconi may have been inspired by Sir Oliver Lodge, a member of a prominent spiritualist society for the inspiration of using "wireless science" to contact the spirit world. The Spiritualist movement was originally thought to be a counter reaction to the rising industrial age, yet ended up looking to emerging technology to help in their quest to communicate with the dead.

But this interest was not just limited to voices and radio. Even the crudest of early cameras were being used to try to capture "astral light" and spectral images long before today's modern ghost hunters cracked open their digital cameras.

When it comes to the original EVP hunters, though, few can argue that George Meek was not an influential figure. Though his device, the Spiricom, which was used by William O'Neil to talk to entities on the other side, has long since been frowned upon, it was undeniably responsible for ushering in a new era of using modified radio waves to attempt to extract EVP. In his book *The Ghost of 29 Megacycles*, author and investigator John G. Fuller documents the research done by Meek and O'Neil as they tested the Spiricom and even communicated with a dead electronics engineer, Dr. Mueller, who prompted them to use multi-frequency audio tone instead of incidental random white noise to capture incoming voices with more clarity.

Mueller suggested utilizing the carrier range frequency between 29 and 31 MHz for best results, and O'Neil reported much more accurate voices coming through on EVP experiments emerging over background white noise. Fuller quotes Meek as saying, "Anybody would think we were crazy, designing and building equipment from instruction coming from someone who was no longer on this world. We had to remind ourselves that both Edison and Marconi had tried seriously to bridge the gap between the living and the dead by electro-magnetic means."

One has to only take a look at the "sophisticated electronic technology" now available in the 21st century to understand why paranormal researchers look to EVP as a potential source of solid evidence of life after death. With the types of sensitive recording equipment being designed today, it's only a matter of time before everyone owns a machine for talking with dear departed Aunt Jane on a rainy afternoon. Fuller ends his examination of Meek and O'Neil's long journey to prove that EVP are real with a telling statement: "The interesting thing about the Spiricom development and the whole field of EVP is that it is there, in tangible form, and can be repeated and examined objectively." Although the results are often muddy, weak, or highly questionable because of their fragmentary nature, the experiences are not hallucinatory and occur repeatedly. Whether scientists will one day accept the EVP field as legitimate, only time, and further studies in controlled environments, will tell.

The work begun with the Spiricom may have shifted, become more scientific in methodology, and more adapted to our modern knowledge of radio, sound, and electromagnetism in general, but the idea that there is life after death is as cogent as ever, and continues to drive paranormal researchers and scientists alike toward the possibility of undeniable proof beyond that which is experienced on a subjective level. A person hearing an EVP recording may believe—getting the entire scientific community to come on board is a matter yet to be resolved.

In addition to sound, even light can be used to induce sensations of the paranormal, or at the very least, hallucinations. When pulsed at a particular frequency, light can cause the brain to perceive images, intricate patterns, shapes, and colors. Slow rates of pulsation produce nothing extraordinary, but when pulsed faster, many test subjects of an item called the Dream Machine, a stroboscopic flicker device described in "Key to Hallucinations Found" on LiveScience.com, experienced visual apparitions that were not really there. There is actually a disease, called Charles Bonnet Syndrome, in which patients experience geometrical patterns and hallucinations of figures, faces, and other objects.

In one test, using six male subjects with no history of epilepsy, the men underwent functional magnetic resonance imaging (fMRI) and Electroencephalography (EEG) experiments to measure brain activity while exposed to high-frequency repetitive light exposure. Subjects were told to press a button if a hallucination occurred, and then they had to draw what they hallucinated.

These and other studies show a direct correlation between light frequency and the mind's ability to "see what is not there," and also corresponds with the many studies showing how many video games, filled with strobing light and pulsing imagery, have been shown to induce seizures and fits in certain people. The brain clearly does not respond the same to all forms and frequencies of light, just as it does not respond the same to all forms and frequencies of sound. But although we do have a general understanding of which parts of the brain are involved in hallucinatory activity, what brain scientists don't fully understand are the pathways involved that might help them come up with ways to pinpoint the "relevant brain networks" to treat those suffering from ongoing hallucinations.

What all of this suggests is that the paranormal might merely be a reaction of our brains to stimuli of light and/or sound, in the form of resonance, which causes us to see and hear things, or experience sensations, just beyond the norm of what we are used to dealing with. Our five senses drive our day-to-day existence, but if the light is just right, or the sound just so, could this trigger a new sense of awareness to another layer of reality? Has the answer been with us the entire time?

The fact that animals are able to discern light and sound frequencies that are beyond the physiological capabilities of humans may explain why dogs and cats and other animals often react to things that we can't discern, including coming earthquakes, volcanic activity, and, as some paranormal investigators insist, the presence of unearthly entities.

Even the human brain has its own frequencies for differing brainwaves. We know that a change in brainwave patterns can cause increased calm, deep meditative sleep, even increased awareness, causing shifts in moods, attitudes, and even thought patterns. Perhaps the brain must find a perfect resonance with that of a ghost or spirit to be able to "see" or sense the apparition. Later in the book, we will look at the brain and how it perceives, and receives, information, and ultimately may be responsible for not only our perceived reality, but also the actual creation of it.

■ ■ ■ ■ ■ ■ ■ ■ ■ ■ ■

The human brain has its own set of frequencies

▶ **Delta, 0.1 to 3 Hz**—Lowest frequencies with highest amplitude and slowest waves. Delta is the realm of deep sleep, non-REM sleep, trance states, and the unconscious.

▶ **Theta, 4 to 8 Hz**—Slow activity, associated with creativity, intuition, and day dreaming. The state between wakefulness and sleep, and the realm of the subconscious.

Children up to age 13 practically live in Theta, which may explain why they appear to be more "psychic" or imaginative.

▶ **Alpha, 8 to 12 Hz**—Relaxed, but alert, the common brain state. Not overly processing information, associated with "good moods" and mind/body integration. A good brain state for healing and balance of the mind.

▶ **Beta, above 12 Hz**—The frequency associated with fast and normal life activity, problem-solving, focused thought, decision-making and analyzing information. High Beta, in the 18 Hz range or above, can lead to agitation and anxiety, or over-alertness and hyper vigilance (as Marie experienced often after big earthquakes while living in L.A.).

▶ **High Alpha and Low Beta (approx. 13 Hz)**—The most common states of the brain during normal activities, with the exception of sleep.

▶ **Gamma, above 36 Hz**—This is when the brain needs to process information simultaneously above various parts of the brain, high-level information processing and thinking, integrating thoughts and ideas, and excellent memory recall. Utilizes every part of the brain, especially at rates over 40 Hz.

■ ■ ■ ■ ■ ■ ■ ■ ■ ■ ■

Even as paranormal researchers test for the right frequencies that might explain how the brain can perceive such things as ghosts, UFOs, and cryptids, the military has another view of the power of sound and vision altogether.

Whenever there is the possibility of changing or altering human behavior or finding the means behind the manifestation of anomalous phenomena, you can bet there will be interest in those mechanisms involved at the higher levels of power.

5

FORBIDDEN FREQUENCIES: THE SHADOWY SIDE OF RESONANCE

When it comes to the future, there are three kinds of people: those who let it happen, those who make it happen, and those who wonder what happened.
—John M. Richardson

Quick—think of Alaska. What is the first thing that came to mind? If you are like most Americans, you probably thought of either Eskimos or more likely the "Pitbull with Lipstick." To others, however, it represents a darker, more foreboding image. Less than 200 miles east of Anchorage there is a secret government facility built by the Pentagon for a very intriguing research program. Yes, you guessed correctly, it has something to do with sound and resonance.

The High-Frequency Active Auroral Research Program (HAARP) cost more than $30 million to construct, but the Pentagon, Navy, and Air Force, all of which are sponsors of the project, hope that it will lead to the development of highly sophisticated forms of surveillance and communications technology that might one day allow U.S. intelligence forces to see deep under water and send signals to nuclear submarines beneath the ocean surface. Or so they tell us...

93

The HAARP project consists of a powerful array of transmitters that beam more than a gigawatt of high-frequency radio waves into the ionosphere. Though some conspiracy buffs have been quick to label this project the "doomsday death ray," Pentagon officials steadfastly assert that HAARP is not even an active pursuit anymore. Still, there are those who insist it is not only active, but has far more sinister applications than simply improving the range and scope of communications.

Figure 5-1. Aerial view of HAARP looking towards Mt. Sanford in the Wrangell-St. Elias National Park. Courtesy of HAARP.

The program is a jointly funded concept that began in 1993 by the Air Force, Navy, the University of Alaska, and the Defense Advanced Research Projects Agency (DARPA). Intended to be operational for only 20 years, HAARP's aim was to control and manipulate the ionosphere with its array of 180-plus antennae, control room, offices, and a housing area for operators. The main instrument HAARP utilizes is the IRI, the Ionospheric Research Instrument (these guys are not very clever at naming things!), which is basically a high-frequency transmitter that sends a signal to the array that "beams" the signal upward, where it is partially absorbed at a distance of 100 to 350 km altitude.

This ionospheric heater transmits between 2.8 and 10 MHz, a range that lies just above the AM radio broadcast band, and immediately below the Citizen's band. The aim of the project is to direct a 3.6-megawatt signal into the High Frequency Band, in both pulsed and continuous waves, then to study the resulting effects with everything from VHF and UHF radars, optical cameras, receivers, and other modes of determining the natural processes that occur in the ionospheric layer. It is in this ionospheric "playground" that HAARP creates irradiated, charged particles that are very similar to the force behind the beautiful, naturally occurring Northern Lights.

The IRI transmits to a bandwidth of 100 kHz or less, and the HAARP system must only beam within specific frequencies. Continuous IRI transmissions are best for ionospheric modification, and short pulses of 100 microseconds or less are best utilized for radar. HAARP, currently managed by the Tactical Technology Office, a branch of DARPA, is one of several such ionospheric heaters built around the world.

Those who work for HAARP maintain that their primary focus and charter is to research the uppermost portion of the Earth's atmosphere. The ionosphere is a thin layer between the atmosphere and the magnetosphere, and is where the sun's UV rays and X-rays are absorbed, resulting in a density of free electrons that decrease closest to the atmosphere's boundary. Research balloons are unable to reach the ionosphere, where the air is too thin, and satellites find the thick air detrimental to orbiting capability. Thus, HAARP is the best bet for truly understanding what goes on in this veil-like layer.

The military implications are obvious. A system that allows deeper, more accurate communication, and a highly sensitive surveillance technology that can keep an eye on domestic and foreign locales are certainly important goals, especially in our current day and age. But to those who believe there is more than meets the eye, or "ionosphere," HAARP has the capability to be used as a weapon of warfare…albeit in unconventional ways. In the mid-1990s, a group of physicists launched a complaint campaign in several popular scientific journals, citing HAARP as a potential weapon that used deadly beams of high-frequency radio waves to disrupt communications systems, disable spacecraft, knock out power grids, and even change the weather. Sounds like just the things that would incite the tinfoil hat–wearing crowd!

Physicist Bernard Eastlund, who worked on the initial stages of the HAARP concept, asserted that this array could be used to beam tons of power toward the heavens. Additionally, Eastlund alleged that this energy could do quite a bit of damage to enemy satellites by disrupting or destroying their microwave communications systems—an application that the United Stated military was well aware of, and quite interested in. Others, such as author and teacher Nick Begich, who in his book *Angels Don't Play This HAARP: Advances in Tesla Technology*, claimed that HAARP could be used to disrupt the earth's own geophysical system, causing earthquakes, similar to the technology developed by Tesla decades earlier. HAARP, they believed, could also alter or block the jet stream and potentially alter the nervous systems of humans and animals with the same pulsing power it could use to knock out a spy satellite. Wow, even more fodder for the conspiracy buffs!

Begich's claim was further enhanced in a book by Jerry Smith titled *HAARP: The Ultimate Weapon of Conspiracy*. Smith wrote, "If HAARP is a TMT [Tesla Magnifying Transmitter], and these researchers correctly understand Tesla's work, we could be in a lot of trouble." Smith went on to state that those working on HAARP might not even know the power they had in their hands, and how it could be abused or worse still, they might know very well what power they wielded and the end result could be manufactured weather patterns and earthquakes by playing on geophysical weaknesses in the earth and environmental instabilities easily manipulated by small amounts of directed energy.

In a 2005 issue of *New Dawn* magazine, reporter Jason Jeffrey wrote an article titled "Earthquakes: Natural or Man-Made?" about some interesting research into the December 2004 tsunami that struck the shores of the Indian Ocean after a megaquake. Some researchers, such as Australian Joe Vialls, commented on just how easy those in the know could "deliver a multi-megaton thermonuclear weapon to the bottom of the Sumatran Trench, and then detonate it with awesome effect." Other researchers, such as Canadian Professor Michel Chossudovsky, suggested that the military might have known about the tsunami far in advance, resulting in no damage to the U.S. Naval base on the nearby island of Diego Garcia. Was this simply an unusual coincidence?

Jeffrey documents some of the recorded instances of human-created seismic activity, and again points to the work of Tesla and his fascination with resonance. We recall from Chapter 2 that resonance was behind the mini-quake that Tesla created. Is it possible that the Tesla Effect and systems such as HAARP could be behind more current seismic activity? Electromagnetic weapons do possess the ability to transmit explosive effects, such as earthquake induction to selected target sites all across the globe with force levels equivalent to a major nuclear explosion. All it takes is someone crazy enough to perfect and utilize the existing technology, and we could be looking at a powerful new terrorist threat.

This idea of HAARP as a geophysical weapon was adopted in 2002 in a report presented to then President Vladimir Putin by the state parliament of Russia. The report, composed of the concerns of the members of high-ranking officers, stated that HAARP could "influence the near-Earth medium with high-frequency radio waves." Interestingly, Russia would go on to develop their version of HAARP, called SURA, near the city of Nizhny Novgorod.

Bernard Eastlund's claim that HAARP could also pick up communications signals for intelligence purposes created a stir among conspiracy theorists, who were already watching for signs of Big Brother while keeping a close eye on the Strategic Defense Initiative (SDI)—the Star Wars missile defense system that was touted so highly during the Reagan presidency. However, the biggest concern came from those who believed that manipulating the ionosphere via radio frequencies could lead to weather disruption, or worse, control.

The actual patent of the HAARP technology system, namely Patent #4,686,605 held by the ARCO subsidiary contracted to build HAARP, states "Weather modification is possible by…altering upper atmospheric wind patterns or altering solar absorption patterns by constructing one or more plumes of particles which will act as a lens or focusing device." The artificial heat could create a laser-sharp focus on vast amounts of sunlight on specific parts of the Earth.

Again, the work of HAARP sounds awfully similar to, and was inspired by Tesla's work projecting electrical energy to a specific location and using it for any purpose, either peaceful or not. And remember, Tesla created not just a man-made earthquake, but also lightning with his technology, something

HAARP critics claim the array in the Alaskan wilderness is also more than capable of doing.

Is HAARP simply the result of expanded development of Tesla's controversial Death Ray? Certain functions do sound reminiscent of Tesla's claims in the July 11, 1934 *New York Times* article that reported that the new invention "will send concentrated beams of particles through the free air, of such tremendous energy that they will bring down a fleet of 10,000 enemy airplanes at a distance of 250 miles...."

Tesla apparently was frustrated when, as war was about to break out in Europe in 1937, he could get no interest or financing for his "peace beam." He drew up an elaborate paper of technical information and diagrams and sent it to the Allied Nations of the United States, Canada, England, France, the Soviet Union, and Yugoslavia. The paper, titled "New Art of Projecting Concentrated Non-Dispersive Energy Through Natural Media," was the blueprint for a modern-day charged particle beam.

Tesla's Death Ray included the unique aspect of a vacuum chamber with one end open to the atmosphere. His proposal also had the description of a unique vacuum seal that directed a high-velocity stream of air at the tip of his gun to maintain "high vacua." A large turbine would provide the pumping action of the air stream.

Regardless of one's beliefs concerning the feasibility of many of his ideas, it is unfortunate that many of Tesla's greatest creations were not taken seriously during his lifetime. Tesla unquestionably left an enduring legacy to all of us who believe him to be one of the true geniuses of our time.

Although there are two other ionospheric heating facilities in the United States, HIPAS near Fairbanks, Alaska, and one located at the Arecibo Observatory in Puerto Rico, only HAARP seems to have garnered the attention of conspiracy buffs.

Fear of electromagnetic resonance weapons prompted a call to action in May of 2005 by David Lamb, working at the behest of American biophysicist and former vice president of the U.S. Psychotronics Association, Lynn Surgalla. This call to action took the shape of a letter asking concerned citizens to prompt the then-current Congressional bill, HR 2977, called the "Space Preservation Act," to include a stipulation that would ban the development of electromagnetic weapons of mass destruction as listed in the 2002

United Nations Institute for Disarmament Research. These weapons included any type of mind control weaponry involving sonics, plasma, laser, ELF, ULF, radiation, or other particle beams or energy beams that could be focused on persons or populations for the purpose of "mood management, mind-control, warfare and disablement." Mood management? Wow, on second thought…could we perhaps design a hand-held version that might be used to change the mood of cranky coworkers?

Termed *electronic harassment*, the concern of these activists was based upon real and tangible research being conducted into all of those potential sources, including microwave, laser, and other forms of Electromagnetic Directed Energy Weaponry. The Space Preservation Act had been introduced in 2001 to ban all forms of directed energy weapons; however, it did not pass, and in 2002, the United Nations Institute for Disarmament Research formally added the new category of weapons of mass destruction that encompassed the darker uses of resonance and vibration.

In a fascinating timeline created by Judy Wall, editor of *Resonance Newsletter*, she documents the interest in EM weapons from 1934 to 1993. Some of the research she cites includes:

- 1934—A monograph by Drs. E.L. Chaffee and R.U. Light titled "A Method for Remote Control of Electrical Stimulation of the Nervous System."

- 1934—"Experiments in Distant Influence" and "Critical Evaluation of the Hypogenic Method" regarding remote control of the brain by Soviet Professor Leonid L. Vaisliev.

- 1945—Allies discover Japanese interest in Death Ray involving ultra short radio waves focused into high-power beam, tested on animals.

- 1958/1962—The United States conducts high-altitude electromagnetic pulse (EMP) bomb test over the Pacific, according to *The Road From Armageddon* by Peter Lewis.

- 1965—McFarlane Corporation develops a "death ray" described as a modulated electron gun with an x-ray nuclear booster, based upon research involving House Subcommittee of Department of Defense Appropriations hearings.

▶ 1965—Reports surface of a U.S. conducted experiment called Project Pandora, involving exposure of chimpanzees to microwave radiation, with the potential for exerting low-level microwave radiation on humans as behavior control.

▶ 1972—Invention of the Taser, the first electrical shock device that delivers barbed, dart-shaped electrodes to human body.

▶ 1972—A U.S. Department of Defense document reveals that the Army has tested a microwave weapon dubbed the "electronic flamethrower."

▶ 1972—The U.S. Army Mobility Equipment Research and Development Center report titled "Analysis of Microwaves for Barrier Warfare" reveals the use of microwaves to immobilize humans by creating third-degree burns on the body using 3 gigahertz at 20 watts/square centimeter in two seconds time.

▶ 1978—Hungarians submit the report on the use of infrasonic weapons to the United Nations.

▶ 1982—The U.S. Air Force reviews the use of specially generated radiofrequency radiation (RFR) fields as powerful antipersonnel military threats from "Final Report on Biotechnology Research Requirements for Aeronautical Systems Through the Year 2000."

▶ 1986—Attorney General's Conference on Less Than Lethal Weapons reviews tasers, stun guns, electrical pulse generators, and other EM weapons, as well as ELF weapons that induce vomiting, discomfort, and disorientation.

▶ 1992—The U.S. Army's Armament Research, Development, and Engineering Center conducts a one-year study of Acoustic Beam Technology.

This is a small sampling of the papers, reports, and research projects that have been declassified or dug up by determined researchers that point to long-standing military interest in the use of resonance in the lethal and nonlethal weaponry of tomorrow. The concept behind nonlethal weaponry is to incapacitate the enemy without causing death, and according to those who research the military's growing interest in this technology, these weapons that utilize infrasound, ultrasound, and electromagnetic energy such as lasers, radio waves, microwaves, and visible light pulses (strobe) should be banned along with more lethal modes of warfare.

In 1982, the Associated Press reported on the LIDA Machine, a device said to alter and tranquilize humans and animals by bombarding the brain with low-frequency radio waves. This machine was apparently designed in the 1950s by the Soviets under a man named L. Rabichev, who understood the biorhythmic pulse rates that created the desired effects on the brain's own electromagnetic current, producing a powerful trance-like state. Dr. Eldon Byrd, a neuro-electromagnetic researcher for the U.S. Navy, stated that a man named Dr. Ross Adey had used the LIDA Machine to put rabbits into a stupor and cause cats to experience REM. LIDA put out an electric field, light, heat, a magnetic field, and sound at a higher frequency, high enough to bring about the feelings of sedation.

The machine, holding U.S. Patent #3,773,049 was also rumored by a biographer of Adey's to deliver pulsed light, sound, and heat in adjustable intensities, and would be applied to patients in a therapeutic sense by placing two disc electrodes on the side of the neck and using an optimal repetition frequency between 40 and 80 pulses per minute to cause the positive benefits.

■ ■ ■ ■ ■ ■ ■ ■ ■ ■

Larry's Experience:

▶ I have conducted personal research of a similar device that utilized pulsed electromagnetic stimulation of the brain primarily for relaxation and meditative purposes. Called the BT-7 Braintuner, and designed by Bob Beck, the BT-7, according to BrainTuner.com is: "An electronic instrument that produces more than 500 harmonic frequencies to rapidly balance and restore the natural energies of your body and mind. Research suggests that these subtle energies may be linked to improved memory, creativity, learning, and intelligence."

▶ The BT-7 features six selectable output settings: 111 Hz, 0.5 Hz, and 7.83 Hz at 550 microseconds pulse-width setting and 111 Hz, 0.5 Hz and 7.83 Hz at 220 microseconds pulse-width setting. The 0.5 Hz and 7.83 Hz settings may be more relaxing, whereas the 111 Hz may be more energizing. The 0.5 Hz setting represents the DELTA brainwave frequency normally associated with deep sleep and release of deeply embedded stress patterns. The 7.83 setting represents the middle ALPHA brainwave frequency, and a relaxed, yet focused mental state, as well as increased creativity, improved memory, intuition, and superlearning.

▶ While using the device throughout an extended period of time, I can definitely assert that it does "something." After carefully attaching the electrode headset, and switching the power on, an immediate "buzzing" is felt throughout the body. After several minutes, an overall feeling of relaxation washes over your entire body. This state seemed to last for several hours. Beyond this extraordinary feeling, I have had some of the most incredibly realistic dreams that I have ever experienced after a short BT-7 session.

■ ■ ■ ■ ■ ■ ■ ■ ■ ■ ■

Though the LIDA and BT-7 may have been developed for beneficial purposes, other devices were under development, many utilizing sound, which had an entirely different motive indeed. The Long Range Acoustic Device (LRAD) is a simple round, black device weighing about 45 pounds that can be placed upon a truck bed or carrier. Developed by American Technology Corporation, the mobile LRAD has but one purpose, and that is to control unruly crowds by emitting a high-frequency beam of sound between 120 and 140 decibels. That is loud!

Sounds louder than 80 decibels are considered potentially dangerous. The extent of damage depends on the amount of noise and the length of exposure to it. A very intense impulse, even a brief one like an explosion, can cause damage to the hair cells of the inner ear and the hearing nerve. And you always wondered why your parents were constantly telling you that your love of blaring rock concerts were harmful to your hearing.

Noise levels considered dangerous are a lawnmower, a loud concert, fire-arms, firecrackers, headset listening systems, motorcycles, tractors, house-hold appliances (garbage disposals, blenders, food processors/choppers, and so on), and some noisy toys. All can deliver sound of more than 90 decibels and some up to 140 decibels. Again, duration of the exposure and the amount of noise determines the damage done.

Figure 5-2. The LRAD mounted on a Naval ship. Image courtesy of the United States Navy.

If you are standing within 100 yards of the LRAD device, you will suffer extreme pain, but effective use (in other words, permanent auditory damage) comes from pulses of more than a few seconds at a time. Usually, the sound emitted from the LRAD is a short warning blast, unless, of course, the unruly crowd gets unrulier…or the operator has had a bad day.

Ironically, earplugs can deplete the LRAD's effectiveness, and the fact that sound reflects off of hard surfaces might actually send the pulse back to its originators. Regardless, many sources believe that sonic weaponry is the direction of the future. Originally used by warships to warn incoming vessels, these devices have been employed throughout the Iraq War in several capacities, as well as to repel Somalian pirates in 2005 from attacking a cruise ship.

In a 2002 issue of *Cabinet Magazine Online*, author Daria Valsman writes in "The Acoustics of War" about the increased interest in the use of sound to permanently disable humans, most notably for riot control means. By 1996, almost $37 million had been invested into this nonlethal technology involving everything from foam bullets to foam sprays to temporarily blinding people. But the military had come to recognize the effects sudden, high-decibel noise could have on people. Valsman states that despite the 1907 Hague Convention, which prohibited any use of arms or materials calculated to cause human suffering, a new question was being asked: could sound disable?

From 1994 to 1999, a number of articles appeared discussing "acoustic weapons," and in a 1997 issue of *U.S. News and World Report* on nonlethal weapons, the CEO of the Scientific Applications and Research Associates, the Pentagon's acoustics research arm, was quoted as saying that acoustic fences and acoustic cannons would be available within one or two years. The use of infrasound specifically was targeted, but further research proved it to be not so easy a task. If you recall from the previous chapter, infrasound has been linked to some very unusual effects on the human body. It is almost comical to think about a weapon being developed that would force enemy combatants to believe they are experiencing a paranormal event.

Infrasound can be effective, but only under the right conditions. One must be especially sensitive to infrasound to become a victim of its ability to create extreme nausea or disorientation. Ultra-low frequencies can cause these symptoms in many people, but large populations appear to be another story. Even ultrasound was looked at, because it is useful in medical arenas for breaking up kidney stones and is cheaper to generate and direct.

Rumor has it that Walt Disney experimented with low-frequency sounds, exposing his team of cartoonists to a tone that had been slowed down from 60 cycles to 12 cycles. As a result of his test, the team became ill for days afterward, mirroring the effects experienced by Vladimir Gavreau, a Russian robotics scientist who in 1957 became nauseous after experimenting with infrasound due to the resonance created in a large duct near where he happened to be seated.

Other rumored acoustic weapons tossed about on the Internet include a gun that shoots 10-Hz "acoustical bullets," a sonic cannon developed by the Nazis, a police club that emits a 120-decibel tone at 30 feet, and something called a Ring Vortex Cannon. Clearly, if the military is not up to creating these devices, the conspiracy theorists and underground tinkerers certainly are.

In *The Acoustics of War*, Valsman discusses a 2001 *New York Times* story about a grad student named F. Joseph Pompei, who created the first acoustic beam utilizing ultrasound, which acted like a long, thin loudspeaker to deliver audible sound. Apparently, the American Technology Corporation was intrigued enough to approach Pompei to discuss the device for evaluation by military contractors.

Though sound can deafen and debilitate, its many critics say that we can easily develop the means to defy the affects. Again, simple earplugs or plugging one's ear, with their fingers can block any acoustic devices that are being used for crowd control purposes. But the military clearly is interested not just in the work of Tesla and his ability to use resonance to shake and bake, but in the role of sound and sound waves to shake and distress the human populace much the same way the Navy's use of sonic waves often results in the beaching and distress of dolphins and whales.

Sonic resonance isn't the only area of interest to both military and conspiracy buffs alike. Anyone familiar with the Philadelphia Experiment and Project Montauk is therefore familiar with the supposed use of resonance to create invisibility. The best weapon of defense and offense in any military strategy would be to have the enemy completely unaware of your location. The quest for the ultimate cloaking device sounds suspiciously like something fresh out of an action hero comic book, or *Star Trek*, but those with a need-to-know certainly know that this is a concept to be taken seriously.

Though no solid proof of either event exists, both the Philadelphia Experiment and Project Montauk have reached near mythological proportions. The legend has become so widespread that the Office of Naval Research even describes the Philadelphia Experiment on its own Website:

Allegedly, in the fall of 1943 a U.S. Navy destroyer was made invisible and teleported from Philadelphia, Pennsylvania, to Norfolk, Virginia, in an incident known as the Philadelphia Experiment. Records in the Operational Archives Branch of the Naval Historical Center have been repeatedly searched, but no documents have been located which confirm the event, or any interest by the Navy in attempting such an achievement.

The ship involved in the experiment was supposedly the USS Eldridge. Operational Archives has reviewed the deck log and war diary from Eldridge's commissioning on 27 August 1943 at the New York Navy Yard through December 1943. The following description of Eldridge's activities are summarized from the ship's war diary. After commissioning, Eldridge remained in New York and in the Long Island Sound until 16 September when it sailed to Bermuda. From 18 September, the ship was in the vicinity of Bermuda undergoing training and sea trials until 15 October when Eldridge left in a convoy for New York where the convoy entered on 18 October. Eldridge remained in New York harbor until 1 November when it was part of the escort for Convoy UGS-23 (New York Section). On 2 November the convoy entered Naval Operating Base, Norfolk. On 3 November, Eldridge and Convoy UGS-23 left for Casablanca where it arrived on 22 November. On 29 November, Eldridge left as one of the escorts for Convoy GUS-22 and arrived with the convoy on 17 December at New York harbor. Eldridge remained in New York on availability training and in Block Island Sound until 31 December when it steamed to Norfolk with four other ships. During this time frame, Eldridge was never in Philadelphia.

Supposedly, the crew of the civilian merchant ship SS Andrew Furuseth observed the arrival via teleportation of Eldridge into the Norfolk area. Andrew Furuseth's movement report cards are in the Tenth Fleet records in the custody of the Modern Military Branch, National Archives and Records Administration (8601 Adelphi Road, College Park, MD 20740-6001), which also has custody of the action reports, war diaries, and deck logs of all World War II Navy ships, including Eldridge. The movement report cards list the merchant ship's ports of call, the dates of the visit, and convoy designation, if any. The movement report card shows that Andrew Furuseth left Norfolk with Convoy UGS-15 on 16 August 1943 and arrived at Casablanca on 2 September. The ship left Casablanca on 19 September and arrived off Cape Henry on 4 October. Andrew Furuseth left Norfolk with Convoy UGS-22 on 25 October and arrived at Oran on 12 November. The ship remained in the Mediterranean until it returned with Convoy GUS-25 to Hampton Roads on 17 January 1944. The Archives has a letter from Lieutenant Junior Grade William S. Dodge, USNR, (Ret.), the Master of Andrew

Furuseth in 1943, categorically denying that he or his crew observed any unusual event while in Norfolk. Eldridge and Andrew Furuseth were not even in Norfolk at the same time.

The Office of Naval Research (ONR) has stated that the use of force fields to make a ship and her crew invisible does not conform to known physical laws. ONR also claims that Dr. Albert Einstein's Unified Field Theory was never completed. During 1943–1944, Einstein was a part-time consultant with the Navy's Bureau of Ordnance, undertaking theoretical research on explosives and explosions. There is no indication that Einstein was involved in research relevant to invisibility or to teleportation. ONR's information sheet on the Philadelphia Experiment is attached.

The Philadelphia Experiment has also been called "Project Rainbow." A comprehensive search of the Archives has failed to identify records of a Project Rainbow relating to teleportation or making a ship disappear. In the 1940s, the code name RAINBOW was used to refer to the Rome-Berlin-Tokyo Axis. The RAINBOW plans were the war plans to defeat Italy, Germany, and Japan. RAINBOW V, the plan in effect on 7 December 1941 when Japan attacked Pearl Harbor, was the plan the U.S. used to fight the Axis powers.

Some researchers have erroneously concluded that degaussing has a connection with making an object invisible. Degaussing is a process in which a system of electrical cables are installed around the circumference of ship's hull, running from bow to stern on both sides. A measured electrical current is passed through these cables to cancel out the ship's magnetic field. Degaussing equipment was installed in the hull of Navy ships and could be turned on whenever the ship was in waters that might contain magnetic mines, usually shallow waters in combat areas. It could be said that degaussing, correctly done, makes a ship "invisible" to the sensors of magnetic mines, but the ship remains visible to the human eye, radar, and underwater listening devices.

After many years of searching, the staff of the Operational Archives and independent researchers have not located any official documents that support the assertion that an invisibility or teleportation experiment involving a Navy ship occurred at Philadelphia or any other location.

Two movies, many books, and a plethora of Websites later, rumors persist of invisibility and stealth experimentation involving the manipulation of light, sound waves, EMF, and microwaves, with alleged further studies leading into the psychological warfare arena. Project Montauk was said to be an offshoot of the Philadelphia Experiment, and involved all kinds of exotic research, including time travel at the Montauk Air Force Station's AN/FPS-35 Radar facility in Montauk, Long Island. UFO researcher and astrophysicist Jacques Vallee wrote about the early Montauk Experiments and believed they originated with a man named Preston Nichols, who may have witnessed the continuing of the "electromagnetic shielding" experimentation first done on board the USS *Eldridge* during the Philadelphia Experiment.

This time, though, the idea of using electromagnetic shielding went far beyond that of invisibility and stealth. The military, according to conspiracy theorists, wanted to know its potential for psy-wars—psychological warfare meant to disrupt and even destroy the enemy by inducing psychosis and even schizophrenia. Clearly, researchers into this project, if they existed, knew of the powerful effects of EM waves on the human brain and body. The equipment being developed at Montauk was alleged to involve a SAGE radar dish operating at a frequency of 400 MHz to 425 MHz…the optimal range to produce effects on the human brain. As Bernie Cropp said in the *Invisibles*, "Coincidence? Perhaps not."

Theories exploded throughout the 1980s, with conspiracy buffs claiming that the military had successfully developed a means of time travel and teleportation. Among these stories were tales of experiments gone awry such as trapping people (à la the crew of the USS *Eldridge*) in some creepy hyperspace warp, from which they would later emerge with major disorientation (think of the abductees returning home from space in *Close Encounters of the Third Kind*) and plenty of mental disorders. The crewmen were then debriefed and studied. Some theorists claim the ship's crewmen died. Others claim they met up with extraterrestrials. Another conspiracy theory even suggests that Nikola Tesla himself was at the base when the Montauk Project took place. If so, his presence was far more important than the experiment itself, as it would have made him more than 120 years of age at the time! The authors of this book do not desire to get into a debate over the validity of the previously mentioned projects, but interestingly, the idea of developing an invisibility cloak has finally met mainstream science in the new millennium.

In October 2006, reports surfaced that scientists at Duke University's Pratt School of Engineering, under team director David Smith, had actually managed to use microwaves to create a cloak of partial invisibility. Smith and his colleagues created a device that could reroute certain wavelengths of light, forcing them around objects like water flowing around boulders in a stream. The cloaked object would appear invisible to organisms that see only microwave light.

Unfortunately, the object would be fully visible to humans, because the device would only be effective within the microwave range, and only in two dimensions, because of its cylindrical nature; however, the promising concept suggested further research could possibly produce a cloak that was three-dimensional, and could hide the object completely. The device was constructed of "meta-materials," artificially engineered materials that have precisely patterned surfaces. These surfaces react with and manipulate light in unusual ways, and the mathematical precision necessary to perfect such a device is incredibly intricate.

The cloak had a radius of about 6 cm and is surrounded by a copper cylinder, and then exposed to pulses of microwave energy of about 10 GHz. The team reported that the cloak absorbed and deflected some of the radiation; however some of the pulses bent around the cylinder and reformed on the opposite side. This cloak was a cylindrical arrangement of split-ring resonators (SRRs) made out of thin strips of copper and resembling a square-shaped ring that is partially split into two rectangles. The SSRs were arranged in 10 concentric rings, each three resonators tall.

The team, by varying the size, shape, and arrangement of these SSRs was able to engineer the electrical permittivity and magnetic permeability at any point within the cloak, effectively resulting in the steering of the microwave radiation around the object.

The fact that some radar systems use microwave radiation made Smith and his team's discovery exciting, but it's only a matter of time before sci-fi and *Harry Potter* buffs see invisibility cloaks that people can wield at will. These cloaks would have to use visible light, something that researchers state would require incredibly small and intricate cloaking devices not yet created (but no doubt on the drawing board!).

In addition, the search for the perfect meta-materials continues, despite the difficulties of finding just the right materials that can do the job. We might look to an "invisibility cloak" concept developed years ago by Japanese inventor Susumi Tachi. This concept involved first "reading" the scene behind the person wearing the device, then projecting the scene onto the front of the cloak—sort of like camouflage, but lots of wires, cameras, and perfect lighting were needed to pull it off. Still, Tachi's idea had merit.

Roger Walser of the University of Texas is credited with coining the term *meta-materials* (sometimes seen as "metamaterials"), and defined it as "artificial composites...that achieve material performance behind the limits of conventional composites." But these meta-materials are not magic, and although they do have the ability to take familiar composite materials and modify them by adding microstructures or even nanostructures, yielding amazingly new properties and materials, they may come very close.

Still, the ability to use meta-materials to render an object invisible needs lots of work, because the materials we have now are "lossy"—they have a habit of absorbing upward of 20 percent of their original input signal, and they are also highly frequency specific, meaning that a different tailored meta-material would be needed for each specific frequency band. As always in the field of cutting-edge technology, we may have the perfect meta-materials to do the job by the time this book hits the shelves—things happen that fast.

As we are finishing this book, we have found an article on Yahoo News titled "Science Closing in on Cloak of Invisibility," documenting the research of a team of Duke University scientists who have succeeded in developing new meta-materials that can deflect microwaves around a three-dimensional object, rendering it invisible. These new materials can cloak more types of objects in a larger range of electromagnetic waves. "The new device can cloak a much wider spectrum of waves—nearly limitless—and will scale more easily to infrared and visible light," says senior researcher David R. Smith. By the time this book hits the shelves, progress will have no doubt been made...and perhaps we will be able to cloak people, too!

Whether or not these new high-tech weapons of resonance are used for lethal or nonlethal means, sound, light, and any other form of resonant vibration does change the human brain and body, create changes to the weather, disrupt the earth's own geophysical makeup, and can even, as current research shows, render an object invisible to radar. Those who are avid fans of the *Star Wars* movies are familiar with the science fictional use of sound in many of the weapons utilized. From Wookiepedia (haha) we get this:

Sonic Weapons: Used extensively by the Corporate Sector Authority, sonic weapons generated highly focused bursts of sonic energy. Like blasters, most sonic weapons offered both stun settings in addition to their more lethal, full power settings."

The cheeky description goes on to say how blasters give off a high-pitched wail that causes disorientation and/or loss of consciousness. The sound is so powerful that it can shatter solid objects, even break bones. Sonic weaponry could also be used underwater, and comes in many forms, usually as sonic pistols or rifles, and require setting adjustments depending on what part of the galaxy you are in, and what types of life forms you are using the weapons on!

Fans of *Star Trek* will recall that the Klingons carried sonic disruptor pistols. And thanks to the folks at Wikibin.com, we have a great list of sonic weaponry in television, movies, and other media:

▶ In Ayn Rand's novel *Atlas Shrugged*, Project X was a sonic weapon with an effective radius of up to 300 miles. It was used in an attempt to keep the population in line.

▶ In the novel and anime *Trinity Blood* the "Silent Noise" system uses the sound of altered church bells as a weapon. It is controlled by playing an organ, and depending on the length of the song, it can destroy a single building or entire cities.

▶ In the book *The Calculus Affair*, in the series of books entitled *The Adventures of Tintin*, Professor Calculus develops a sonic projector that has the potential to destroy entire cities.

▶ In Marvel Comics, the symbiote (a parasitic alien lifeform) is vulnerable to sonic weaponry and fire.

▶ In *The Runelords* fantasy series by David Farland, the Wolf Lord, Raj Ahten, discovers he is able to use his heavily augmented voice to harm enemy soldiers and even—at the proper resonating frequencies—to reduce city walls to rubble.

Film and Television

▶ The David Lynch film features handheld weapons that amplify the user's voice.

▶ Rifles that project sound to knock down or stun are featured in the 2002 movie *Minority Report.*

▶ In *Star Wars Episode II: Attack of the Clones*, the Geonosians use sonic weapons that can reduce solid materials, such as rock and bones, to dust.

▶ A sound weapon is developed by the Germans in the movie *Biggles: Adventures in Time.*

▶ Sonic disruptors and pistols were used by several aliens (most notably the Klingons) in the various *Star Trek* franchises.

▶ Sonic disruptors/sonic stun guns were used by the UEO in the first season of *seaQuest DSV.*

▶ In the television series *Firefly*, Alliance Feds use nonlethal sonic weapons to incapacitate criminals. The Hands of Blue utilized a lethal device that may have been based on the same technology.

▶ In the popular BBC series *Doctor Who*, the Doctor uses a device known as a Sonic Screwdriver, which has been used for quite a few things in the Doctor Who universe. In the episode "The Empty Child" Captain Jack Harkness" reveals he has a weapon known as the sonic blaster. Based on the same technology and by the same manufacturers of the Screwdriver, it functions as a weapon that can digitally rewind the damage it does to solid objects. Apparently, from the return of The Master in Series 3, the upgrade from the Sonic Screwdriver is the Laser Screwdriver. In the original series, the Martian Ice Warriors are also shown to use sonic weaponry.

▶ On the ABC television series *Lost*, a ring of pylons surrounds the camp of the Others. Crossing between two pylons activates a sonic pulse that causes a lethal cerebral hemorrhage.

Animation, Comics, and Manga

▶ The *Batman Beyond* villain Shriek uses a variety of sonic weaponry.

▶ Siryn (Marvel Comics) and Black Canary (DC Comics) have the ability to utter an ultrasonic scream (referred to simply as a "Sonic Scream" for Siryn, and the "Canary Cry" in Black Canary's case). Cyborg (DC) fires soundwaves from his arm attachments.

▶ In the manga and anime series *Naruto*, many villagers from the Land of Sound implement sound into their combat in various ways. For instance, the villager Dosu Kinuta wields a sound amplifier on his arm, allowing the motion of his attacks to create sound waves that disrupt the target's inner ear and thus their coordination and balance.

▶ The Powerpuff Girls have the ability to emit what they call an "Ultrasonic Scream."

▶ Minmei, a fictional pop singer in *Macross*, sings songs that cause an adverse reaction when broadcast against enemy Zentraedi.

▶ In RahXephon, Dolem and the RahXephon sometimes sing while attacking. Some of them turn the song into a weapon that inflicts damage by sonic or other means.

Games

▶ In *Command & Conquer: Tiberian Sun*, the Global Defense Initiative employs a powerful sonic weapon mounted on a tank called the Disruptor, much like the Sonic Tank from *Dune II*.

▶ In the *Dune II* video game, House Atreides has access to a Sonic Tank, with the ability to devastate any vehicle or troop with little resistance.

▶ In the *Warhammer* and *Warhammer 40,000* universes respectively, the rat-like Skaven use sonic weapons in the form of the Screaming Bell (although this is more of a magical effect than a sonic one), while the Emperor's Children chapter of the Chaos Space Marines also utilizes an array of dangerous sound-based portable support weapons. The Centurio Ordinatus superweapon Ordinatus Mars use a highly destructive Sonic Cannon capable of destroying entire units without saves, and even the game terrain.

▶ In *City of Heroes* and *City of Villains*, two villain groups, the Council and the Gold Brickers, utilize sonic guns. Additionally, ranged sonic attacks are available to the primary ranged archetypes of both games.

▶ In *X-COM: Terror from the Deep*, the aliens use powerful "sonic" weaponry that works both above and below water, showing no difference in damage potential in either situation.

▶ In the RTS game *Empire Earth*, the ultra cyber Tempest has a special ability called the Resonator.

▶ In the video game *Star Wars Battlefront 2*, the Geonosians have sonic weapons (hand weapons and defensive turrets) that damage enemies and knock them down, and the Imperial Officer has a sonic blaster that damages enemies.

▶ In *Mortal Kombat 3*, Sindel has the ability to create sonic screams, which she calls "Banshee Scream," and uses as a powerful weapon against her foes.

▶ In the computer game *War Front*, the Third Reich can build Sonic Tanks, which mount a large sound weapon capable of easily ripping through almost any ground unit or building.

6

GOOD VIBRATIONS:
THE HEALING POWER
OF RESONANCE

O trumpeter, methinks I am myself the instrument thou playest,
Thou melt'st my heart, my brain—thou movest, drawest, changest them at will.
                        —Walt Whitman, "The Mystic Trumpeter"

Less than 100 years ago, the concept of laying in a tube-like structure and having a camera take a picture of your inner organs or brain was thought to be the stuff of pure science fiction. Could you imagine describing this technology to someone of that time period? It would be like trying to show a cavewoman how to use an iPod.

But for the thousands of patients who have gone for a magnetic resonance imaging (MRI) this "fantasy" is an accepted reality. Magnetic resonance imaging involves the combined use of a powerful magnetic field and radio frequency pulses to produce a detailed computer image of inner organs, bone, tissue, blood vessels, and even the brain. An MRI is one of the most critical non-invasive diagnostic tests for evaluating a variety of diseases such as cancer and heart disease—conditions that cannot otherwise be accessed via the typical x-ray, ultrasound, or CAT scanning.

MRIs do not use ionizing radiation or x-rays. The typical cylindrical-shaped unit is composed of a tube surrounded by a powerful circular magnet. While the patient lies in the magnetic tube, radio waves redirect the axes of spinning protons within a powerful magnetic field, created by the passing of an electrical current through embedded wire coils in the walls. A second electromagnetic field using radio waves is then activated, allowing the protons to absorb the energy. Other coils send and receive radio wave signals (which accounts for the clicking sounds heard during the exam) that are then processed on a computer, resulting in the final images that are given to a doctor or specialist. The doctor looks for diseased tissue or organs, which are detectable due to the protons in different tissues returning to their equilibrium state at different rates, allowing contrasts between types of body tissues.

MRIs use a static magnetic field. The energy difference between the nuclear spin states corresponds to a photon at radio frequency (rf) wavelengths. Resonant absorption of energy by the protons due to an external oscillating magnetic field occurs at what is called the Larmor frequency for the particular nucleus. The Larmor frequency is what happens when a magnetic moment is placed in a magnetic field. Its natural tendency is to align with the field. A magnetic moment is like a current loop, and the influence toward alignment can be called the torque on the current loop exerted by the magnetic field. It is all very technical, but the end result is an imaging machine that can detect a variety of diseases and save lives.

Man's use of resonance and sound to heal the body is probably one of the oldest treatment modalities in existence. The idea that the body responds to different sound and light frequencies is not new, and serves as the underlying foundation of many ancient healing traditions. From the drumming of shamans, to chanting, music, humming, and pulsating light, many techniques involving sound have been used throughout the ages by healers and religious leaders. Even in today's modern, technology-centric world, scientists are re-evaluating the use of sound and light in aligning the body's own vibratory frequencies with those of a body vibrating at optimal health.

Archaeologists have recently discovered small, clay, skull-shaped whistles buried with human remains in unearthed Aztec temple cities. These "whistles of death," which can also take shapes other than skulls, were at first dismissed as ancient noisemakers and toys by archeologists, but new research by a mechanical engineer named Roberto Velazquez points to a much different use.

Figure 6-1 and 6-2. An example of Ehekachichtli or Death Whistle, ancient noise generators believed to have been used in Aztec and pre-Columbian tribes to entrain the human brain into altered states of consciousness, as well as for treating illness. These belong to Larry Flaxman's personal collection of archeological artifacts. Images courtesy of Larry Flaxman.

Velazquez, who has produced hundreds of replicas of these whistles and other flute and wind-type instruments found in Mexican ruins, suggests that, among other purposes, they were used during mourning to help assist the dead in their journey to the other side. He is working with musicians, archeologists, and historians to take a new look at these ancient artifacts, and what they were capable of. In a June 2008 story for LiveScience.com by Julie Watson, Velazquez says "We've been looking at our ancient culture as if they were deaf and mute, but I think all of this is tied closely to what they did, how they thought."

Watson reports that many pre-Columbian tribes had utilized similar whistles, including noisemakers made of turkey feathers, sugar cane, and frog skins for a variety of purposes including religious rituals, to fend off enemies, and even to heal. Though the primary use was thought to be helping the deceased make the journey to the underworld, a clearly Shamanic influenced practice, the whistles are also thought to have been used to treat certain illnesses among tribe members. The sounds produced by some of the whistles fall within the maximum upper range of human hearing. It is certainly possible that the users may have known exactly which whistles could produce sounds that altered the brain, changed the state of consciousness, or even affected the rhythm of a person's heart rate.

Velazquez has traveled extensively across Mexico to examine newly unearthed instruments. Frequently, he has to spend significant amounts of time trying to figure out just how to blow into them in order to recreate the specific sounds for which they were made. Some of the noisemakers had to be put inside his mouth in order to produce the right sound, and one, a frog-shaped whistle, took nearly a year for Velazquez to figure out how to operate. The end result for many of the objects is a combination of good and bad. According to Arnd Adje Oth, a pre-Hispanic music expert, some of the instruments emit a positive tone; others sound clearly negative. "Surely, sounds were used in all kinds of cults, such as sacrificial ones, but also in healing ceremonies."

Today's New Age mentality has certainly put a new spin on the use of sound and light to heal, but the basic theory remains the same. There are good vibes—those that make you feel good—and bad vibes—those that make you feel awful. Sick. Diseased. Perhaps the Beach Boys in their Grammy-winning song "Good Vibrations" were alluding to the effect of positive vibrations upon the human mind?

The use of sound and resonance in holistic healing has led to a multi-million dollar business of products, techniques, and machines that use varying frequencies of radio waves, dubbed Sound Wave Frequencies, supposedly to help the body re-attune itself to optimal health. Those involved in the field suggest that they can heal physical, mental, emotional, and even spiritual "diseases" using sound waves to restore the body's natural harmonious balance.

One of the pioneers of this concept is Nicole La Voie, a French-Canadian mother who used her own experience to launch a healing technology company. After being exposed to numerous x-rays during her employment as an x-ray technician, La Voie's son was born with many health problems, including glandular system failure as a child. La Voie went on to study everything from homeopathy to sacred geometry and even became a Reiki Master. Her intense interest in helping her child led to her developing a sound therapy system based upon a specific system of vibrational frequencies, called Sound Wave Energy, which she claims healed her son and many others.

The idea behind La Voie's program is that the body is like a symphony, with each cell taking part in the orchestration of harmony. "When a musician (organ or system) produces a sour note, we bring them back into harmony by helping them to retune their instrument, or refocus their attention." This may sound very "New-Agey" and metaphysical, but we have to remember that the body is an electrical system of sorts. The frequency ranges used in the Sound Wave Energy system are between 15 and 33 Hz, and "sound like a cat's purr or an engine's hum," with the purpose of achieving balance and peace of mind.

Dr. Hans Jenny, author of *Cymatics: Volume Two*, writes that sound is "the creative principle. It must be regarded as primordial...." The Old Testament begins with "In the beginning was the Word, and the Word was with God, and the Word was God." In Sanskrit, "Nada Brahma" states the world is sound. Jenny's research involved the use of this creative power found in tone and sound to create three-dimensional shapes that corresponded with the sound frequency. Much of Jenny's work involved transforming powders, pastes, and liquids into patterns that were mirrored in nature, art, and architecture (à la sacred geometry!). These patterns were created by the use of specific vibrational frequencies of sine waves, the majority of which lay within the audible range. The waves act to excite the inanimate powders, pastes, or liquids into lifelike forms. Light is projected up through the lens to provide a glimpse of the amazing standing wave patterns that suddenly emerge from the proper pitch or tone, and amplitude of sound directed at the inert object. Jenny's methodology suggests that sound provides a foundational and fundamental basis for all matter; a sort of a vibrational matrix, which, in future chapters, we will compare to the concept of the Zero Point Grid. Perhaps the grid itself is composed of sound.

In an article for *Kindred Spirit* magazine's Autumn 2002 issue, Cymatics expert Jeff Volk writes about the power of sound to change and shape matter. "Imagine hearing a tone, and watching as sound waves involute an inert blob of kaolin paste, 'animating' it through various phases in a nearly perfect replica of cellular division." Volk claims these types of experiments "vividly reveal certain universal principles which lend credence to the proliferation of sound therapies that are rapidly emerging at the forefront of the holistic health movement." In a video titled *Of Sound Mind and Body: Music and Vibrational Healing*, Rupert Sheldrake is quoted as stating that human bodies are "nested hierarchies of vibrational frequencies" that are part of an even larger, more complex system of vibrational structures. Again, this speaks to the concept of a grid of layered vibrational realities that are both macrocosmic and microcosmic in nature.

Volk refers to the work of Dr. Peter Guy Manners, a British naturopath who, in the 1950s, applied the principle of entrainment, in which weaker pulsations fall under the influence of stronger ones, to his theory that every form, unique in size, shape, and density, has its own range of vibrational frequencies. "Manners correlated the resonant frequencies of healthy tissues and organs," Volk continues. "He devised a way to project these vibrations via sound waves, directly into distressed areas." The process is called "sympathetic resonance," and the distressed areas are brought back to their original, healthy vibrational levels. The continued research and development of the EEG and EKG increased the possibilities of using audible sound waves on the brain, and the work of Robert Monroe in the 1960s solidified the use of specific sound frequencies to modulate brain waves, research that was again continued by the Monroe Institute in Virginia, devoting years to the study of using specific frequencies to entrain brainwaves.

These concepts were not outlandish to those of a spiritual bent. As mentioned in an earlier chapter, the use of Tibetan Singing Bowls are used to calm the brain with tone, as does meditation, chanting, and shamanic drumming, all of which can induce an altered state of consciousness and take the brain from a normal Beta state (14–20 Hz) into the deeper Theta and Delta states (8 Hz to 0.5 Hz). One new healing modality, called Unified Field Healing System, correlates the Earth's Schumann Frequency with that of the "light of consciousness" to create an integration of resonance and light. Even the ancient Egyptians were aware of this connection between the vibration of the planet and that of the body, as discussed in an earlier chapter.

To review a little, the Schumann Frequency occurs because the space between the surface of the Earth and the conductive ionosphere acts as a waveguide. The limited dimensions of the Earth cause this waveguide to act as a resonant cavity for electromagnetic waves in the ELF band. This cavity is naturally excited by energy from lightning strikes. Schumann Resonance modes are observed in the power spectra of the natural electromagnetic background noise, as separate peaks at extremely low frequencies (ELF) around 7.8, 14.3, 20.8, 27.3, and 33.8 Hz.

Recall that the fundamental mode of the Schumann Resonance is a standing wave in the Earth-ionosphere cavity with a wavelength equal to the circumference of the Earth. This lowest-frequency (and highest-intensity) mode of the Schumann Resonance occurs at a frequency of approximately 7.8 Hz. Further resonance modes appear at approximately 6.5 Hz intervals, a characteristic attributed to the atmosphere's spherical geometry.

In another article for *Kindred Spirit* magazine's July 2002 issue, Volk also discussed the use of cymatics to tone up the body and tune up the mind. He states that "cymatherapy" uses "specific overlays of frequencies all within the audible range" to provide everything from a "sonic facelift" that tones and tightens the skin while removing toxins, to using the sound wave therapy to heal bone chips and ligament tears in a football player's ankle. He points also to the more well-known use of this therapy on a racehorse named Rarely Found, who used the technique to heal a torn flexor tendon and achieve full recovery, something at which other therapies failed. Volk's work has led to a plethora of modern-day devices that use both sound and light to heal.

Jenny studied the earlier works of Rudolf Steiner and of Ernst Chladni, "the father of acoustics," and contributed his own knowledge to a body of work that is growing each year. Volk points to the progress of technology in engineering and electronics behind the more recent "Cyma Glyphs" of contemporary researchers Alexander Lauterwasser and John Reid, who have created "sound figures" in water and sand. Reid, an acoustic engineer, did research in the sarcophagus of the King's Chamber in the Great Pyramid, transforming it into a giant resonator. He applied electronic frequencies to a membrane stretched over the opening to create a resonant vibration and explored the various acoustic properties of the chamber and surrounding passageways.

In his book *Vibrational Medicine*, Dr. Richard Gerber posits the difference between physical matter and etheric matter as simply a difference of frequency. He posits that MRIs are utilizing the same principle of applying resonance to reveal and image physical distress within the human body. He also believes that energy imbalance in the subtle or etheric body always leads to disease in the physical body. The idea is that, from an energetic standpoint, when the human body is weak or off balance, it oscillates at a less harmonious frequency than when healthy. "This abnormal frequency reflects a general state of cellular energetic imbalance within the physical body." By further applying certain vibrational frequencies, Gerber maintains that the body can restore itself to the balance of health and rid itself of the "toxicities of illness."

Gerber's believes this new paradigm of healing views the human body as more than just a machine with parts. Instead, the body and its various systems act more as energy fields within which the life force moves. This more harmonious and holistic view of the body and its systems is shared by many doctors and researchers, including Deepak Chopra, Andrew Weil, and Bernie Siegel. In Cynthia Logan's *Healing Vibes*, her essay in *Forbidden Science: From Ancient Technologies to Free Energy*, Gerber is quoted as stating his intention to create a "kind of Mayo clinic of healing research." He firmly believes that "Western technology has now evolved to the point that we are beginning to get confirmation that subtle energy systems do exist and that they influence the physiologic behavior of cellular systems." Though vibrational medicine is still not considered a scientifically accepted area of research, Gerber and his colleagues continue to put forth the idea that because the body is a vibrating field of energy, the way we look at healing must acknowledge that new view of what it means to be human.

Modern sound healing modalities have even embraced the use of sound in conjunction with acupressure, as in the Alphatouch treatment method. Alphatouch claims that through the use of a proprietary AlphaSonic sound wave machine, acupressure points along the body are activated helping to alleviate pain and inflammation. Acupressure has long been considered a viable alternative health modality, so it seems like a natural progression to introduce the element of sound into the mix. Sound waves can amplify the effects upon the acupressure points to relax muscles, increase circulation, and even reduce inflammation just by holding a transducer a few inches from the body and moving it slowly across the body's meridian, where acupressure points are located.

A more New Age concept involves finding the resonant frequencies of the body's chakras, or seven energy points, and aligning them back to wholeness. Supposedly, if even one of the chakras is not vibrating at the proper frequency, the person can experience a variety of disease and distress, both mental and physical. Thus, if the body is nothing but vibrating energy, and sound is nothing but vibrating energy, to achieve the synching of both would lead to perfect "soundness" of body and spirit. But what are the chakras exactly? Other than hearing about your favorite movie star espousing her latest "feel good" chakra treatment, do you know "what" or "where" they are?

Chakras are the body's energy centers through which life energy or life force flows into and out of our aura. They serve to create a harmony of energy throughout the body, mind, and spirit, and when one chakra is blocked, it can cause disease or distress to the entire physiological and psychological system. Okay, that sounds reasonable enough, but what does a chakra look like? Chakras have been alternatively described as a wheel-like vortex, or similarly shaped to a lotus flower. Various colors are assigned to the chakras, as are associations with the particular organ, gland, and body system they are connected to. The heart chakra, for example, governs the thymus gland and is in charge of the functioning of the heart organ, lungs, bronchia system, lymph glands, secondary circulatory system, immune system, and arms and hands. The heart chakra resonates to the color green.

The seven main chakra centers are aligned along the spinal column. If there are disturbances on any level, this shows in the chakra's vitality level. Also, each of the seven main chakras is its own intelligence center. This means that each chakra is not only associated with our physical health, but also controls aspects connected to our emotional, mental, and belief system.

The body itself is incredibly sensitive to sound, from the slightest whisper to a shocking scream. Our ears are able to discern sound vibrating between 20 and 20,000 cycles per second. Our bones and skin can even perceive sound through a process called conduction—in fact, do you remember the "Bone Fone" from the 1980s? This device would "resonate through your bones—all the way to the sensitive bones of your inner ear."

Native cultures recognized the therapeutic nature of sound, using gongs, bowls, didgeridoos, rattles, and other objects to align the body and correct disturbances in the physical vibratory mode. Those objects have now morphed into sound discs, resonator plates, sound tables, frequency modulators, and other high-tech machines that produce frequency ranges that correspond with the human body's own transducing waves. According to the Center for Neuroacoustic Research and the California Institute for Human Science, scientific studies have shown that the sound vibrations of dolphins, Tibetan bowls and even musical choirs can have a healing effect. They have even discovered that the sounds made by the rings of the planet Uranus are virtually identical to those produced by the Tibetan bowls! NASA recordings of "outer space noise" sound almost just like the sounds made by the ebb and flow of ocean tides. Perhaps sound patterns are far more prevalent than we ever imagined, creating a virtual symphony that links outer space with inner space.

People who meditate can attest to the vibratory healing of using a simple mantra, such as "om," which they claim heightens consciousness and brings about a deeper awareness, as do Buddhist and Gregorian chants. The repetitive nature, the rhythm of a word repeated over and over, or a chant sung or spoken, seems to have a profound effect on the body as well as on the mind. One has only to listen to a decent high school marching band banging on the drums to experience how this rhythmic resonance can move the body. Watch people dancing and it becomes clear that music moves the body (although not always in a good way. Think Elaine on *Seinfeld*).

In an article for the December 2008 *O Magazine*, noted neurologist Oliver Sacks, MD, discusses the healing power of singing. He refers to the "profound bond between music and our brains, and how the simple act of singing can be good medicine—especially as we age." Sacks further explores how every culture uses music and singing in ritual as well as in play. Think of Christmas carols and African drumming rhythms. Music is one of the ways we bond as humans, often through memories associated with it, such as a favorite song from childhood that still has the power to soothe us as adults.

Music involves the use of many parts of the brain, and Sacks feels this is why it is so important to us in terms of building memories and even learning. He has also seen proof of it healing diseases and making profound changes in those stricken with neurological diseases. "I have seen this over and over again in my practice as a neurologist," he states. "The right sort of music can literally unlock someone frozen by Parkinson's disease, so that they may be able to dance or sing, even though, in the absence of music, they may be unable to take a step or say a word."

Music is a fundamental way of expressing what it means to be human. And when music resonates with us, it heals, inspires, and lifts us. Again, we refer to the concept of entrainment, which exists both as a concept of physics and in the human brain. In physics, entrainment is the tendency for two oscillating objects to lock into phase, or synchronization, so that they have similar vibrational frequencies. They are said to oscillate in harmony, pulsing in synchrony. This principle also appears in chemistry, astronomy, biology, and even psychology, and the brain itself can be trained to certain brainwave frequencies that are in phase with outside vibrational rates.

In music, there can be entrainment of rhythm, vibration, harmony, and tone, and it has a direct effect on the listener by either resonating positively, or sounding like an awful cacophony that does not promote a state of calm or well being. Dutch scientist Christian Huygens, who has a long history with resonance studies, discovered the concept of entrainment in 1665 working with pendulum clocks, which would eventually end up swinging at the same rate when placed near one another. This synching of the pendulum swing was repeatable. The swings did not stabilize in synchrony, but in anti-phase instead. Entrainment occurred, however, because the swing rates had the same period, even though they had opposing phases. When two systems achieve entrainment, they assume a stability that gradually reduces the expended amounts of energy. The systems are then said to be in resonance.

Brainwave synchronization is the entrainment of the brain's wave frequency with that of an outside stimulus, creating a different brain state. For example, the two hemispheres of the brain synchronize to binaural beats, which occur when audio signals to the brain cause a response directly related to the frequency of the introduced signal. Two tones that are close in frequency then generate a beat frequency at the difference of the frequencies, which is generally in the subsonic range. For example, a 500 Hz tone and 510 Hz tone will produce a subsonic 10 Hz tone, roughly in the middle of the alpha range.

Figure 6-3. Clockwise from top left, these are the sound and light machines owned by Larry Flaxman, with Websites where available for purchase. Pzizz—*www.pzizz.com*; Nova Pro Light & Sound Machine—*www.photosonix.com*; Braintuner—braintuner.com; Zapper Z4e—zapperguy.com; Zapper Z3i—zapperguy.com; Neurotrek Digital Pro—wellnesstools.com; Dream Maker—wellnesstools.com" Image courtesy of Larry Flaxman.

This new subsonic tone can have effects on the mind of the person experiencing it. Also, the normal "carrier frequency" (for example, the 500 Hz in the previous example), may have the same such effect. The way it works is that the brain experiences the pulse by combining the two tones. Each ear hears only a steady tone.

These entrainment frequencies may provide health benefits in treating certain medical conditions, but as of yet, the medical community is reluctant to adopt brainwave synchronization for emotional/mental disorders. Although the effects and efficacy can certainly vary from person to person, there are a variety of helpful brainwave synchronization techniques available that can have beneficial effects on individuals, such as classical neurofeedback or learning meditation.

Coauthor Larry has had personal experience with one of these entrainment devices, which he describes here.

■ ■ ■ ■ ■ ■ ■ ■ ■ ■ ■

Always the voyager, "inner space" represents the next horizon of exploration for me. Imagine a personalized world of untapped, never-before-seen or experienced things that are created solely based upon one's life experiences, beliefs, and attitudes.

After pondering the possibilities, my first thought was, "I wonder what is out there that can help me explore the inner recesses of my mind." Drugs were definitely out of the question (I don't even take aspirin!). Pain would likewise not be in the equation. Hmm, so, what else? Yoga or transcendental meditation? Sorry…I don't have the patience. Drumming or chanting? Nope, the effects seem entirely too subjective. Since I am an avowed technology and gadget freak, I immediately began my search for an electronic device that could help facilitate my journey into Larry land.

My first stop was the information highway, and our Internet heavy-hitter, Google. I immediately found quite a few devices primarily marketed and sold by alternative health vendors. Many of these seemed more "hype" and pseudoscience than legitimate possibilities. Violet ray wands…magnetic mattress pads…orgone generators and chi energizers. Do you want to live forever? Believe it or not there are magnetic rings that you place on your fingers and toes each night that guarantee it! It's all out there. Oh, and if you believe those things work then remind me to tell you about the beautiful oceanfront property I have for sale in Arkansas.

So, with such a plethora of options, how does one separate the wheat from the chaff? Again, the Internet to the rescue! Spend some time in the vast folds of the Web, and you will run across a variety of informative Websites, message forums, and blog posts. I spent several months meticulously studying real people's experiences and thoughts regarding different devices and modalities. Several immediately stood out.

The first tool that seemed to receive rave reviews was a device called a "light and sound machine." Due to the fact that studies have shown that specific brainwave frequencies are linked to one's mood and mind-state, these devices utilize sound and light to "entrain" your brain into specific states that are conducive to mediation, concentration, dreaming, or even altered states of consciousness.

Mind machines, called in some countries "psycho-Walkmans" are nothing more than devices that use pulsing rhythmic sound and/or flashing light to alter the brainwave frequency of the user. Mind machines are alleged to induce deep states of relaxation, concentration, and in some cases, altered states of consciousness that have been compared to those obtained from meditation and Shamanic exploration. The idea is for the machine to move the brainwave frequency from a high level to a lower level by ramping down in several sequences. Target frequencies typically correspond to Delta (1–3 Hertz), Theta (4–7 Hz), Alpha (8–12 Hz), or Beta brain waves (13–40 Hz), and can be adjusted by the user for desired effects.

Mind may be utilized along with biofeedback or neurofeedback equipment in order to adjust the frequency quickly. Target frequencies that effect the brain are:

- Delta (0.1–3 Hz)—deep sleep, lucid dreaming, increased immune functions, hypnosis.
- Theta (3–8 Hz)—deep relaxation, meditation, increased memory, focus, creativity, lucid dreaming, hypnagogic state.
- Alpha (8–12 Hz)—light relaxation, "superlearning," positive thinking.
- Low Beta (12–15 Hz)—relaxed focus, improved attentive abilities.
- Midrange Beta (15–18 Hz)—increase mental ability, focus, alertness, IQ.
- High Beta (above 18 Hz)—fully awake, normal state of alertness, stress, and anxiety.
- Gamma (40 Hz)—associated with information-rich task processing and high-level information processing.

Mind machine devices utilize these frequencies, in pairs of "binaural beats" in combination with visual stimulation.

Binaural beats are auditory brainstem responses that originate in the superior olivary nucleus of each hemisphere. They result from the interaction of two different auditory impulses, originating in opposite ears, below 1,000 Hz, and which differ in frequency between one and 30 Hz (Oster, 1973).

For example, if a pure tone of 400 Hz is presented to the right ear and a pure tone of 410 Hz is presented simultaneously to the left ear, an amplitude modulated standing wave of 10 Hz, the difference between the two tones, is experienced as the two waveforms mesh in and out of phase within the superior olivary nuclei. This binaural beat is not heard in the ordinary sense of the word (the human range of hearing is from 20–20,000 Hz). It is perceived as an auditory beat and theoretically can be used to entrain specific neural rhythms through the frequency-following response (FFR)—the tendency for cortical potentials to entrain to or resonate at the frequency of an external stimulus. Thus, it is theoretically possible to utilize a specific binaural beat frequency as a consciousness-management technique to entrain a specific cortical rhythm.

Binaural beats are heard at low frequencies (< 30 Hz) that are characteristic of the EEG spectrum. Many people who use binaural beats report altered states of consciousness, and a number of research studies have shown that changes in consciousness associated with binaural beats do actually occur. Depending on the listener, some people find binaural beats either relaxing or stimulating, depending also on the frequency of the binaural-beat stimulation.

Binaural beats in the Delta (1 to 4 Hz) and Theta (4 to 8 Hz) ranges are associated with reports of more relaxed, meditative, and creative states, and even aid sleep. Binaural beats in the Alpha frequencies (8 to 12 Hz) have increased Alpha brain waves, and binaural beats in the Beta frequencies (typically 16 to 24 Hz) have been associated with reports of increased concentration or alertness and wakefulness.

The device I selected for my personal journey was the Photosonix Nova Pro. This "mind machine" includes a pair of white LED glasses and stereo headphones that work by generating gentle flickering lights and pulsing binaural sounds that are tuned to help one reach various states of consciousness. My first session using the device was absolutely incredible. Call me a pessimist, but I had little expectation that a $400 device could catapult me from one reality to the next. I absolutely could not have predicted what would soon unfold.

After selecting the program, putting on the headphones and glasses, closing my eyes, and lying back, the swirling lights and binaural beats immediately took me aback. It was a fantastic rush of color, sound, and feelings. Red, blue, green, yellow. Where was I? Was this real? What the hell was going on? I saw, heard, and felt images from my childhood. I felt the wind on my face from my first bicycle ride. I saw the first girl I kissed in third grade. I smelled my mother's pot roast simmering on the stove. Wow! Was that the cave at the edge of my parent's property in Connecticut that I spent many a day exploring? These brief experiences were as real as they had been when I first lived them so many years ago. It was like a dream—only vastly more realistic, and completely enveloping.

Faster and faster the visuals came to me. The speed and intensity was explosive. There was no control over my journey—I was being pulled and pushed into reliving these experiences whether I wanted to or not. At some point, I fell asleep, and when I awoke it was morning. The device was neatly laid on the night table next to my bed. Did I put it there? My normally OCD nature seemingly had vanished, as I did not obsess upon that question. What was immediately evident to me was that I felt a sense of incredible euphoria. I felt energized. Renewed. Extraordinary. For the next few days I was on cloud nine. Nothing could bring me down. Had I discovered the "Holy Grail?" Was this relatively simple system the key to exploring my inner space?

Although I realize that my experience may not be typical, I am a true believer. Technology to the rescue! Unfortunately, due to a recent move, and the ensuing chaos that followed, all of my fun stuff was temporarily lost in the shuffle. Note to self—in the future be sure and label boxes! As a result, I have been unable to explore my inner realms since. It has been on my mind for months, and I've mounted many unsuccessful searches for my mind machine.

Update: Thankfully, while cleaning the attic a few weeks ago in anticipation of a neighborhood garage sale, I came across a box that had not been opened. Could it be? WOOHOO! I found it! You can be sure I will be embarking on many, many more explorations of the mind soon!

■ ■ ■ ■ ■ ■ ■ ■ ■ ■ ■

Entrainment in the brain, when it comes to memory, just got a boost in a new study. *USA Today* reported on January 27, 2009, that researchers at the University of California-Irvine have found the possible source of "super-memory," revealed in the MRIs of a woman named Jill Price. Price's brain scans revealed two areas of the brain, the caudate nuclei and the temporal lobe, that are linked to the formation and storage of memory. The research team noted that these two parts of the brain may be working in synch in a way never before examined, to create "detailed recall" of memory entrained in the brain that could one day be retrieved as automatically as brushing one's teeth. "What we are looking at is a new chapter in the book on memories and the brain," stated neuroscientist and researcher Larry Cahill.

But sound is not the only way to use good vibrations for health and enhanced overall well-being. Bio-resonance uses electric, magnetic, or electromagnetic fields to cure disease. Described as an offshoot of "electro-acupuncture," bio-resonance involves reactivating the natural resonance of human cells by utilizing a machine that employs magnetic mats to pulse electromagnetic energy into the affected areas of the body.

Even healing cancer with electrical frequencies is not a new concept, thanks to the work of Royal Raymond Rife in the early 20th century. Rife can be credited with designing several cutting-edge medical devices, including the incredibly complex Universal Microscope in 1933, which had nearly 6,000 different parts, and was capable of magnifying objects 60,000 times their normal size. This microscope allowed Rife to view living viruses, and until quite recently, was the only piece of equipment that was capable of doing so.

Royal Raymond Rife was a brilliant scientist. He studied at Johns Hopkins, then went on to develop technology that is still commonly used today in the fields of optics, electronics, radiochemistry, biochemistry, ballistics, and aviation. Although his techniques were often controversial, he focused on refining his method of destroying tiny killer viruses. He used the same principle to kill them that made them visible in the first place: resonance.

By increasing the intensity of a frequency that resonated naturally with these microbes, Rife increased their natural oscillations until they distorted and disintegrated from structural stresses. Rife called this frequency "the mortal oscillatory rate," or "MOR," and it did no harm whatsoever to the surrounding tissues.

Today's Rife instruments use harmonics of the frequencies shown on the display screen. The wavelength of the actual frequency shown (770 Hz, 880 Hz, and so on) is too long to do the job.

This principle can be illustrated by using an intense musical note to shatter a wine glass: the molecules of the glass are already oscillating at some harmonic (multiple) of that musical note; they are in resonance with it. Because everything else has a different resonant frequency, nothing but the glass is destroyed. There are literally hundreds of trillions of different resonant frequencies, and every species and molecule has its very own.

Though many of Rife's inventions did not succeed, his ideas were certainly ahead of their time, and are now being reexamined by a new breed of holistic researchers eager to use sound and EMF to eradicate cancer cells.

Vibrational Therapy involves the use of resonance and vibration to stimulate the five senses and restore balance. This involves the belief that "like attracts like" and that when a certain note on a harp is struck, anything else that vibrates on that very same note will be in resonance with it. Tune the body up, tune up the life. By consciously stimulating the five senses with things such as color, light, aroma, food, art, and touch, this therapy posits that the body can then be healed of trauma and pain. Other therapies involve laying on "tactile sound tables" that vibrate and send sound and music waves into the body of the patient, zoning you out and creating a slightly altered state of consciousness to encourage healing. Remember our previous comment regarding the vibrating beds found in some motels back in the1970s and early 80s? Just imagine—the vibrational fun may in fact be your ticket to resonance and wholeness. So drop in those quarters and lay back!

Light is also widely used to support healing. Anyone who suffers from Seasonal Affective Disorder (SAD) or the winter blues can attest to the power of light to influence one's moods. Light therapy involves exposure to bright artificial light of a specific wavelength that brings about similar benefits to natural sunlight (the best healer of all!). Using light boxes that mimic outdoor light, the patient's circadian rhythms are altered and corrected, and the body's natural melatonin is suppressed to bring about biochemical changes to the brain.

Phototherapy, consistent exposure to daylight, or the wavelengths of natural light via a full-spectrum lamp, can bring about healing of more than just depression. Targeted wavelengths of light can be used to heal acne, psoriasis, eczema, sleep disorders, and even jet lag. Those with infants suffering from jaundice likely know that exposure to light can heal that affliction as well. Monochromatic infrared light that has a specific wavelength of 890 nanometer waveband is used to heal wounds and improve ulcerous conditions, even improving blood flow in patients with diabetes.

Heliotherapy involves the use of tanning to treat a variety of conditions. Exposure to light in the UVA/UVB range, either by direct sunlight or the use of tanning beds, improves skin conditions and are often prescribed by doctors and dermatologists. Light therapy in general can be described as a mood-altering therapy, and can have negative effects if abused or used too much. This especially applies to the use of tanning beds, which seem to release endorphins that help with depression and mood disorders, but again, too much of a good thing can cause mania, extreme anxiety, and an obviously over-tanned, leathery look very similar to the old lady in the movie *There's Something About Mary.* So, go to the light…but, go easy!

The use of LEDs or light-emitting diodes have been shown to grow exposed cells 150 percent to 200 percent faster than normal. The light arrays from the LED "wash" seem to speed up healing processes by increasing the energy level within the cell. In an article titled "Healing With Light Moves Beyond Fiction" for *HealthLink*, Dr. Harry T. Whelan, professor of neurology, pediatrics, and hyperbaric medicine at the Medical College of Wisconsin, states "the potential is quite endless." He describes the history of medicine as being too focused on poisons and knives—a.k.a. drugs and surgeries—and sees the possibilities of using light and LED light specifically to enhance cells normal biochemistry. "I consider that to be a paradigm shift in the entire approach to medicine that has the potential, therefore, to alter all kinds of disease processes, particularly any in which there's an energy crisis for the tissue."

Clinical studies using LEDs to treat cancer patients after bone marrow replacement have shown significant success in diminishing the painful side effects of mucositis, which often accompanies the transplant surgery. New trials are underway with young patients undergoing transplants. LED efficacy is of such interest that even the Food and Drug Administration is collaborating with Whelan on research into the positive uses of his handheld light-emitting diode arrays.

The article states that while not all cells will react in the same way to the LED, Dr. Whelan and fellow researchers are working on LED therapy for organ and tissue regeneration, stroke, brain tumors, spinal cord injuries, and Parkinson's disease. Whelan feels that the use of near-infrared light could mean the difference between "a small stroke and a large stroke."

One particular energy healer, Julie Motz, believes that "matter as highly organized as human tissue would not only give off distinctive and identifiable wave patterns, but also be able to receive and identify them." She equates this with human emotion, as Cynthia Logan writes in "Energy Medicine in the Operating Room" from *Forbidden Science.* Motz, author of the book *Hands of Life,* is one of the first nontraditional healers to work alongside surgeons at major hospitals, including Stanford University Hospital in California. She has lectured widely at medical schools, discussing her belief that when she touches a patient, their bodily energy begins to align itself vibrationally with hers, and the resulting meridians she is touching will then shift. She also believes that when she touches a patient with a loving or healing intent, that point of contact becomes a magnet for ambient energy in the room, entering the patient's body through her fingertips. This may suggest that she is actually attracting a flood of neutrinos that interact with other subatomic particles inside the body and thus "alter the energy flow."

Those who heal with touch may indeed be manipulating the life energy of the patient, balancing negative frequencies and aligning cellular structure back to a normal state. Though this modality is in no way scientific, millions of people swear by the effects of healing touch and the shifts in their vibratory state that lead to feeling better physically, mentally, and spiritually.

One form of touch therapy that plays upon the body's subtle energies involves tapping specific points along the meridians also utilized in acupuncture. Emotional Freedom Technique (EFT) is a psychotherapeutic alternative modality that suggests that when one taps these meridian points while thinking of a negative emotion, it then restores the body to balance by providing a "distraction" from the negative emotion that becomes embedded as a new association. Some psychologists suggest this is nothing more than a glorified way to play up the importance of distraction from negative thought used in cognitive therapy, but those who work with EFT insist it can do wonders and perform miracles.

EFT was created in the mid-1990s by Gary Craig, who based his modality on the prior work of Roger Callahan's Thought Field Therapy (TFT). Because EFT is still quite new, no major long-term studies exist to support or denounce it. EFT differs from TFT in that it uses the same sequence of tapping points for a variety of problems, where as TFT is very specifically matched to the problem and must be predetermined using applied kinesiology.

The whole idea behind tapping your way to balance rests on the concept that negative emotions or disturbing memories are originally caused by disturbances in the body's energy field. Thus, by tapping on the meridians while at the same time thinking the negative thoughts, one can alter one's own body's energy field back to a state of equilibrium. Those who support EFT say it can cure depression, anxiety, addictions, and phobias.

As with light, color can likewise provide therapeutic benefits. Each color has a different light frequency, and as many people who have their favorite hue can attest to, color can affect mood—sometimes in very significant ways. Using color frequencies to match the desired mental or physical healing outcome seems natural, especially because we are constantly exposed to different colors throughout our day, usually with little or no knowledge of how those colors influence our brain chemistry. The resonant frequency of red, for example, creates an entirely different mood than that of a deep blue. Shocking pink vibrates at a different rate than cool forest green. Just as color pleases or displeases the eye, those who believe in color therapy contest that it also pleases or displeases the brain, the mind, the body, and the spirit.

Even thought. We often talk of having dark thoughts or light thoughts. Do thoughts have their own vibration? That we will explore in the next few chapters, but it may not be too "out there" to posit that thoughts can not only give off their own vibration, but also in turn be affected by sound, light, and other thoughts. In fact, the work of Dr. Masaru Emoto, author of *The Message From Water* and *The Hidden Messages in Water*, shows the amazing results of his experiments using words to affect the shapes of water crystals. Positive, loving words create beautiful, symmetrical crystal shapes. Violent, negative words do the opposite, proving that sound is not even needed to have a resonant reaction on an object. The water was reacting to a word shown to it, as if the water was somehow picking up on the "thought vibe" and not a specific sound frequency.

President Emeritus of the International Water for Life Foundation, Emoto has been criticized by skeptics and his work dubbed pseudoscience, but he and other researchers working with water claim that prayer, spoken words, music, and they even words written on paper can result in either beautiful or disturbing crystals, and have provided hundreds of photographs from experiments that have continued to this day.

Though often harshly criticized for his lack of scientific methodology and the potential for human error, Emoto's theory that water can be affected by directed emotion is actually mirrored in earlier studies involving plants reacting to positive and negative verbiage. Mainstream science, mainly in the arena of medicine, might benefit from giving Emoto the benefit of the doubt regarding his claim that external influences can change the shape of something as sensitive as water. After all, remember that the human body is primarily composed of water, and we all know how it feels to be yelled at, hated, and disgraced.

Bad vibes.

Aside from helping to achieve optimal health, radio waves are being used to do something every single one of us can benefit from—fight the signs of aging. A new technology called CRF, for capacitive radiofrequency, promises to make the facelifts of old obsolete. CRF works by delivering concentrated radio waves to the face to tighten sagging skin, lift sagging eyelids, and improve the tone of facial muscles that cause droopy jowls, and it involves nothing more than moving a wand-type instrument over the skin for a process that takes about an hour. There are no scalpels or stitches, and recovery time is nil. You can do it on your lunch break!

The basic idea is that the wand carries CRF into the deepest layers of the dermis, or skin, and heats the collagen layers underneath the skin. The skin is smoothed and tightened, and the only sensation is that of hot and cold on the skin as the wand's tip does its thing. Non-invasive cosmetic procedures such as this are becoming commonplace as cosmetic surgeons discover the power of radio and light waves to undo years of abuse to the skin.

Sound...light...thought. Everything has a frequency, and thus a resonance.

7

The Reality Machine: The Brain as Perceiver and Receiver

On the contrary, we have seen that there is considerable support at top scientific levels for the notion of the brain as a receiver that my be temporarily retuned by hallucinogens to pick up frequencies that normally fall below the threshold of our senses.

—Graham Hancock, *Supernatural*

We are all familiar with the old axiom of "which came first, the chicken or the egg?" Well, is the brain the originator of what we see, hear, feel, smell, and taste? Is our personal gray matter responsible for the creative and constructive design of our perception of reality—both the seen and unseen?

Or is our "wetware" nothing more than a receiver; a type of radio tuner that picks up broadcasts from out in the aether, then processes and accepts them as real, solid, certain, and sure?

This question continues to intrigue researchers of brain and consciousness theory who are anxious to identify the roles each plays, or does not play, in our individual and collective experiences of reality. In a 1997 article titled "Radio Head: The Brain Has Its Own FM Receiver," Alison Motluk discusses how changing frequencies of neurons allow the brain to pick up the information sent by our five senses in the same manner as an FM radio picks up specific radio station broadcasts.

Pointing to research by Ehud Ahissar of the Weizmann Institute of Science, Motluck describes how constant oscillations in the neurons of a monkey's cortex may play a significant role in sensory perception as signals such as touch, taste, or smell pass from the nerve endings, in the form of electrical pulses, through the thalamus, and on to the processing area of the cortex. This oscillation factor has also been studied in rats with similar findings.

Cutting-edge brain research promises to further the understanding of the links between the brain and consciousness, as well as how the two appear to operate autonomously. Zack Lynch, executive director of the Neurotechnology Industry Organization, believes that we are on the verge of a massive new revolution in brain science. "Just as information technology has affected everything from the way we do business to human communications, it will be the science of the brain that drives the fundamental changes of the future," Lynch told reporter Tim Jarvis in a November 2008 article for O titled "The Brain Age." Jarvis documents the many predictions on how the new science of the brain will change our lives, including:

▶ Neurolongevity—cures for diseases of the aging brain.

▶ Neuroentertainment—gaming systems that read brainwaves, and video games in real time of which the player can direct the outcome.

▶ Neuroeducation—sculpting teaching materials for brain-specific functions and tailored teaching materials for different learning types.

▶ Neurofitness—drugs and devices designed to stimulate the brain to augment physical performance and mobility.

▶ Neurospirituality—tools such as fMRI (functional magnetic resonance imaging) to deeply access meditative/spiritual brain states.

The idea is that one day, everything from shopping to choosing a mate will change when we begin to unlock the mysteries of neuroscience. One neuromarketing company, FKF Applied Research, uses the fMRI technology, which measures neural activity, to scan consumers' brains as they respond to different advertising images and brands. fMRI has even been used to document the process someone goes through when they fall in love; from the first passionate stage of shared lust to the later more emotionally attached stage of true love.

Brain scans are also being used in courts of law to defend alleged criminals. Jarvis stated that in 2005 the Supreme Court struck down the death penalty for anyone under 18, as brain scans and research have shown that the brain was still developing during that life stage. Neurological evidence is often used in the courtroom.

Even as we come to rely more and more on our brainpower to drive our world, we have to admit that much of what we perceive as "our world" may not actually be coming from the brain and its neurons at all. Processed through it, received into it, perhaps. But not coming from it. The brain might just be receiving information from somewhere else altogether.

In an extremely intriguing experiment conducted by a team from the University of Copenhagen in early 2008, the question of what, and where, "awareness" is challenged. Researchers took a group of 11 healthy people and focused a beam of magnetism directly on their visual cortex, at the back of the brain, temporarily blinding them. But before they did, they showed all 11 test subjects three lights in a row with buttons beneath each light. The subjects were asked to push the button *next to* the center light each time they saw it come on. Some trials were tricky, with researchers switching off and on lights just as the subjects were reaching to press the right button. Other subjects got the blinding zap of magnetism just as the light was being switched. Yet, the subjects were still able to almost instantaneously detect the correct button to push, suggesting that the unconscious mind acts of its own accord without the total awareness of the active, conscious mind.

Other experiments, documented in the October 2008 *Discover Magazine* article "Is There an Inner Zombie Controlling Your Brain" point to the idea that we do not always have to be consciously self-aware to think, act, and react. Reporter Carl Zimmer tells us that researchers have discovered that we are deeply influenced by perceptions, thoughts, feelings, and desires about which we have no awareness. "Their research raised the disturbing possibility that much of what we think and do is thought and done by an unconscious part of the brain—an inner zombie."

Another fascinating experiment had people react whenever they saw an image of money on a computer screen. Brain scans showed that even when the images raced by, people were able to react, suggesting that the reward-judging part of the brain, the ventral palladium, activated when the people were both consciously and unconsciously seeing the images go by. Other researchers suggest that there are some things that the brain requires full consciousness to do, as in solve word puzzles or complex problems that the unconscious could help process, but not complete. Maybe the inner zombie is our friend in disguise, freeing the conscious mind to focus on more interesting things, such as giving us the gifts of free will and awareness. So much for being of two minds!

Even when it comes to the storage of memories, controversy continues as to the true function of the brain. Current theories posit that memory is not just stored in the brain, but in consciousness as well. The idea is that the brain may not be a good enough "storage unit" to hold all of the information that it is required to process. Studies by Simon Berkovich, professor of engineering and applied science at George Washington University, propose that the brain is more like an accessing unit, with the actual storage place of information, and thus, memory, being somewhere else.

In his paper "On the Information Processing Capabilities of the Brain: Shifting the Paradigm" for the Department of Electrical Engineering and Computer Science at The George Washington University, Berkovich wrote, "However, trying to understand the brain by incremental adjustments of the existing paradigms may be condemned to Sisyphus labor." Perhaps an entire change in the paradigm of how we see the brain and what it does is needed. Berkovich suggests we begin with the holographic mechanism of information processing in the brain by Karl Pribram and the interpretation of quantum mechanics by David Bohm to create an integrated view on "the transcendental phenomena of Nature."

Berkovich was referring to the research of Karl Pribram into the holographic nature of the human brain. Pribram, a Stanford University neurophysiologist, believed that holography could explain the brain's ability to store so many memories in such a small space. In his seminal book *The Holographic Universe*, Michael Talbott explores the idea, that like the universe, the brain may operate as a hologram, and thus "holograms possess a fantastic capacity for information storage. By changing the angle at which the two lasers strike a piece of photographic film, it is possible to record many different images on the same surface."

Using Pribram's work into the holographic theory, Talbott continues to say that recalling and forgetting memory can be explained by the specific angle of the lasers striking the film. "When we are unable to recall something, this may be the equivalent to shining various beams on a piece of multiple-image film, but failing to find the right angle to call up the image/memory for which we are searching."

Pribram's work with rats convinced him that memory was stored not in a specific part of the brain, but all over it. He surgically removed the portions of the brain thought to store memory, then tested the rats in a maze. Pribram discovered that certain cognitive abilities of the rats were maintained, and they were able to remember their way around.

Surprisingly enough, this happened no matter what part of the brain was removed. Even human patients who had certain parts of their brains removed could still retain specific memory functioning. Amazingly, removing the temporal lobe led to no loss of memory! Pribram was sure that memory was not localized, but evenly distributed throughout the entire brain.

Or was it?

Intriguingly, the holographic model of the brain suggests that, similar to virtual reality, the "mind/body ultimately cannot distinguish between the neural holograms the brain uses to experience reality and the ones it conjures up while imaging reality." It seems that the only one doing the imagining limits the power of the imagination. During the dreaming stage, even dreams can be perceived as a type of reality, with the actual body reacting to sensations and images even as it lies still in a bed.

But we may have to take that holographic theory one step further. We must, as many suggest, ask the question of where holographic information can be stored. One suggested paradigm states that the main information processing takes place outside of the brain. "The role of the material formations of the brain is to provide an access to these facilities. With the arrangement of accessing to the information outside of the brain the inscrutable properties of human memory—unlimited storage capacity and reliability—

becomes immediately clarified." The brain therefore is expected to be more a source of processing information from this outside storage facility.

In another paper, "A Note on Science and NDE: A Scientific Model Why Memory a.k.a. Consciousness Cannot Reside Solely in the Brain," Berkovich talks about similarities with our DNA. DNA, he suggests, might be more of an "information marker," while the actual information that dictates how our body will look and function is stored elsewhere. He likens it to a card catalog system in a library. The brain acts in this way, as part of the informational infrastructure of the physical reality/world. Or think of logging on to the Net. Could the brain be just one of many computers in a vast and linked network of shared information? "In other words," he states, "the human brain is not a stand-alone computer but rather a terminal at the 'Internet of the physical universe.'"

The suggestion that consciousness, and even the ability to store memory, may reside outside the brain itself is not a new one, especially to the metaphysical community, which has long believed that consciousness was supreme to the more human and mundane activities of the brain. Yet the two are interactive, and one might wonder if it would be a correct analogy to look at the brain like the computer this book is being written on. The authors represent consciousness, and their Mac computers are the brains that receive their talent, wisdom, and knowledge, and process it into the reality of a published book.

Consciousness could be thought of as the higher arena of knowledge, because in many ways, it is just too easy to fool the brain into thinking something is real. Think of virtual reality. For anyone who has been on the *Back to the Future* ride at Universal Studios, the brain's perceptions of the images and movements of the car cause you to hurtle to the side, scream in fear, and, in Marie's case, need an extra two doses of Dramamine, even though you know you are just on a ride. Even hypnosis can affect the brain's ability to perceive reality and influence the processes of the body thought to be from the subconscious, such as sneezing, blood flow rates, and nearsightedness! A placebo acts in the same way, tricking the mind and the body into thinking a healing dose has been delivered.

Sometimes the mind knows better, but a part of it still reacts, as if what it is seeing is real. Virtual reality can be thought of as a possible reality based upon the processing of information. Without that information, virtual reality does not exist. Objective reality, on the other hand, exists as a constant, with or without the influence of the outer processing of information. It is self-contained, yet the brain will perceive each type of reality as being real at the time it is being experienced.

The virtual reality world does not exist independently. It requires someone to program it, and someone to observe it with a helmet, computer, or on a nasty vomit-inducing ride at a theme park. It stops being perceived when the programming stops, or the perceiver takes off the helmet or falls off the ride. Are we living in virtual reality, the illusion of "Maya" Buddha spoke of? A holographic reflection of the more objective reality operating just beneath the surface?

Just watch the *Matrix* movies to get an idea of what this might be like. Are we caught in the Matrix, with no concept or idea that something else might be real beyond what we know? Could this explain why some people perceive the paranormal, and others do not? Would it depend entirely on who took which pill?

Though we have had a general scientific understanding of which part of the brain was responsible for certain functions and how the regions work together to create perception, knowledge, speech, and action, we still do not entirely know everything about the stuff between our ears. Despite all of the advances in neurological research, our brains are still one of the greatest mysteries.

Yet one of the most basic facts of the field of neuroscience is that nerve cells in the brain that fire together, wire together, meaning that once you do something there is a group of neurons that form a network to respond to what you are doing. If you only do it once, that network vanishes, but if you do it again and again, a "track" is carved in the brain as fine, stringy dendrites spread out like a web and connect with other dendrites, creating a stronger connection in the neural pathways. Until you make that new action a regular part of the brain's neural track, that new action may just disappear and leave no record. We learn this way.

It all comes down to neural connections, or neuroplasticity, which also drive memory, and even in someone with only half a brain (we mean literally here, folks), these functions can be spread out enough over the pathways of the brain to make up for the lost half. The brain is an amazing thing, but it can limit us, as when we fail to make the strong neural connections associated with seeing something new that we do not understand, or understanding something we have never before seen—like a ghost. Every new experience causes chemical changes within the brain, and when those experiences repeat themselves, they become a part of our general perception of life around us.

The "plasticity" of our neurological system allows us to adopt new ideas, adapt to new experiences, create and retain memories, and possibly even "see" things we didn't see before, such as the pink tuxedo we had custom-made, thinking it the only one on earth, only to find pink tuxedoes are everywhere. We just never made the neural connections before. Now that we have, our plastic brain has permitted us the joys of seeing an abundance of pink tuxedoes. Not!

Sometimes, the greatest breakthroughs in brain science come from those who have experienced firsthand when the brain does not work well. Strokes, aneurysms, and brain injuries often lead to amazing new ideas about the brain. One perfect example happened, ironically, to a brain scientist named Jill Bolte Taylor, PhD.

Taylor documents her own journey into the inner workings of the brain in her book *My Stroke of Insight: A Brain Scientist's Personal Journey*. In 1996, at the age of 37, Taylor, a Harvard-educated brain scientist, suffered a massive stroke as a blood vessel on the left side of her head exploded. Her book discusses her work as a neuroanatomist and how she used her vast knowledge to literally observe her own mind reacting to the stroke, even as she was becoming unable to walk, talk, or function. She struggled to maintain cognizance as her ability to read, write, and solve basic problems evaporated.

What Taylor observed during the downward spiral of the stroke's effects was that the damaged side of the brain, the literal and rational left side, was shut down to the point that her right brain was given a chance to express itself. She experienced euphoric senses of well-being and peace, and even a sort of spiritual "nirvana," as her left brain comprehended her fate and helped her seek help before the damage was irreversible. As she progressed, she began to understand on a deeper level how the two sides of the brain worked to create her reality. "After a childhood of information processing through sensory, visual, and pattern association strategies, the tapestry of my knowledge was all intimately inter-linked."

Despite being unable to form words, Taylor felt "an enveloping sense of being at one with the universe." She had to force herself to comprehend the damage to her left brain, though, and pay attention to what was happening to her so she could find the physical strength, and the mental ability, to call for help. She had a damaged brain, but somewhere a door opened to a higher sense of herself and her place in the universe. She sensed what might arguably be considered the most important of all—the importance of living in the present moment. In the book, she even shares some of the wisdom she used to achieve a sense of inner peace by calming the monkey mind and staying in the now. "My left mind thinks of me as a fragile individual capable of losing my life," she shares. Her right mind focused instead on feelings of being at one with all, of an eternality. She was fully aware that recovery would most likely return her to her usual three-dimensional perception of the world, but the memory of the euphoric sense of unity would stay with her in the form of gratitude.

Taylor's entire journey to recovery has led her to numerous TV appearances, including *Oprah*, where she emphasizes the importance of allowing the right brain to occasionally step forward and offer its gifts of peace and insight, even as our left brains threaten to drown us in chatter and trivia. Her experience of a sort of omniscient state of being during the stroke helped her come out of the experience with a newfound sense of her own connection to spirituality. Interestingly, she began working on a virtual reality system to help other stroke survivors use "visually directed intention" to neurologically rehabilitate themselves.

For those who are more driven by the right brain, the future looks so bright, they may have to wear shades. Wow, that was a total flashback to the 1980s—and the band Timbuk 3. Daniel Pink, former Al Gore speechwriter and author of *A Whole New Mind: Why Right-Brainers Will Rule the Future*, writes extensively about how right-brain aptitudes complimented by left-brain thinking result in "a whole new mind." The right brain, however, will be playing a much more important role in our future, simply because the faculties of the left brain, including linear thinking and intellectualism, may be falling in power, so to speak, to the characteristics of the right brain, including empathy, inventiveness, and big-picture thinking. With the world in the shape it's in, Pink and others believe that the future will be driven by right-brain talents and abilities much more so than in the past, when having a left-brain job or attitude served the public well. "The right brain is finally being taken seriously," Pink comments, pointing to the work of brain researchers like Taylor, who are learning more about the powerful and profound roles the right brain will have in a job market once driven by spreadsheets and statistics.

Pink points to "design" as one of the right-brain abilities important to future success. Design is the ability to create something that has significance as well as usefulness. He gives examples of how design is being used in hospital settings to aid healing and save lives. Pink also discusses "symphony," which is the ability, again of the right brain, "to see the big picture, connect the dots, combine disparate things into something new." These skills are going to be critical to our future as we watch more and more left-brain skills outsourced or replaced by computers and robotics. Even empathy is seen as a critical force of the future as we strive to reach out to the world and make it a better place and pursue economic well-being.

At last, the right brain is getting its day in court. As Pink summarizes, "The kingdom changes based on who's holding the keys. In our world now, those with right-brain skills will flourish." In no way does this mean that left-brainers such as computer programmers are going to be forced to look for work at a fast food joint, but it does mean that those programmers will have to develop more people skills and treat different parts of their business in a "symphonic" way. Oh yes, the last right-brain skill of the future was being able to tell stories, and create stories about our lives and build connection through those stories. This is good news for those of us who have chosen writing as a profession. Maybe now we will make some good money.

Having a violent brain injury similar to Taylors, though, is not the only way to recognize the understanding that there is more to the brain than we think—no pun intended. This realization can happen during a spiritual awakening, but also through a simple "aha" moment that points out to us how our past programming of thoughts and behaviors often leads to our future perception of reality. All of human perception begins in the brain's center, where sights, sounds, and tastes are passed, as sensory information, along the brain highway from the thalamus to the neocortex, where the information is processed as "reality." But reality is not made up of just what we see, hear, taste, feel, or smell in an objective sense, because our own "perceptions of our perceptions" help shape the way we continue to see and experience the world. In a sense, just as the metaphysicians and New Agers tell us, we really may be creating our reality as we go along.

Again, as if we are of two minds, we have the objective reality that tells us all that a tree is a tree, but also the subjective reality that tells one of us that we can communicate with the dead through latent psychic ability, and another that we can see auras around living things. Subjective reality may tell another person that she cannot sing, resulting in a screechy voice that closely resembles a small rodent getting its tail caught in a meat grinder, when in fact she has perfect tone and pitch. The subjective nature of past programming, perhaps parents telling her to "shut up" or a friend saying "you can't sing that song very well" colors her own belief, thus reprogramming her "singing" brain into one that cannot carry a tune to save her life.

In a healthy, functioning person, both realities work together to create a brain that recognizes what is, but also imagines what can be. Dysfunction occurs when one remains captive to either the subjective or the objective, with no middle ground.

The question becomes, is one reality more real than the other? To answer this question, we need only look at our own lives. What we experience in our left brain is just as real as what we experience from the right brain's influence, even if we tend to give more credence to one over the other. What we see objectively can hold just as much truth as something we experience subjectively, as long as we recognize whether that truth is a personal one or a collective one.

The brain takes in sensory stimuli through receptive fields—regions of space where the presence of stimuli alters the firing of sensory neurons. Our ability to hear comes from the auditory system's receptive fields of auditory space or frequencies. Our visual acuity comes from the receptive fields of volumes in visual space, identified as the section of the retina where incoming light alters the neuron's firing. And when we touch or feel something, it is the receptive fields associated with our somatosensory system at work on our skin and in our internal organs.

But what about other types of sensory stimuli that are hitting the brain other than the five senses? Extra-sensory stimuli?

In a speech before a distinguished audience of scientists at the University of Utrecht, Nobel Prize Winner Sir John Eccles stated: "The brain is only a useful instrument to serve the mind. This doesn't mean to underestimate the brain. The computer is a child's toy in comparison. The point is that the mind is superior to the brain. This is essential to know for the understanding of life."

By this point, you may be wondering, is any reality truly real? Do external signals—sound, resonance, or vibration—somehow manifest reality within the inner sanctum of our brains? Perhaps the answer is much more obvious. What if our conscious mind was an electromagnetic field?

According to the Daily University Science News Website, Professor Johnjoe McFadden believes our conscious mind could be an electromagnetic field. His theory would solve many previously intractable problems of consciousness and could have profound implications for our concepts of mind, free will, spirituality, the design of artificial intelligence, and even life and death. Most people consider "mind" to be all the conscious things that we are aware of. But much, if not most mental activity goes on without awareness. Actions such as walking, changing gear in your car, or peddling a bicycle can become as automatic as breathing. We tend to do things on automatic, in a bit of a zombie state, often without thinking. It sometimes takes an event, like a car crash, to wake us back into that present conscious awareness.

The good professor presents some intriguing ideas! He has formulated a theory known as the "Cemi Theory" which is the acronym for Consciousness Magnetic Field Theory. Consciousness makes us human. It encompasses such things as language, creativity, emotions, spirituality, logical deduction, mental arithmetic, and our sense of fairness, truth, and ethics. But what is consciousness made of? What Professor McFadden realized was that every time a nerve fires, the electrical activity sends a signal to the brain's electromagnetic (EM) field. But unlike solitary nerve signals, information that reaches the brain's EM field is automatically bound together with all the other signals in the brain. The brain's EM field does the binding that is characteristic of consciousness.

Perhaps the brain's EM field is consciousness. Perhaps this field does more than just take in information; rather, it also influences behavior and action, and governs which neurons will fire or not fire, resulting in the manifestation of our conscious will in the physical realm. This may not be as far-fetched as you might initially think. McFadden's concept actually has a precedent, and he states that this concept of information encoded as an electromagnetic field is actually a very familiar one, and that we are always encoding information from the images and sounds in EM fields that we transmit to our TV and radio sets.

The brain may be both transmitter and receiver of its own electromagnetic signals in a feedback loop that generates the conscious EM field as a kind of "informational sink." This informational transfer, through the conscious EM field, might have many advantages over neuronal computing in the rapid integrating and processing of information distributed in different parts of the brain. The EM field might also provide an additional level of computation that is wave-mechanical, rather than digital; one that allows for free will and the very human ability to make decisions.

On McFadden's Website (*www.surrey.ac.uk/qe/*) he has attempted to provide answers to several intriguing questions. He does not believe that Cemi Theory accounts for telepathy, stating that the EM field outside of the head is too weak and that another brain most likely could not detect it. Nor does he see any connections with Cemi Theory and ghosts, stating that if ghosts were made up of EM fields, they would then be very easy to detect. We should be able to locate the source of the field they create, which results in charged molecules, but we cannot.

He does believe that our heads act as an effective cage of sorts that screens out most of the external electromagnetic fields in our environment. MRIs, he states, can penetrate the head, but do not change the firing patters of neurons. The same can be said for mobile phones and the high-frequency fields they give off, which do go through the head, but most likely do not interact with lower frequencies of brainwaves.

When asked the intriguing question of whether or not the Cemi field can survive after death, McFadden answers, "My hypothesis is that consciousness is the experience of information, from the inside. There is a postulate in physics that information is neither created or destroyed—the conservation of information 'law.'" If this law is proven to be true, McFadden feels it might suggest that "awareness [associated with that information]—in some form— might survive death."

Besides McFadden, there are several researchers engaged in the study of the brain and consciousness, specifically in regards to localized EM fields. Certainly, one of most intriguing is Dr. Michael Persinger, whom we discussed earlier. A neuropsychologist at Canada's Laurentian University in Sudbury, Ontario, Dr. Persinger believes that there is a definite link between EM fields and the brain's ability to experience religious epiphany, spiritual awakening, or even the "sensed presence," which may be an explanatory agent for ghosts, aliens, and other "paranormal" phenomena. Persinger has even created a device that has been affectionately nicknamed "The God Helmet," which looks like a dorky motorcycle helmet and offers its users a unique glimpse inside themselves. The helmet is described as a device that generates weak electromagnetic fields and focuses them on particular regions of the brain's surface. The helmet's modus operandi sounds eerily familiar to something that we all take for granted and use daily—the cell phone! Just think— your last alien abduction may have actually been in your head, and caused by your cell phone!

Persinger's team has trained their device on the temporal lobes of hundreds of people for several decades, inducing in most of them the experience of a sensed presence—a feeling that someone (or a spirit) is in the room—or of a profound state of unity or cosmic bliss that reveals a universal truth. Using three-minute bursts of stimulation, subjects were asked to translate the cosmic feelings into their own worldview or religious belief system, as say, God, Buddha, or a benevolent presence—The Source.

Persinger believes that religious experience and belief in God are merely the results of electrical anomalies in the human brain. Visions and beliefs in religious entities can, according to him, be triggered by such neural stimulation. Some of Persinger's research involved putting subjects into a dimly lit room, telling them they might experience some strange phenomena, then using infrasound to create a spooky atmosphere. By altering the lighting and creating the sound waves, some subjects did indeed report feeling a presence or entity or hearing voices. Just by adding the infrasound alone Persinger was able to create the perceptions of supernatural events. But perhaps we need to also ask if the disclosure to the subjects may have influenced their experiences. Can the suggestion that something might happen make it happen? Will you see it if you believe it, to paraphrase the title of a best-seller by Dr. Wayne Dyer?

Maybe there is a scientific basis to that concept after all.

An October 2008 *Newsweek* article titled "Why We Believe" suggests that belief in the paranormal can be ascribed to normal brain activity carried to an extreme. Sharon Begley writes that researchers studying the processes of the brain and the mind agree that the belief in paranormal and supernatural events must first be preceded by an "open mind." Scientists who undertake the serious study of the paranormal hold the opinion that belief requires an open mind: "one not bound by the evidence of the senses, but in which emotions such as hope and despair can trump that evidence." Research that once showed the brain constructs reality from the "bottom up" starting with perceptions has been proven wrong. Instead, it seems the brain's sensory regions are much more affected by the higher-order systems that run attention and emotion than once thought. Thus, we may miss something that is right in front of our face if we are not "wired" in these systems to see it.

Interestingly, Begley also said that we may find this pervasiveness of belief in the supernatural and paranormal odd in an age of science. But we also live in an age of anxiety, a time of economic distress and social stressors. Historically, such stress-filled and fearful times increased the public's belief in astrology, ESP, and other paranormal phenomena, which often give people a sense of hope. It may also give them a sense of connectedness, as people who believe in something else "out there" often do so as a means of feeling a part of a bigger whole, and one that continues beyond physical death. This certainly explains the abundance of paranormal media available now, and the onslaught of ghost-hunting groups all over the country eager to find proof of the unknown.

Because our eyes and ears are only able to take in a specific amount of "information" out there, it is highly possible that we rely on our brains to fill in the blanks of what perception cannot complete on its own. Think of those crazy optical illusions and how the brain makes patterns that the eye cannot at first pick up on without a little help. The brain is actually doing the majority of the work involved in seeing an object or hearing a sound, as well as giving interpretation and meaning to what is sees and hears. This is also why we tend to see patterns and synchronicities in coincidences and chance encounters. Even the act of wishful thinking is linked to brain activity associated with daydreaming and the imagination.

Similar to belief, wishful thinking or "attractor thinking" focuses on the meaning and perceptions we attach to the world of our senses, depending on our hidden needs and desires. And, similar to belief, especially hysteria and fear-driven belief, wishful and positive thinking has a kind of contagious nature, spreading to those around us who then pattern their mental processes from others. Moods spread quickly, as does the common cold. Belief in the power of thought, especially positive thoughts such as affirmations, or negative thoughts such as curses, drives the behavior of many a culture, from the tribal rituals to fend off evil to today's obsession with *The Secret*.

So, if the brain is behind a lot of what we see and believe we will see, why is it that everyone with an open mind is not seeing ghosts and spirits? Why isn't everyone who believes in UFOs seeing strange objects scooting across the night sky? Why can't Marie or Larry ever succeed in psychically picking the winning MegaMillion lottery numbers? Maybe there is something other than a willing brain required to have a paranormal experience. Maybe that extra link involves a level of consciousness some of us have more access to than others…and some none at all.

We wanted to end this chapter with an interesting personal example of resonance at work related to Persinger's findings. The following is a true story courtesy of Larry himself, who experienced this while on an actual paranormal investigation.

■ ■ ■ ■ ■ ■ ■ ■ ■ ■

Larry's Experience

"Have you ever had something happen that truly makes you go "hmmmm?" Something so inexplicable that you are left scratching your head in utter disbelief, and wondering if you were perhaps dreaming?

Like many folks of a scientific (and often skeptical) mindset, I can probably count the number of truly "weird" or unexplained occurrences that I have personally experienced in my life on one hand. In fact, this can be reduced further to only a few fingers on that one hand!

I have traveled the world, experienced many "close calls," and have seen, heard, and felt some incredibly unique and interesting things. Past life regression? Done. Archaeological dig? Check. Sensory deprivation tank? Yes. Acupuncture? Oh yeah. Ghost hunting? Yep. For as long as I can remember, I have been interested in pushing the envelope. Researching hidden and forbidden knowledge. Studying that which is not commonly known. Experiencing things that would cause most sane people to run and hide. Basically, my interests can be summarized as anything that challenges the generally accepted tenets of conventional scientific knowledge and wisdom.

One of my more interesting experiences occurred in October 2008 during an ARPAST-sanctioned paranormal investigation. This particular site was reported to be extremely haunted, and, in it's previous incarnations had an extremely storied past. At one time it was a hospital run by a fanatical doctor who supposedly derived personal pleasure from performing unconventional experiments on his patients. The location had been completely renovated and converted into retirement condominiums. We were contacted by the property manager, who believed that activity was present in several of the units; however, one particular unit seemed to be a virtual hotbed of activity. According to the owner, she had experienced a variety of phenomenon including seeing an apparition of a young boy, having unusual feelings in one particular area, and seeing shadows and dark shapes out of her peripheral vision. Due to this, we focused the majority of our efforts on this unit.

As with all of our investigations we utilized strict scientific methodology, while looking for natural or man-made variables that are commonly (and often mistakenly) associated with paranormal phenomenon. Usually, we are able to rule out a significant number of events in a relatively short period of time by meticulous observation and utilization of some very impressive equipment. On this particular investigation we ran the usual gamut of baseline environmental assays—radiation, electromagnetic, barometric pressure, temperature, air/ion count, airborne particulate count, and a battery of other tests. Although we found highly elevated electromagnetic field levels in three specific areas within the residence, it certainly did not raise any red flags for me at the time, because we often see similar issues. Many homes have insufficient electrical grounding, breaker boxes that are unshielded, or incorrect-gauge wiring being utilized. Mostly, these are safety issues.

Before attending their first field investigation, all ARPAST members must undergo a mandatory training regimen. This training program is quite extensive, and covers a wide variety of topics such as scientific method, equipment use, data analysis, environmental factors, and psychology. One of the instructional blocks covers EMF and the known effects upon the human body. To be completely honest, when I was putting together the curriculum for that lesson I had no real-world experience with the effects. That was about to change!

Before I actually talk about the experience, let's explore some of the theories regarding EMF and paranormal phenomena, as well as what science knows about its effects on the human body. Many paranormal researchers buy into the belief that ghosts emit an electromagnetic field and that their presence can be detected by EMF meters. Although we do not necessarily believe this to be the case, EMF activity is but one variable that is logged during our investigations.

Although there is quite a bit of disagreement regarding the actual effects of EMF, according to the National Institute of Environmental Health Sciences, for many years scientists have suspected that long-term exposure to extremely-low-frequency electromagnetic fields (EMFs) may be associated with increased risk of neurodegenerative diseases such as Alzheimer disease, Parkinson's disease, and amyotrophic lateral sclerosis. Some studies have shown that EMF exposure can even damage the DNA of human and animal cells, whereas others have shown no significant effect. Recently, Henry Lai and Narendra P. Singh of the University of Washington offered their support to the speculation that environmental exposure to EMFs is hazardous and that the effects may be cumulative.

The National Association of Certified Home Inspectors goes one step further in defining an actual condition (electromagnetic hypersensitivity): "Electromagnetic hypersensitivity (ES) is a physiological disorder characterized by symptoms directly brought on by exposure to electromagnetic fields. It produces neurological and allergic-type symptoms." These symptoms may include headache, eye irritation, dizziness, nausea, skin rash, facial swelling, weakness, fatigue, pain in joints and/or muscles, buzzing/ringing in ears, skin numbness, abdominal pressure and pain, breathing difficulty, and irregular heartbeat. Affected persons may experience an abrupt onset of symptoms following exposure to a new EMF, such as fields associated with a new computer or with new fluorescent lights, or a new home or work environment.

In addition to the primary investigative location, we also deployed equipment in several other condominium units on the first, second, and third floors. Once this was completed, we proceeded to conduct the investigation per our standardized procedures. For the most part, the first half of the night was interesting, but uneventful. Because I had spent the majority of the evening walking around with the property manager and supervising my team's hourly rotations, I decided to spend the remaining time in the "hot" residence doing an EVP session. I settled onto the most comfortable area—the bed, and immediately began to feel disoriented and weak. I had a sense that something was in the corner of the room watching me, and, out of the corner of my eye, I thought I saw a dark, shadowy object materialize, then almost immediately disappear into the wall.

There was a buzzing—a resonance—within my head, which felt like nothing I had every experienced before. The feeling was unbelievably intense, all-encompassing, and immediate. In fact, it was so powerful and so sudden that after this point I have no recollection whatsoever. I am certain that I did not black out, and according to the other investigators who were present in the room, I was fully cognizant and awake. Although I have no memory of the event, we have more than an hour of "interesting" audio footage. In the recording, I can be heard "hallucinating" and commenting about several nonsensical subjects. It was mostly gibberish, and quite comical to listen to myself in this state. I'm generally a man of few words, and babbling is not something I do!

Looking at my experience from a purely objective, scientific view, I believe the high EMF fields can explain my incident. As we have previously discussed Dr. Michael Persinger's work, an interesting commonality appears. In his study, he was able to duplicate (with astonishing similarity) the "effect" of a paranormal event by bombarding the test subject's temporal lobes with elevated EMF energy. After hundreds of test subjects, he was able to prove that even short-term EMF exposure can cause frontal-lobe hallucinations—both auditory and visual. Study participants reported effects that were remarkably similar to my experience— the feeling of a presence, seeing dark figures out of the corner of their eyes, being watched, fear, general paranoia, and hearing unexplained noises.

■ ■ ■ ■ ■ ■ ■ ■ ■ ■ ■

Can a machine make us experience the paranormal? Does it all come down to simply triggering one part of the brain to see things we don't normally see, or hear things we don't normally hear? The devices mentioned in this chapter certainly seem to suggest that anyone can hook up to a machine and turn it on and see their dead Auntie Janie, or feel the presence of an angel, or have a psychic experience. If that were the case, imagine the commercial aspects. We could open bars and restaurants where people could eat, drink, and see a ghost. Larry and Marie might open a franchise called "Encounters"— sort of a "McDonalds," but instead of a burger, we give you a ghostly encounter with your fries.

The brain, though, might need a little help from another mechanism in order to have experiences that are outside or beyond the norm. And rest assured, you don't have to spend $500 on eBay to get ahold of one.

8

PARACONSCIOUSNESS

"On campus, a student said, God—
I find it exceedingly odd
That a tree, as a tree,
Simply ceases to be
When there's no one around in the quad."

—Old limerick

Beyond the realm of everyday consciousness, there is a level of awareness that overrides the five senses and oversees the dark and murky depths of the subconscious. Paraconsciousness is the location of intuition, psychic abilities, synchronicity, and mystery. It is the stomping ground of what we call the "perception of the paranormal."

"It's all in your mind," someone might say to a friend or colleague who claims to have seen a ghost, or have psychically predicted an earthquake's exact location. Yet, what might be a sarcastic insult, even when laced with affection, could really have more truth behind it than we ever imagined. If consciousness creates our daily reality, or at least our perception of it, then could paraconsciousness create other realities? Perhaps providing us access to realities and realms that we rarely encounter? The ones we label "otherworldly," like some distant *Twilight Zone* or *Outer Limits*...a borderlands we spend little, if any time in?

To tell someone who has had a paranormal experience that what he or she saw was not physically real might be a stretch, as we do know of thousands of cases of solid objects in the sky, monsters in the woods, and ghosts in the hallway. But perhaps physicality is not the entire story, and just as in quantum physics, an observer is required to determine a specific outcome of a perceived experience—even one that ends up with an antique vase flying across a room of its own accord, or a late-night, static-filled phone call from dearly departed Uncle Dominick.

In his book *The Origins of Psychic Phenomena*, author and researcher Stan Gooch states "We should probably never finally close the door on the possibility of discarnate or spirit beings existing independently of ourselves...however, with that cautionary note and despite the dramatic evidence of apparently discarnate entities or forces noisily breaking up rooms, starting fires, attacking and severely bruising human beings, and causing some of them to burst into flames, we have, nevertheless...seen persuasive evidence that these entities or forces are directly associated with, and indeed directly produced by, certain individuals."

Gooch refers to the "alternative consciousness" as the origin of many psi phenomena. The dark and shadowy realm of the unconscious holds layers that we cannot access upon demand, or at least most of us cannot, and can contain within those layers all sorts of paranormal anomalies. Although we seem to understand which part of the brain is associated with the conscious mind, the cerebral cortex being the main contender for what we experience as waking consciousness, we still struggle to locate the seat of the unconscious, with some, including Gooch, seeing the cerebellum as the primary residence. He likens it to a brain within a brain, or a complete organism within the organism that has full informational access to the sensory and motor systems, and full executive control of them as well. Along with the cerebrum and the primal brain, we may one day find the true location of the unconscious.

But aside from where it is housed, or at least paying rent (for the verdict is still out as to whether consciousness is part of the brain or separate from it), we do understand there are different layers to our awareness. The most closely associated with spirituality, religious experience, and paranormal manifestation is called superconsciousness, the metaconsciousness, and paraconsciousness, and describes a higher realm of awareness above that of our everyday wakefulness.

The Hindus describe the superconscious mind as the all-knowing intelligent soul-mind, and is associated with divine consciousness, non-dual consciousness, and spiritual consciousness. This level of conscious awareness is beyond even the states of deep sleep and dreaming, and is an omniscient state that offers a universal sense of oneness with all. Hinduism goes one conscious level above that of the "turiya," or superconsciousness, with the final and highest state of "turiyatita," or complete transcendence.

Another way to break down these layers is body, mind, and spirit, also known as individual consciousness, intellectual consciousness, and God consciousness—that which is far above the ordinary and personal. Interestingly, mainstream Christianity likens this same state to the Holy Spirit, or spirit of truth, the gift of which is complete communion with the Father, or union with the divine. We can even simplify this further with the subconscious, the normal conscious state, and the superconscious.

When we ask the question, "does consciousness survive at death?" perhaps it is this last and highest level we are referring to that continues on without us. Near-death experiences (NDE) are ripe with imagery of the continuation of the soul and of awareness, including the presence of many paranormal entities as angels and guardians and the spirits of loved ones. This is also the realm of intuition, higher guidance, and mental clarity, the level of consciousness that sees the bigger picture and sees solutions to problems our conscious mind struggles to find.

The deep perceptions of the superconscious, or from this point, the paraconscious, can be glimpsed during meditation, hypnosis, or trance states, when our attention is off the daily chatter and activity, and relaxed or lulled into a more receptive state. Dualistic thinking gives way to a sense of oneness, and we become far more attuned to what lies beyond our normal sensory experience.

■ ■ ■ ■ ■ ■ ■ ■ ■ ■

Marie's Story:

I was fortunate enough to have had a very profound experience during a deep meditation many years ago, when I somehow managed to open my eyes in a very relaxed state, and saw everything around me as waves of light, rather than solid objects. I could sense where my bed was, or the window, or a table, only because the vibratory rates were more dense for solid objects, and much faster for, say, the light coming in through the window. But it was all vibrating, and although the sensation lasted only about a half a minute, if that long, it was enough to convince me that all is vibration until the wave function is collapsed and objects become fixed and solid. I had that subjective glimpse between levels of reality. I cannot prove it, or even duplicate it, but it mirrored all of my later studies in quantum physics and particle/wave duality. Was I getting a look at what reality looks like before my own act of observation turns it into something tangible, with form and position? It was such a deeply profound experience, I immediately signed up for ministerial courses at the local Science of Mind church! In later years, as I studied quantum physics, I had a subjective experience of my own that I could look back on to help me understand the more complex ideas of wave/particle duality and superposition. You believe it when you see it!"

■ ■ ■ ■ ■ ■ ■ ■ ■ ■

In the world of quantum physics, the phenomenon of non-locality states that two particles of a complementary pair can be separated by vast spatial distances, yet still remain in instantaneous communication with one another, as if they are psychically sharing information faster than the speed of light. One of the particles may spin vertically, and its paired particle will immediately spin horizontal at the exact same time. Again, this proven principle occurs over light-years of distance. Classical physics have continually ingrained within us the knowledge that this simply could not happen, and even Albert Einstein refused to believe in what he called "spooky action at a distance." But he was proven wrong after his death, and the concept of non-locality hints at the bizarre nature of reality at the most minute levels.

We also know that the observer is paraamount to the outcome of an experiment at the quantum level, where particles are waves and particles at the same time, until the wave function is collapsed and a fixed particle is positioned in time and space. This state of superposition, before the wave function collapse, is parallel to the paraconscious landscape of unity and oneness, from which matter and form arise as thought and experience. Before that wave function collapses, we can say that stuff exists only as a probability in the quantum brain, just as a thought exists only as a probability in the human brain before being turned into a specific action or expression. If the wave is not under current observation, it simply remains a wave, expanding throughout the space-time continuum, and thus any particle of that wave could be anywhere at any time until the second it is observed…and fixed.

The idea that information can be shared faster than the speed of light applies to the process of mind and thought as well, suggesting that there is a very implicate connection between the mind and the body, and between particles and the quantum field in which they exist. The personal consciousness of the individual is to the paraconscious as the brain is to the mind; one being a more individualized aspect of the greater, more connected other.

When it comes to the paranormal, it seems our consciousness as well as the brain has its blind spots. Dean Radin, author of *Entangled Minds,* wrote in his article "What Gorilla? Why Some Can't See Psychic Phenomena" for the Jan./Feb. issue of *New Dawn Magazine*, that "inattentional blindness" describes the phenomenon of how our perceptual system "unconsciously filters out most of the information that is available to us. Therefore, we actually really experience a tiny amount of the remaining information, possibly as little as a trillionth of what is actually out there for us to perceive. From that tiny amount, our mind then constructs what we expect to perceive."

That final line is most telling. *Our minds see what we expect to see.* As if wearing blinders, we have no peripheral vision of the things that may be standing "just off to the side" of our reality—things such as ghosts, aliens, angels, and spirits. But were we to turn toward that previously filtered information, we might finally see that there is more out there than meets the eye. Radin states, "An important class of human experience that these blinders exclude is psychic phenomena, those commonly reported spooky experiences, such as telepathy and clairvoyance, that suggest we are deeply interconnected in ways that transcend the ordinary senses and our everyday notions of space and time."

Radin humorously refers to the fact that often evidence is there, yet we fail to "see" it, in a sense. He suggests we imagine a UFO landing smack on the White House lawn. Normally, we are not able to have such a big piece of evidence to work with or one that would no doubt be all over YouTube in a matter of seconds. The evidence that we do have available is, rather, in the realm of reports of UFOs repeatedly flying over the U.S. Capitol, captured on film and detected simultaneously by radar, jet pilots, and hundreds of witnesses on the ground. Radin asks, would this kind of evidence not capture the interest and attention of millions of people? Yet such a UFO sighting actually *did* occur in Washington, D.C., in 1952. Tunnel vision, or selective evidence, as he calls it, stops real research from advancing knowledge of the paranormal, just as does the quest for constantly producing repeatable effects "on demand" when we want them, and in the harshness of a sterile laboratory environment.

Whether or not we can repeat a ghost sighting over and over in a lab doesn't take away from the fact that zillions of people claim to have had a ghostly experience—many of the visual variety. So if perception has the power to put a ghost in our path, or not, consciousness appears to be the driver of the oncoming car. The brain has a say, too, and can be considered a backseat driver. Supernatural belief, or nonbelief, can trigger the act of pattern-seeking in the brain, whereby we give more credence to the concepts of ghosts and aliens than we otherwise might. The brain finds patterns wherever it can, even in those acts that cannot be explained by the known laws of nature. For example, in the fog of a shower door someone might spot the image of the Virgin Mary, or in the discolorations of a burnt tortilla one sees the face of Jesus Christ. Or maybe someone sees the face of a deceased relative looking back at them from a plate of nachos. This may be a part of an evolutionary trait based upon our behavior as infants: As soon as an infant can see, it recognizes faces, a skill hardwired into the human brain. Perhaps, infants who were once unable to recognize a face would not smile at that face, and thus were less likely to win the hearts of their parents, and less likely to prosper or be cared for. These days, nearly every infant is quick to identify a human face, and to respond with a toothless smile.

Cognitive scientists have found that the brain's processes behind our ability to reason and perceive are the same processes involved in belief in religion and the supernatural. Our brain takes in a ton of information (yet leaves out much more, as mentioned previously) and has to make sense of the chaos, using patterning as a ways and means to do so; this includes paranormal events that have no basis in scientific reasoning. The brain does not care—if it can find a pattern to it, it will, and it will continue to believe in that pattern. This serves both as a physical truth, as the brain makes new neural connections in relation to that new pattern, but also an emotional truth, as it may also seek a pattern of meaning in the repetition of perceived information.

But aside from the brain's role in perceiving or experiencing paranormal phenomena, even religious phenomena, the consciousness plays the most vital key. Both Sigmund Freud and Carl Jung ascribed meaning to the levels of consciousness as follows:

▶ Conscious—the awareness of both internal and external states, and wakefulness.

▶ Preconscious—buried memories, latent memories, habitual thoughts, automatisms, and censored thoughts (the censor).

▶ Unconscious—repressed memories, forgotten knowledge and memories, and the true non-ego self.

▶ Collective Unconscious—instinct, intuition, race memory, genetic memory, foundational mind, and common mind.

In his book *Transcending the Speed of Light: Consciousness, Quantum Physics and the Fifth Dimension,* Marc Seifer, PhD, uses this model to suggest that the deeper parts of the individual mind have the most transcendent qualities. He also states that paranormal activity could possibly arise "through the same psychic apparatus as normal memories when appearing in consciousness. They all come up from the unconscious through the same pathway, that is, through the preconscious to awareness in the conscious." This can make it difficult to distinguish a paranormal thought from a normal one. Similarly, paranormal information arising in a dream may suffer distortion by this same censor, such as appearing in symbolic form, similar to what occurs in normal dreams. This makes it difficult to realize that a dream may, in fact, have been telepathic and not just a strange dream that haunts us for reasons we cannot put our finger on.

Furthermore, the collective unconscious would be in a "resonant frequency" that connects all individual consciousness, and is responsible for shared thought, ESP, remote viewing, and other forms of psi abilities that involve the transference of information or the awareness of information one does not have normal access to. All people are linked at the source, and in the next chapter, we will describe what we authors believe that source is.

Jung particularly described the collective unconscious as the link that may unite all individual human minds. Telepathy between twins suggests a link between their own individual consciousnesses that is more dramatic because of a shared genetic origin and brains that are often almost identical. Physicist David Bohm referred to this mental realm of connectedness as the implicate order that was beneath and in between, and throughout all of the explicate, manifest reality. This invisible realm was where everything interacted with everything else, yet this connectivity was not visible on the explicate level where we see, touch, taste, feel, and hear in 3-D.

Seifer also posits a resonance model to allow for things such as telepathy and synchronicity, involving the structure of the brain and how certain brainwave frequencies can act "as carrier waves for various kinds of ESP phenomena." Take Alpha EEG waves, which have a frequency of 8 Hz. Alpha waves correspond with a deep, relaxed state, and research by Michael Persinger has shown that ESP occurs more frequently during this state of Alpha. Alpha is identical to the Earth's own resonance rate as well, and those who have psi abilities may be picking up on that very low EMF resonance within their very sensitive temporal lobes.

An even more intriguing theory of Seifer's that describes the possible mechanism of transfer of "psi information signals" involves water. The brain's content is largely water, and Seifer posits that the electronic frequency of the brain would no doubt be affected by this, with individual water molecules held to each other by an H-bond, a weak attraction between the positive side of one molecule and the negative side of another. Rapid H-bond shifts account for the fluid property of water. The H-bond-shift frequency, which would also be in harmonic resonance with water molecules in the air or ocean, could potentially act as a carrier frequency for direct brain perception (DBP)—the transfer of information from one brain to another. Certain neurotransmitters could be in synch with this frequency.

Synchronistic phenomena may involve the idea of mutual vibrations. Resonance. Even the principle of harmonics plays into the brain's ability to access other dimensions of consciousness and reality. Through brainwave resonant effects, identical or similar information may be arising in the consciousness of two individuals who have in common "neurophysiological characteristics." The fact that the collective psyche or unconscious exists in "an all-pervasive hyperspatial realm" suggests that it can initiate synchronistic phenomena in the same way that one twin can initiate it in the mind of his or her twin sibling. Non-locality shows that particles can do this. Why not thought?

And because the collective unconscious is the realm of symbol and archetype, it would explain why ghosts, aliens, demons, and angels always seem to have similar morphologies, and are often said to look the same—depending on the current mindset of the collective populace—and why paranormal events, though hard to repeat or make happen on their own, tend to be quite the same when they do happen. A ghost is a ghost. A UFO is a UFO. And an alien is an alien…until the collective psyche shifts and then we go from faeries to benevolent contactees with long blond hair and blue eyes, to those mean nasty anal-probing grays and their buddies, the Men in Black (MIB), to the sinister reptilians that want to eat our brains. Some researchers and psychologists suggest that even Bigfoot and the Loch Ness Monster may be constructs of the collective psyche, materializing up from the murky depths of shared belief.

Jung once stated that these manifestations seem externalized because they are foreign to the ego. In his book *The Psychological Foundation of Belief in Spirits* he states, "Thus we admit the existence of independent psychic complexes, escaping the control of our consciousness and appearing and disappearing according to their laws." The act by which they appear and disappear could use resonance as the physical medium of telepathic transfer of information.

Rupert Sheldrake, author of a number of books about cutting-edge science and consciousness, believes that paranormal phenomena are worthy of further investigation. In his 2003 book, *The Sense of Being Stared At*, he argues that unexplained human abilities such as telepathy, the sense of being stared at, and premonition are not necessarily paranormal, but a normal part of human biological nature. His widely accepted concept of "morphogenic fields" states that there are fields that evolve in correspondence with the systems they organize. A field is described as a sphere of influence, and these fields exist around everything from the cells of our bodies to the entirety of an ecosystem.

Built within these fields are events and patterns that create memory, or "morphic resonance," which may explain things such as instinct and behavior similar to the homing seen in pigeons, or how a dog knows ahead of time that its owner is on his/her way home. A morphic field can influence the behavior and movement of "cells within a body or members within a group," closely mirroring that of David Bohm's levels or reality, including the implicate order or underlying field that is invisible, but present throughout the manifest world.

Paraconsciousness may be the state of awareness necessary to perceive the morphic fields, or access them. Altered states of consciousness are most often associated with accessing mystical experiences that are beyond that of everyday experience. Trance states, meditation, chanting and drumming, rhythmic movement, music, and even hallucinogenic drugs are means by which these levels of consciousness may be achieved. On rare occasions, the brain can trigger them on its own, but more often requires the assistance of one of the afore-mentioned modalities to move from alert wakefulness to the deeper states where thought and perception take on a whole new light, and where consciousness leaps.

Meditation and chanting have long been associated with altered states of consciousness, used for thousands of years by ancients eager to access higher levels of knowledge and wisdom. Mystical traditions, including those associated with the major religions, have long understood that meditation and prayer, or any activity that created a trance-like state and changed brainwave patterns, could create a state of resonance such that the person meditating achieved perfect union with all. Paraconsciousness might also be accessed by accident, as a result of environmental effects, such as the often high levels of electromagnetic field anomalies typically associated with paranormal experiences, even telekinesis.

But divine union with the God at the center of everything is not the only result of accessing altered states of consciousness, especially in terms of the paranormal, or the ability to perceive the paranormal. Sometimes the result is a plethora of strange and alien entities with often archetypal foundations. And the tool of choice is not calming the mind, but taking a drug.

The use of both natural and man-made hallucinogens is not new to those seeking to move beyond the veil, or walk along the Grid into other realms or dimensions. Shamans have long made use of Ayahuasca, a potent plant-based hallucinogen, to journey to other worlds to retrieve lost souls, find healing for diseases, and access totem and power animals. Their visionary states appear to be timeless, as even modern native Shamanic tribes have created imagery in the form of paintings that show the various supernatural entities encountered during a journey to another world. Intriguingly, some of those entities are almost identical to those found on cave and rock art from prehistoric times!

And, as Graham Hancock, author of *Supernatural* and *Fingerprints of the Gods* discovered, these ancient images mirror those of test subjects given mescaline in laboratory settings today. Similar to many other researchers devoted to understanding the inner workings of the universe, Hancock has taken such drugs and seen the very images that both medicine men in the Amazon and college test subjects in American universities have reported as well.

Hallucinogens seem to tap into a part of the paraconsciousness that creates symbolism and imagery, yet for those who have experienced these "trips," there is every indication to suggest these symbols might actually be real entities that exist in a parallel dimension or another level of reality. Stone Age art has incredible similarities with the drawings of angels, faeries, large-headed aliens, and insect-like reptilians we hear so much about in more recent times, suggesting that there is a foundational, archetypal well of knowledge that these drugs tap us into.

Hallucinogens, broken into three categories of psychedelics, dissociatives, or deliriants, are simply drugs, whether natural or chemical, that affect a person's brain by altering perception, emotion, thought, and sensation. Of the synthetic, or manufactured forms, LSD, or d-lysergic acid diethylamide, is probably the most notable. Although it is found in a fungus that grows on rye and grains called "ergot," it is made from lysergic acid and sold in tablet, capsule, and sometimes liquid forms. LSD, discovered in 1938, is a mood-changer, and is known for, in overdose quantities, causing such horrific hallucinations as to sometimes alter a person's behavior long after they come off the "bad trip," creating paranoia, psychosis, and other mental disorders. These feelings often return later as flashbacks, adding to the original trauma of the negative trip.

Contrary to their names, though, hallucinogens don't actually cause hallucinations, which are described as perceptions with no basis in reality, but are perceived as such. Instead, these poorly named drugs cause visual images and altered perceptions, but the "user" is aware that it is not reality, but illusions driving that imagery. Only deliriants like muscarine and nicotine can cause "true" hallucinations and cause effects similar to delirium.

Drugs such as LSD also change physiology, causing dilated pupils, increased heart rate, raised body temperature, tremors, and appetite changes. Heavy usage can result in actual signs of brain damage (or "dain bramage," as we children of the 1960s and 1970s once said). Of course, the potency depends on not only the amount taken, but also the quality, and some street LSD has been known to be low grade.

Phencyclidine, which is commonly referred to as PCP or angel dust, is another manufactured drug with hallucinogenic properties. It is considered extremely dangerous, and is known to cause effects similar to LSD. PCP can create bizarre behavior and mental disturbances in users, and affects memory, perception, and even judgment when used regularly. PCP is classified as a hallucinogen and has many of the same effects as LSD, but can be much more dangerous. In the 1950s, PCP was investigated as an anesthetic, but due to its severe side effects, its development for human use was discontinued. PCP is known for inducing violent behavior and physical reactions such as seizures, coma, and death. There is no way to predict who will have a bad reaction to the drug. Maybe this is because PCP acts as a hallucinogen, stimulant, depressant, and anesthetic—all at the same time.

In its original state, PCP is a white crystalline powder. It is available in tablet, liquid, and powder forms, and is either ingested orally or smoked by applying the liquid form to tobacco or marijuana cigarettes. Sometimes cigarettes can be laced with herbs, such as mint or parsley, or with PCP powder.

Mescaline is a manufactured drug from a natural source, derived from the peyote cactus, with effects similar to LSD, although normally not as intense. Native American medicine healers have long used peyote as a means of both healing and sacred divination. When used for religious or healing purposes, these drugs are labeled "entheogens" and have been used by the ancient Mayan, Incan, and Aztec civilizations, as well as the ancient Egyptian, Vedic, Greek, and Pagan cultures.

Mescaline is one of the oldest psychedelics known to man. It is the major active component of the small dumpling cactus known as peyote growing wild in the southwestern United States and in northern Mexico, and has been used as a part of religious traditions among the native Indians. The cactus is recognizable by its small round shape and the appearance of tufts of soft fuzz in place of the more conventional spines. The dried plant material has been used with anywhere from a few to a couple of dozen of the hard tops, called buttons, being consumed in the course of a ceremony.

Another natural-based hallucinogen is psilocybin, derived from mushrooms. The mushroom can be fresh, dried, eaten, or taken in tablet or capsule form, and again acts on the brain in a similar fashion to LSD. Mushrooms also have a long history as a healing and/or divination agent in native traditions. Mushrooms have been taken for religious rituals in indigenous cultures in Mexico and Central America for thousands of years. Today, recreational users take them as a hallucinogen that is considered more natural and gentler than LSD. Commonly reported feelings include mild euphoria and tingling physical sensations, mood swings, perceptual distortions, as well as increased sensitivity to visual stimulation and music. In relatively small doses (4 to 8 mg), effects are produced within 30 minutes, and may continue for up to five hours.

One psychotropic drug, Ayahuasca, is still popular today in many native rituals, and is the "drug du jour" for those seeking a Shamanic experience. There are actual tours for the upscale person to locations where Ayahuasca is used in native traditions to give the "white man" a chance to get away from his mind-numbing white collar job and go on a trip unlike anything Club Med has to offer!

Ayahuasca, made from plants containing dimethyltryptamine (DMT) and harmine, is usually taken in the form of a bitter brew that helps to release the potent hallucinogens and create a sensation of being taken to another world or dimension rampant with entities and images.

■ ■ ■ ■ ■ ■ ■ ■ ■ ■

Hallucinogenic Organisms

Nature can make you see things that aren't there…or are they? The following is a list of some organisms known to contain hallucinogens:

Plants

Psychedelics

▶ Ayahuasca (contains DMT and an MAOI, commonly *Banisteriopsis caapi* with *Psychotria viridis*).

▶ Epená (*Virola sp,* contains 5-MeO-DMT and DMT).

▶ Hawaiian baby woodrose (*Argyreia nervosa*, contains ergot alkaloids).

▶ Ololiuhqui/Coaxihuitl (*Turbina/Rivea corymbosa*, contains ergot alkaloids).

▶ Tlitliltzin/Badoh Negro (*Ipomoea violacea*, contains ergot alkaloids).

Cacti psychedelics

▶ Peruvian Torch cactus (*Trichocereus peruvianus*, contains mescaline).

▶ Peyote cactus (*Lophophora williamsii*, contains mescaline).

▶ San Pedro cactus (*Trichocereus pachanoi*, contains mescaline).

▶ Quasi-psychedelics.

▶ Cannabis (contains THC).

▶ Nutmeg (*Myristica fragrans*, contains myristicin).

Dissociatives

▶ Iboga (*Tabernanthe iboga*, contains ibogaine).

▶ *Salvia divinorum* (contains salvinorin A).

Deliriants

▶ Deadly nightshade (*Atropa belladonna*, contains tropane alkaloids).

▶ Floripondio (*Brugmansia sp.*, contains tropane alkaloids).

▶ Henbane (*Hyoscyamus niger*, contains tropane alkaloids).

▶ Mandrake (*Mandragora sp.*, contains tropane alkaloids).

▶ Thorn Apple/Jimson Weed (*Datura sp.*, contains tropane alkaloids).

Fungi

Psychedelics

▶ Psilocybe mushrooms (*Psilocybe sp.* and some *Conocybe*, *Panaeolus* and *Stropharia*, contain psilocybin and psilocin).

▶ Ergot fungus (*Claviceps purpurea*) not hallucinogenic in itself, but contains ergotamine, along with deadly poisons.

Dissociatives

▶ Fly Agaric mushroom (*Amanita muscaria*, contains muscimol).

Animals

Psychedelics

▶ Psychoactive toads (*Bufo alvarius*, contain 5-MeO-DMT and bufotenine).

Courtesy of Wikipedia

■ ■ ■ ■ ■ ■ ■ ■ ■ ■

The word *psychedelic* comes from the Greek "psyche" and "delien," meaning "mind" and "to manifest." The primary goal of taking a psychedelic is to access and develop parts of the mind that are normally unused. Part of the larger grouping of hallucinogens, these drugs offer an experience many claim similar to that of being in a hypnotic trance or dream state, disabling the brain's ability to filter information and perception even as they expand the mind.

Salvia, or salvia divinorum, which is a plant-derived "dissociative" ethneogen that blocks signals to the conscious mind and inhibits perception and sensation of the physical body, is a popular choice for today's seekers. Sold on the Internet in various forms including leaf, tincture, and extract, Salvia, also known as "Diviner's Sage," or "ska María Pastora," when smoked or consumed orally, offers a milder psychedelic experience rich with imagery and symbolism that users swear offers profound meaning and transformative qualities.

Figure 8-1. Salvia in plant form.

Salvia is a unique psychoactive, containing *salvinorin A,* and is the most potent naturally occuring psychoactive compound known. Long used by Mazatec Shamans, who crushed the leaves to extract juices that were then mixed into a "tea" with water, salvia is now estimated to be used by more than 1.8 million people, most of whom buy it through the World Wide Web. Salvia is native to the Sierra Mazateca in Oaxaca, Mexico, where it is still used to facilitate Shamanic journeying and visions, as well as for medicinal relief from anemia, diarrhea, and other maladies.

Many of the effects of salvia use include accessing past memories from childhood, being encompassed in membrane-like structures, the perception of being in more than one place at a time, sensations of movement, and merging with objects. Some salvia users report seeing entities such as guardian spirits, cartoonish characters, beautiful angelic beings, and wise sages, but just as many users report feeling more frightening sensations such as loss of control and claustrophobia. The presence of a sober and mature "sitter" is required for anyone using salvia to assure the person's safety, and, in some cases, maybe their sanity once they come off the experience!

Salvia divinorum is an uncontrolled substance in the United States by federal law, but it is controlled in some states. This means that all parts of the plant and its extracts are legal to cultivate, buy, possess, and distribute (sell, trade, or give) without a license or prescription. If sold as a supplement, sales must conform to U.S. supplement laws. If sold for consumption as a food or drug, the FDA would be tasked with regulating it, though the Internet makes it quite easy to get ahold of the stuff. Recent YouTube videos featuring salvia users talking about their magical salvia "trips" have come under fire for promoting usage in areas where it might not be legal.

These herbal hallucinogens, when used in the hands of experienced medicine healers or vision questers, can produce profoundly transformative experiences. During vision states, many have even reported encounters with "beings" that we might think of today as alien and paranormal. But many neurologists and scientists argue that what is really happening is not the accessing of a higher or deeper state of conscious reality, but the simple effect on the brain of a substance or chemical that in no way, shape, or form suggests anything more than a subjective shift in the brain's ability to perceive.

The authors of this book are not going to get into a philosophical argument about the legalities or moralities of using substances to change consciousness, whether for religious purposes, healing methods, or to just plain get high, but we must state that our own brains do carry within them the means of accomplishing this on their own, without any external help. Graham Hancock, in his research, was led to a stunning conclusion: the brain has its own natural psychedelic: DMT.

DMT, or dimethyltryptamine, is not only a psychedelic drug, but also one that occurs naturally in the human brain, albeit in trace amounts. Though neurologists don't quite understand the role of DMT in the brain, the extracted and synthesized form has been used as a psychedelic in many tribal and indigenous cultures for decades. DMT was first extracted from the Mimosa hostilis in 1946 by chemist and ethnobotanist Goncalves de Lima, and first synthesized by chemist Richard Manske in 1931. It occurs naturally in many plant species, and is part of the potent hallucinogenic drink Ayahuasca, widely known for triggering visions, often of a prophetic nature. Psilocybin is a close chemical relative found in mushrooms that even contains a DMT molecule.

DMT must be smoked, injected, or taken orally in conjunction with a monoamine oxidase inhibitor (MAOI) to get the powerful effects that include visions, true hallucinations, and out-of-body experiences. In his book *Supernatural*, Hancock writes about the experimental use of DMT in a lab setting courtesy of Dr. Rick Strassman, author of *DMT: The Spirit Molecule*. In the question-and-answer interview, Strassman reveals that many of his test subjects, having taken DMT, report the same types of entities and beings that are part of the imagery painted by indigenous cultures. In fact, these entities and beings often mirror imagery reported by UFO abductees, as well as the older elves and faeries of folklore and localized legends.

Strassman's clinical research, done at the University of New Mexico, posited that DMT not only might be revealing repressed existing memories in the brain, but actually accessing something else on a deeper level. Nor would he qualify the reports of his test subjects as simple hallucinations. "While certainly there are just 'releases' of previously, or normally, repressed, or suppressed images, thoughts, feelings, and the like—particularly at lower doses of these drugs, or in those with reduced sensitivity to them (for either biological or psychological reasons)—in the more nether regions where these drugs may lead our consciousness, something else may happen. That is, we are forced to clothe, or engarb, the external forces, or beings, or influences that otherwise might be invisible to us, in a manner that we are able to recognize."

This profound statement suggests that what we talk about as paranormal might actually be these external forces, or beings, being made "understandable" or "acceptable" to our sensibilities. Therefore, beneficent beings may be seen as angels, malevolent forces as demons, or as strange forces taking on strange appearances and emotional colorations that assume the nature of forces or information they are representing or conveying. This implies a very subjective element of the supernatural: that people will see what they are culturally, socially, or even emotionally prepared to see. Yet it also implies that this is happening on a larger, more collective level, as many people report similar entities and experiences.

The previous statement alone is probably more critical to the understanding of paranormal phenomena than any thermal imaging camera or EVP recorder can ever give us. If the brain contains trace amounts of DMT, is it possible that with the right environmental effects, the right mindset, and with the right resonant frequencies present, someone could see the same being or entity they might see if they were to inject DMT in a controlled setting? Could there be external, or even internal triggers that cause our own natural DMT to kick in and produce for us the sensations of ghosts, aliens, angels, and demons?

Is this your brain on DMT?

When asked about the huge range of commonalities of entities and beings reported by different peoples of different backgrounds throughout the course of history, the response of many researchers points to whether or not these phenomena are internally generated, externally generated, or a bit of both. Many of these commonalities do show up when test subjects used DMT, but also with subjects who were not on psychedelic drugs at all, and had elevated levels of endogenous DMT generated by various means such as meditation, stress, and sleep disorders. Thus, the drug was not necessary for the experience of the beings and entities to take place, although it certainly helped.

Hancock's own research into the commonalities of UFO abduction reports with the lore of elves, faeries, and other types of beings reported by various cultures during various times in history led him to suggest that perhaps the human brain has been programmed with these images at the genetic level. For people all over the world to have massively recurrent shared cross-cultural experiences involving massively recurrent shared external real-world events is one consideration, but we kick things up a notch when people all over the world have massively recurrent cross-cultural experiences in situations where there is no provable scientific real-world stimulus for these experiences.

Even Jung speculated that this collective imagery might hint at the presence of parallel realities, or even the parallel universes of the quantum physics world. Perhaps even a field of "all reality" that consisted of an "unknown substrate possessing material and at the same time psychic qualities." Hancock speculates that these spirits and aliens are real, and that they may have found ways of manifesting in our reality in a variety of quasi-physical forms (of which "aliens" are the most recent). They have been appearing to us for a long, long time, which explains why reports of the paranormal don't seem to ever go away (and are even becoming more the norm).

The commonalities of these experiences might even be hard-wired into every animal or creature that has DMT in the brain, blood, and spinal fluid. DMT is found in many plants, as well as in fish and invertebrates. On the material biological realm, DMT seems to be the mechanism of action by which this spiritual nature is made manifest, and also serves to give the effect of a connection with the Divine nature. Research with DMT even intersects with NDEs, or near death experiences, and it produces the associated images with NDEs of the dark tunnel, the divine light, and the presence of loved ones and guardians. Those images, common as they are, are what we experience when we think we are dying, and DMT is the trigger or mechanism by which this occurs. NDEs are not hallucinations at all, but rather what our consciousness actually experiences as we die, which accounts for the amazing consistencies of NDE reports from all over the world.

DMT is indeed the brain's own trip to other worlds, and other levels and layers of the Grid of reality. And by "tuning into Channel DMT," our brains themselves begin to see the unseen realms usually ignored by mainstream science, despite the millions of reports throughout recorded history of such realms, and the amazing creatures that inhabit them. And for those who do not have the means, natural or otherwise, to access or trigger their latent DMT trip, maybe that explains why some see ghosts and aliens, and others don't.

Yet on a larger scale, we are all going to eventually encounter what exists in these worlds. Possibly only 2 percent of the population seems to be born to "trance," as Hancock calls it, and because the rest of us can be made to trance through substances found in nature, it might be expected that sooner or later every culture will experience the characteristic experiences, landscapes, and intelligent otherworldly beings that these trance states reveal.

We know that every culture at every period of history has had these supernatural visions, images, and experiences, and there is plenty of corroboration provided by such different and completely independent witnesses, suggesting a very real experience that does not yet fit the scientific methodology that seeks to measure or prove it. Too many people for too long have been collectively reporting these strange events, strange beings, and strange images—far too long and far too many for science to simply sweep under the rug. The time has come for science to take a good, hard look at these experiences, whether they be subjective or objective, and begin to examine their importance on both levels.

Yet modern, cutting-edge science may actually be less exclusively "this world"—focused than Hancock thinks. With some of the amazing new discoveries into quantum and theoretical physics, we are now hearing murmurs of possible universes that exist alongside our own, additional temporal and spatial dimensions, which some may already be traveling within, and even the "mother of all fields"—the infrastructure that ties all that was, is, and ever will be together. An all-encompassing framework. A grid.

Ahhhh…the Grid. And you thought we would never get around to it, didn't you?

9

INFRASTRUCTURE
OF REALITY

In some sense man is a microcosm of the universe; therefore what man is, is a clue to the universe. We are enfolded in the universe.

—David Bohm

Take an onion and cut it in half. You will see it has many layers—one upon the next—which, when peeled back, reveal only more layers. Take a star, or our planet, and do the same, and it looks very much like the onion, with layer upon layer making up the whole. Yet, an onion, or a star or planet, is a solid object for all intents and purposes. Reality, or the whole of all that is, just might be the same, proving that the creative force knows a good design when it sees it.

Even the most rational thinkers would be hard-pressed to deny the presence of a level of reality that exists beyond what our five senses can perceive. There are hints of this other level, or perhaps levels, throughout religious texts, ancient writings, and the journals of science and physics. What you see is not always what you get. If life has a form, a structure, there must also be a structure to those hidden realms; a foundation or infrastructure, like that of a building or architectural complex before the cement is poured and walls are erected and painted.

There have been many theories and ideas and names for such an infrastructure, but the most fascinating is the Zero Point Field. This field is described by physicist Hal Puthoff, a pioneer in zero-point energy research, as a "kind of self-regenerating grand ground state of the universe" that constantly refreshes itself and connects all matter in the universe. Lynne McTaggart, in her groundbreaking book *The Field: The Quest for the Secret Force of the Universe*, refers to the ZPF as "a repository of all fields and all ground energy states and all virtual particles—a field of fields." She also calls it "an ocean of microscopic vibrations in the space between things."

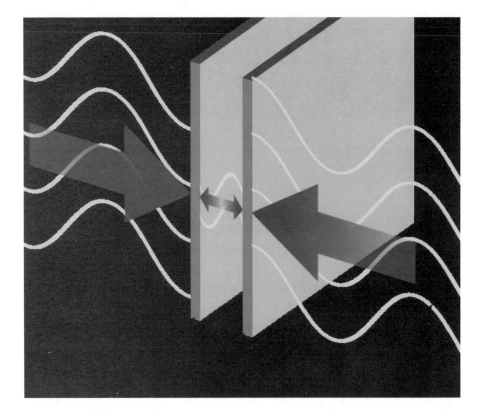

Figure 9-1. Dutch physicist Hendrik Casimir proved the existence of the vacuum energy of the Zero Point Field in the 1940s when he conducted experiments with metal plates. When placed close together, the zero-point waves between the plates cause an attraction and disturbance in the equilibrium of the field. There is less energy present between the plates than in the outer empty space. The greater energy outside pushes the plates together. Image courtesy of Wikipedia.

This underlying entity obviously mirrors what physicist David Bohm called the Implicate Order, and has been called many other names throughout time: aether, quintessence, vacuum energy, and the Force! A vast underlying ocean of energy with waves that, as Puthoff states, "drive the motion of subatomic particles and that all the motion of the particles of the universe in turn generates the Zero Point Field, a sort of self-generating feedback loop across the cosmos." Puthoff likens it to a cat chasing its tail.

Former astronaut Edgar Mitchell writes in *The Way of the Explorer* about this field as well: "Energy, we know, is the foundation of all matter; information is the foundation of knowing. Both were present at the moment of creation, whether in a big bang, or in a continuous process of creation in galaxies. It is likely that just as energy produced the physical structure that we recognize as waves and particles in our macro-world, the seeds of consciousness were also present to produce awareness and intentionality." These fundamental attributes of nature are dyadically coupled in our universe and have their basis in the very ground of existence—the Zero Point Field, which exists outside of space and time.

This field has no shape or form and cannot be seen; there are no spatial or temporal signposts that have been measured, no beginning or center point or end point, and non-locality and locality emerge from the same place within the field. All energy and all being and all thought and all matter in the physical universe originate and exist within the Zero Point Field.

McTaggart emphasizes the importance of this field: "If all subatomic matter in the world is interacting constantly with this ambient ground-state energy field, the subatomic waves of the Field are constantly imprinting a record of the shape of everything." Because everything then is imprinted in the field, all wavelengths and frequencies, the field becomes a sort of shadow to the universe, but one that is eternal and infinite and without beginning or end. A mirror image. A record of all that ever was and will be.

This stunning concept mirrors the Akashic Fields of Edgar Cayce and Ervin Lazlo. The word *akasha* means "sky" or "aether" in Sanskrit, and the Akashic Records refer to a theosophical concept of a collection or record of all knowledge that exists and can be accessed by those with psychic or mystical abilities. This sort of "universal filing system" contains every action and thought, every word and deed, every idea and imagining that ever was or will be. The akasha is the actual substance these recorded thoughts and actions are imprinted on, and can sometimes be accessed during dream states, meditations, trances, and other altered states of consciousness.

There are many names for this concept: collective unconscious, divine mind, collective mind, cosmic mind...and now, the Zero Point Field. Hindus believe that this akasha is the primary natural principle from which fire, water, air, and earth spring forth. Akasha is the womb from which physical form is created and birthed, and to which it will one day return. Ervin Lazlo, in his book *Science and the Akashic Field: An Integral Theory of Everything,* stated that the Akashic Records were the metaphysical equivalent of the more scientific Zero Point Field. Again, this A-field holds within it all form, matter, thought, and action, past, present, and future. This "quantum vacuum" is the fundamental energy and information-carrying field that informs not just the current universe, but all universes past and present, and is collectively called the Metaverse, a vaster, more fundamental universe behind and beyond the universe in which we exist.

Lazlo (also spelled as Laszlo) believes this informational field may explain why our universe is so improbably fine-tuned as to be perfect for the formation of planets and galaxies and even life itself, and why evolution is an informed, not random, process. Lazlo suggests this hypothesis may also potentially solve some of the quirkier problems that emerge from quantum physics, especially non-locality and quantum entanglement.

Lazlo, considered a world-class philosopher and systems theorist, also believes in the possibility of a "psi field," or a psychic field. In his book *Consciousness In the Cosmos,* he compares this psi field to gravitational and electromagnetic fields, and it is here in which all individual experience could be accumulated and deposited at the universal level. Lazlo stresses that such a psi field would have to possess a "mental dimension." In essence, this special psi field would represent the "mental dimension of the universe."

The great seer and healer Edgar Cayce referred to the Akashic Records for his healing sessions, drawing upon library of wisdom and information to make his assessments. His subconscious would link to every other subconscious mind within the field during his sleeping trances. He would then use his conscious mind to interpret the subjective information and make a medical assessment for healing purposes.

Similar to the biblical Book of Life, these records even contain the future, for linear time is only a construct of human reality and does not exist on a cosmic scale. Other mystics and individuals who have claimed to access this field for metaphysical knowledge are Rudolf Steiner, Dion Fortune, Manly P. Hall, Madam Helena Blavatsky, and Annie Besant. There are many who believe past life regression is the accessing of memories of former lives that are imprinted in the field. Even Nikola Tesla believed in a field of information that formed the very soul of the universe, claiming the field was able to create matter when acted upon by cosmic energy.

The energy within this field of all fields, oscillating at the lowest possible energy state detectable in temperatures of absolute zero, could, if we learned how to extract it, fuel the cities and nations of the future. Thus, the field not only has scientific and metaphysical implications, but purely practical ones as well. Imagine this free, unending source of energy. We could be free of fossil fuel dependency forever.

Though Mitchell, McTaggart, and others suggest this field of all fields is formless, that does not mean it is without structure. A thought has no form. You cannot hold a thought in the palm of your hand. But it does have structure: a beginning, middle, and end. And look at a love relationship: It is not an object you can put on a shelf. It has no form. But all relationships have a structure. Infatuation, deep attachment, and hopefully happily ever after...or hell on earth! It is a structure that is not defined by visuals, but a structure nonetheless, and it allows us to better imagine just what this thing they call the ZPF really is.

To begin with, maybe this field is really more of a grid, with varying levels of reality that exist with little or no interaction with other levels. It is almost like a skyscraper where each floor is part of the whole building, but people on each floor have little interaction with those on other floors, either because they can't, don't yet know how, or don't want to. Though it may very well be a field, it is easier for us to imagine varying layers within the constructs of a grid, with levels of reality above and below, whereas in a field we visualize only a flat, two-dimensional area with width and length.

Thus, the authors of this book propose we think about this field as a grid with layer upon layer upon layer, field upon field upon field, with no top or bottom or sides. Infinite and never-ending. A never-ending onion skin of layers.

The idea of a structural component of reality allows us to form a visual interpretation of what might be the building blocks from which our life experience, and the meanings we ascribe to it, arise. Can something come from nothing? According to traditional physics, this is an impossibility. Likewise, if the Zero Point Field is real, then no. Something comes from a field, or sea, of virtual quantum foam from which particles leap into and out of existence, and there is no such thing as empty space. Every inch of space is filled with something, some vibrating form of energy even as low as baseline zero value. A jiggle of primordial Play Doh from which all matter and form and reality is molded.

So, what about this grid? What is in it? Is it just particles and matter and energy that are unformed and unrealized? We speculate there is more. In fact, the Zero Point Grid could be instead filled to the brim, even overflowing, with information. Data. Like a library of books filled with all of the knowledge ever compiled and experienced and gleaned and discovered and uncovered—yet we, with our limited life perspective, tend to check out very few books from that library within one lifetime. This seems such a shame given the potentiality of the information one might glean!

But that does not mean other books, other realities, are not available to us. Consider the Grid a card catalog of everything, and we have the ability, whether conscious or not, to use the card catalog to locate the information we need to fulfill our life needs and goals. Okay, so, newer libraries have their books cataloged on computer, but we as the readers are still in control of which books we choose to check out in the end, and few if any of us could ever read every book in a library in one lifetime. Imagine a library that is filled with constantly updated information, getting new shipments of books in by the trillions on a daily basis. Remember Henry Bemis, played by Burgess Meredith, in the old *Twilight Zone* episode titled, "Time Enough at Last"? Bemis worshipped books, but hated those who would prevent him from having the time to read them. Then the world came crashing to an end and he, surviving the end, found himself with all the time he needed to read and read and read…until his reading glasses broke. Not even Bemis could even come close to reading all the books in the Grid, glasses or no glasses.

Physicist David Bohm (yes, we quote him often, as he is one of the few popular scientists that Marie admires!) referred to the eddys and whirlpools that form a river. These eddies give the appearance of being separate, with their own characteristics and sizes and speeds and measurements, but when we look closer, we see that they are so much a part of the river, it is almost impossible to see where the eddy or whirlpool ends and the river begins.

Living within the Grid, we are generally blissfully unaware of the larger picture of our reality, of all the layers that hover below and above us, to the side of us, through us. An excellent analogy to this would be the plethora of electromagnetic waves floating around us 24/7/365. AM, FM, shortwave, TV, cellular, microwave, UHF, VHF. It's all there for us to experience, but, unless we are properly tuned in, we are ignorant of their existence. Yet, even though we see them not, they are there and they are separate in the sense that they may have their own laws and rules, yet they are also such a part of the whole we cannot see where we end and they begin.

In McTaggart's book, she talks about the field with a reverence often reserved for religious topics. "All living things are a coalescence of energy in a field of energy…this pulsating energy field is the central engine of our being and our consciousness, the alpha and omega of our existence. The field is, in other words, our brain, heart, and memory."

We understand from traditional physics that matter and consciousness are connected. Quantum physics tells us that the building blocks of reality are more like bits of information, or quanta—bundles of energy and not really matter per se. We hear that our act of conscious observation influences the outcome of our perception. Yet most of us continue to live under what psychologist Charles Tart calls "Consensus Reality Orientation," or CRO, which enslaves us to a consensus perception of reality that is difficult to break out of. Perhaps being aligned with this trancelike state of general consensus is what allows us to function in our day-to-day lives. We don't have to think much, just go along to get along.

Unfortunately, it also constrains us to one perspective. Like the quote from Alexander of Persia, "A wolf and a dog each other constrain, but in the end only one shall remain," we cannot seem to hold two worldviews at one time. The trance of our own worldview is far more powerful than anything we do consciously with suggestion or hypnosis. We have held this rather materialist worldview for more than 300 years, ingraining the cultural conditioning into the mainstream. We are brought up with this worldview, go to school to have it hammered into our minds and souls, and find most attempts to escape it filled with resistance from within and without.

We rise through levels of conscious awakening as we move up from one CRO to a new one, yet when we adopt that new CRO as reality, dismissing the one that came before it, we are still not seeing the entirety of the whole. Just another level. We might speculate that beyond death we will reach the final level, the end game. Or perhaps that journey will require a million lifetimes. That is the mystery of life itself. Walking the Grid may be one infinite marathon, for as one level comes to completion, we step up to the next.

By expanding our perception, we walk a new level of the Grid. Here is a simple exercise for shifting your CRO. This exercise gives the experiencer the feeling of being a part of the Grid, with intentional influence upon an outer source. Find a radiometer, which is an instrument that looks like a light bulb with a movable vane suspended inside a near vacuum. Take your radiometer and put it on a flat and stable surface under a light source. You will see a whirring movement. You can then stop the movement with your mind. Focus on the spinning vane, quieting the mind and calming the body. If you do this, the vane should slow down, perhaps even stop. Proof of the power of intention. Ahh, intention—that all-powerful, seemingly New Age concept that has been forever linked with the law of attraction thanks to the now infamous book *The Secret* by Rhonda Byrne. In fact, the concepts of utilizing intention and attraction are not new!

But what it really might be is evidence of the power of the consciousness acting on the vibratory nature of the object, all of which are connected within the field of all fields. There is nothing that is not connected. Thought is connected to the spinning vane in the field. In the Grid.

Like a giant quantum computer, the Grid acts as a machine, but one that is self-learning, evolving, and intelligent—always expanding exponentially as it takes in and spits out more and more information, which then is reprogrammed and creates even more information. An endless progression of computation that has it's own dynamical evolution, as author Seth Lloyd states in *Programming the Universe: A Quantum Computer Scientist Takes on the Cosmos*.

Information theory posits just this: The entirety of reality, the Grid, is made up of "its and bits" of information, and the universe programs itself into existence constantly. All matter and form is a result of this programming. Lloyd tells us, "Every atom, every particle registers information. Every collision between atoms, every dynamic change in the universe, no matter how small, processes that information in a systematic fashion." Like the field, or our Grid, it is all about information and its creation and exchange. "To see this universal information-processing technology in action, one need only open one's eyes and look around. The machine performing the 'universal' computation is the universe itself," Lloyd states.

The general nature of the universe as a computer is to generate complex systems, such as life. But even on the quantum level, it appears the universe supports computation, as long as the laws of quantum mechanics are obeyed. This explains the complexity of all we see around us, which most information technology scientists believe did not just happen by chance, but by intricate programming of information intending the perfect symmetries that led to life as we know it; all of this in a universe that started out very simple, and very unsymmetrical.

This does not mean the universe, or the Grid, is alive and thinking. The authors of this book put forth the idea that the Grid is indeed a sort of "biological machine" that acts as a quantum computer, yet has the ability to evolve and encompass intelligence and consciousness. Lloyd also states that some of what the big universal quantum computer does is process thought, in the form of our own human thought. But that does not necessarily imply that it is capable of thinking itself. In this sense, the Grid is like a self-learning computer, one that can program thought, but not think it on its own in a consciously aware sense.

Still, lest we think we are so special, we are reminded that we are nothing but information. We are unique information, in that we have that certain something that makes us human in all its misery and glory. But that certain something is simply information. We, as Lloyd reminds us, are made of atoms, just like the rest of the stuff out there. "It is the way that those atoms process information and compute in concert that makes us what we are. We are clay, but we are computational clay."

Organic in that it evolves and grows and appears to learn, but not a living thing, the Grid is all life and all inanimate matter and even matter and life that has yet to be formed. Wrap your human mind around that!

If the Zero Point Field is laid out in a grid-like fashion, how many of these layers are there? There may be an infinite number, as the universe is said to be infinite, and of course, when one takes into consideration the possibility of an infinite number of parallel universes, we can say there are infinite grids that make up the whole of all. Except, that whole of all is infinite and has no finality or boundaries. Yet the grid levels themselves may have boundaries. Like an underground parking facility, it is a whole, but made up of many levels, and you had better write down which level you parked your car on.

The Grid level we are on, our manifest reality, obeys particular laws of nature and physics, and has at its foundation certain mathematical concepts. Perhaps one grid above us is a universe that obeys far different laws, or laws very close to our own, but tweaked just so as to form a noticeable difference from our own comfortable reality.

Just as there are levels of consciousness, we may be talking about levels of manifestation that would allow for all kinds of "paranormal" and anomalous stuff to exist, albeit usually out of reach from the primary grid we call home.

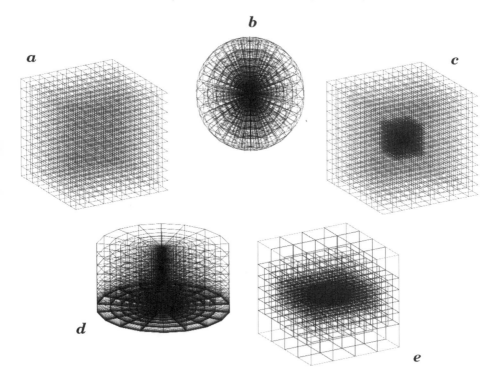

Figure 9-2. Grids come in different sizes, shapes, and levels.

Think of the possible ramifications! Ghosts…UFOs…Bigfoot! Perhaps they all simply inhabit an alternate level of the grid, and are as real as you and I!

If a field can be described as a region of influence, either electromagnetically, gravitationally, or via some as yet undefined force, then the ZPF is the ultimate region of influence, which permeates where one force field ends and another begins. There is no break in between, but there are different individual fields.

The word *grid* is defined as:

▶ A framework of crisscrossed or parallel bars; a grating or mesh.

▶ Something resembling a framework of crisscrossed parallel bars, as in rigidity or organization.

▶ A pattern of regularly spaced horizontal and vertical lines forming squares on a map, a chart, an aerial photograph, or an optical device, used as a reference for locating points.

▶ An interconnected system for the distribution of electricity or electromagnetic signals over a wide area, especially a network of high-tension cables and power stations.

In all these definitions, the concept of layers or levels is clear, creating a framework that encompasses all layers into an infrastructure. Again, think of a skyscraper with dozens of floors, a basement, parking garage, and rooftop deck. Each level may exist as a separate entity; say, one floor for accounting, one for legal, and the rooftop deck for lunch breaks. But together they are all part of the same building. Also, think of a map, and how the use of a grid helps to locate specific points and locations, something most helpful to those of us still living in the dinosaur era without a GPS (Marie still uses her own sharp, hawklike sense of direction, and rarely gets lost).

Except with the Zero Point Grid, we are talking about a building that may have an infinite number of floors. (Sounds like the basis for a great sci-fi series—*Levels.* Marie and Larry have dibs on the copyright!) Or a 3-D map that has pages below it and above—layers upon layers.

And just as big cities have more than one skyscraper, the Zero Point Grid would have more than one "access point" in space and time. Look at an image of a city skyline. If the city is all of reality, and each building represents a different universe or dimension or both, and each of those buildings has numerous floors or levels, you get an idea of the amazing infrastructure we call the Zero Point Grid. Oh, there are so many places you can go (to para-phrase a popular children's book title). Just stay away from where those wild things are.

If we look at typography, a grid is a system by which one lays out a page with different-sized rectangles and such to align words, diagrams, and im-ages. This is used in all types of design, including art and architecture, interior design, graphics, and computer design. There must be a workable structure to the objects that are laid out upon the grid. This book was most likely designed on a grid made just for publishers.

We have all heard of the grids on our own bodies, such as acupressure points, meridians, and other healing modality references that refer to the mapping out of physical points of energy and flow. These meridians are like ley lines of the body, directing energy and power, and requiring balance for optimal health and well-being.

Other more metaphysical grids include:

▶ **Curry-Hartmann Lines**—a mystical and theoretical geophysi-cal phenomenon attributed to German authors Manfred Curry and Ernst Hartmann. These lines form east-to-west and north-to-south grids across the Earth's surface and involve a field of radiation that can be detected by dowsing, but not scientific instrumentation. The human body, when placed upon a C-H Line, can experience either beneficial or detrimental effects, de-pending on the radiation flow.

▶ **Ley Lines**—In 1921, amateur archeologist Alfred Watkins coined the term to describe the alignment of ancient megalithic structures and monuments. Though this could be described by the fact that these lines were common routes of travel and trade, and could have totally mundane meaning, many people believe ley lines are lines of power that link sacred sites.

▶ **Dragon Lines**—similar to ley lines, but ascribed to the Chinese feng shui, this type of geomancy, or ancient form of divination using soil and materials scattered in patterns on ground, is used to locate power sites where *chi* energy is in harmonious

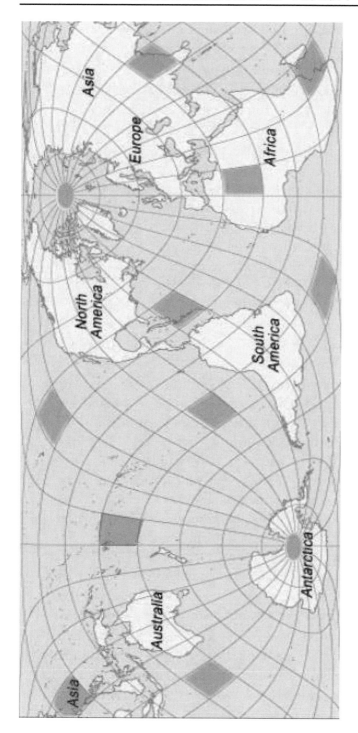

Figure 9-3. The 12 vile vortices of Ivan P. Sanderson.

192 THE RESONANCE KEY

balance. Also known as **dragon current**, these were lines of magnetic force that were designed to balance the negative current of *yin* with the positive current of *yang*.

▶ **Black Lines**—alleged "negatively charged" lines of "black" energy that are said to be naturally formed, and perhaps localized in nature.

▶ **Becker-Hagens Grid**—William Becker is a professor of industrial design at the University of Illinois, Chicago, and Bethe Hagens is a professor of anthropology at Governors State University. Becker and Hagens created an Earth Grid, which they called the Unified Vector Geometry 120 Polyhedron, or the UVG 120 "Earth Star." This "cosmic energy" grid is alleged to crack the code of the positions of the Platonic Solids on Earth. They ascribe this discovery to the work of Ivan P. Sanderson, who was the first to make a case for the structure of the icosahedrons at work in the Earth.

▶ **Vile Vortices**—Ivan P. Sanderson, naturalist, author, and founder of the Society for the Investigation of the Unexplained, discovered what he referred to as 12 "vile vortices," areas of the Earth where mysterious disappearances, mechanical failures, and time-space distortions happen more frequently, as in the Devil's Triangle and Bermuda Triangle. These vortices were marked "Devil's Graveyards," and were thought to be responsible for the many disappearances of people who crossed their boundaries, perhaps due to conflicting air or sea currents, or something even more paranormal in nature. He made this discovery while researching ship and plane disappearances linked to paranormal activity in the late 1960s. Later, in 1973, three Soviet scientists (Goncharov, Morochov, and Makarov) backed up his vile vortices claims by suggesting a matrix of cosmic energy made up of 12 pentagon-shaped plates covering Earth.

Sanderson's vile vortices form the vertices of an icosahedron, and five of them are within the Tropic of Cancer, five within the Tropic of Capricorn, and two at each of the Poles. These vortices are said to be hot spots of electromagnetic anomalies and unexplained phenomena. David Hatcher Childress, author of *Mapping the World Grid*, writes "…we are speaking about an intelligent geometric pattern into which, theoretically, the Earth and its energies are organized—and possibly in which the ubiquitous megalithic sites are also positioned."

■ ■ ■ ■ ■ ■ ■ ■ ■ ■

Vile Vortex Locations	
Tropic of Cancer	**Tropic of Capricorn**
Mohenjo Dara	Megaliths of Zimbabwe
Devil's Triangle, Japan	Wharton Basin
Hamakulia near Hawaii	Hebrides Trench near Fiji
Bermuda Triangle	Easter Island
Algerian megaliths	South Atlantic Anomaly
North Pole	South Pole

Source: Paranormal-Encyclopedia.com.

■ ■ ■ ■ ■ ■ ■ ■ ■ ■

These more mystical concepts of planetary grids emphasize the influence of the grid or matrix pattern as a way for us to make sense out of a chaotic and often disharmonious reality by giving form, structure, and even meaning to the location of people, places, and things. The entire science/art of sacred geometry is founded upon these power points in nature, which take on structure and show amazing design—possibly divine design. Power may be meted in specific measurements, not just on the earth and our bodies, but in the universe and beyond as well.

But grids exist in more mundane ways. Unless you truly are old school, and prefer reading by candlelight, more than likely you are enjoying this book by the light of a modern light fixture. If so, you are likely aware of the power grids that crisscross the planet, giving us the energy we need to heat and light our homes. When one of these grids is down, due to a computer malfunction or natural disaster, thousands, if not millions, are left "in the dark."

Are you an aficionado of maps? Do you fancy yourself an amateur cartographer? If so, then you are intimately aware of the importance that grids play. Anyone who has ever used a map relies on grids to find their destined location, although today GPS systems are slowly making printed maps obsolete.

To describe the Zero Point Grid, it might be most helpful to start not from bottom up, but from the top down.

▶ Infrastructure.

▶ City.

▶ Building.

▶ Floors.

Infrastructure is nothing more than the physical organizational system to describe the operation of a system, society, or enterprise. There are several kinds of infrastructures, but the one that we think most closely describes the Zero Point Grid is that surrounding a major city. Within the infrastructure of say, MarLar, a mythical city created by Marie and Larry, there are technical structures put in place to support the functionality of that city and its suburban areas. In MarLar, there are transportation facilities and roads, power generation and transmission, water resources and supply, public works, communications, social services such as schools and medical facilities, and government operations facilities. Other types of infrastructure may include civil defense and military, construction, waste management, and nightclubs. Oh wait, scratch the nightclubs.

All of these lesser forms of infrastructure create the larger urban infrastructure of MarLar and keep it running smoothly and efficiently, with people coming to and from, goods being exported and imported, and the necessities of life being produced and transmitted to those who live in our fine city.

Any disruption of one part of the infrastructure is felt all over the whole city, for if water availability stops, or power goes off, everyone is affected.

Infrastructure not only holds a city together, but it also holds the people together who live in it…when it works well. One of the most important facets is transportation. We have roads and freeways, airports and train stations, buses and walkways—all designed to get us from Point A to Point B. In a city, this infrastructure is critical to the flow of business and commerce as well. Without a way to get to and from our city to another, or just to get around our own city, we must have a solid infrastructure of transportation.

Think of the Zero Point Grid as the Ultimate Infrastructure.

The infrastructure of an urban area usually involves land outside the actual city, linking roads to other cities. The city is a part of this greater infrastructure, but is also an individual entity. Now, we look at MarLar itself, the several actual blocks that make up the city of cloud-touching buildings and fancy eateries, mid-town parks and hi-rise apartments. We are leaving the suburban areas out of the picture and staying within the boundaries of MarLar city limits.

The city bustles and hums with activity, some of it self-contained, as people who live and work there go about their business within the proximity of the city limits. But like any city, there is also interaction with people in other cities, even other countries, via meetings and lunch dates, phone calls and video conferences, and even texts and e-mails. No city is an island. To engage in this thing called life, we must at some point reach out and touch someone outside the city limits.

Within each city are many, many buildings. Let's take the Umpire State Building (or USB for short). In MarLar, that's what it's called, because, well, copyright issues and all. The USB is 20 stories high and, yes, retrofitted for earthquakes. On each floor, there is a separate business, but some businesses take up more than one floor. So, people can often be seen going up and down elevators and stairs to get to the floors they need, or, in the case of lunch and end of the workday, to get the heck out of the building and go home (or to the suspiciously missing nightclubs and bars). Some people manage to hit every floor, especially those who exercise at lunch running up and down the stairwells listening to their iPods.

But the building is a hotbed of activity, and some people stay all night working. There is always action, the movement of matter and form, although sometimes that movement and form is denser on some floors than others.

Think of our particular universe in the Zero Point Grid as the building we all work in. Heck, let's just say we live there, too. We are all workaholics it seems. Imagine just going into the office right from your bedroom. (Hey…Marie already does that.) Our universe is the Umpire State Building, from basement parking level to the rooftop deck.

Then, in our building, the one we can never escape from, we have floors. Each floor consists of different kinds of activity. The first floor could be Information Services. The fifth floor is all that legal stuff. The ninth floor is popular—that's where the cafeteria is located. The 20th floor is the penthouse suite for the CEOs of a major energy corporation specializing in the extraction of Zero Point Energy. Oh, and the roof has a Jacuzzi and pool. And of course, every floor has bathrooms.

Those who work in legal rarely visit those who work in accounting, and yet at some point they all visit the cafeteria floor. The bums down in human resources on the eighth floor wouldn't be caught dead talking to the bums up on the 17th floor that work in waste management. But they all work in the same building, and at some point, they all come into contact with one another. There are floors that operate autonomously, and floors that require quite a bit of inter-floor communication.

Think of the floors as individual levels of reality in our universe in the Zero Point Grid.

From the macrocosmic nature of the Grid itself, to the finer inner workings of its many components, we are left with an infinite infrastructure in which we exist. Some of the points along the Grid are not easily accessible to us in a general sense. There is no linear time in the Grid, but for those of us locked into a particular building in MarLar, we cannot just cross our arms and blink to access the past, or the future. Although theoretical physicists tell us there are parallel universes and alternate dimensions beyond those we are aware of, we can't just wrinkle our noses and blink out of one and into another.

Or can we?

In every infrastructure, there are roads and airways and waterways. In every city there are buses and taxis and cars and streets we can walk on. In every building there are elevators and stairs to get us from floor to floor. Some people even like to use the fire escapes.

The modes of movement with the Zero Point Grid may be much more theoretical and complex, yet at the same time, just as simple. If you have to get from one point to another, there is always a way to do so.

If we look simply at our building, our universe in the city of MarLar, we could take the stairs, or the quicker elevator. In case of a fire, we could jump, unless there was a fire escape outside the building. No matter which way we choose, we can get from one floor to another.

In the Grid, we could one day take a wormhole.

The idea of a shortcut through space and time was once the stuff of science fiction novels and TV shows, but today wormholes are a widely accepted potential for traversing the universe we live in, and possibly traversing the many universes we live among. Wormholes would provide us with a mode of travel that is faster than light speed, and could get us from different regions of space and even of time throughout the Grid, once we can figure out how to turn theory into fact.

Wormholes were originally called Einstein-Rosen Bridges after the work of Albert Einstein and Nathan Rosen in 1935. The two scientists posited that the theory of general relativity did indeed allow for the existence of these space-time bridges or shortcuts, which we might visualize as big tube-like structures with widened openings at either end. There was once a belief that some kind of exotic matter, as yet to be discovered, would be needed to keep a wormhole's throat open so that something could pass through it without the wormhole collapsing inward, but new research points to the possibility that nothing more exotic than what is already out there is needed.

Inter-universe wormholes are those that can link up *one universe with another universe*. Intra-universe wormholes connect two points in *the same* universe, either spatial or temporal. Traversable wormholes, those that would allow for actual travel from one mouth to the other, always fall under the category of Lorentzian wormholes, which are studied in relation to general relativity and semi-classical gravity. There are other types of wormholes, such as Euclidean, which relate to particle physics.

Schwarzschild wormholes describe those that connect closed universes, with a "black hole" and a "white hole" at either end. They are not thought as yet to be traversable. Krasnikov wormholes suggest hyper-fast interstellar travel. A Morris-Thorne wormhole is a traversable wormhole with its mouths held open by the presence of exotic matter.

Wormholes could allow for time travel as well as spatial short-cuts. By accelerating one end of the wormhole at a high velocity relative to the other end, then later bringing the first end back, one would achieve relativistic time dilation with the accelerated end of the wormhole aging at a lesser rate then the stationary end. If you were to enter the accelerated end and come out the stable mouth, you would exit in the past.

Although time travel is certainly within the realm of science fiction at this point, are we that far off from time machines made from wormholes? Remember, television was something our cave-dwelling ancestors could never fathom…especially some of the shows on network TV. University of Connecticut Physicist Ronald Mallett predicts that human time travel will be accomplished within this century. Mallet's solution is elegant, but intricate. According to the *Daily Mail*, "He thinks he can reverse time by using just a circulating beam of light. Light is energy, and energy can cause space-time to warp and bend, just like gigantic spinning cylinders," he explains.

In 2000, he published a paper showing how a circulating beam of laser light could create a vortex in space-time. It was, he says, his eureka moment.

The details are complex, to say the least. But, in essence, Mallett believes it is possible to use a series of four circulating laser light beams swirling space-time around like "a spoon stirring milk into coffee."

Are Mallett's idea's impossible or forbidden by the laws of traditional science? "In physics," says physicist Michio Kaku of the City College of New York, "that which is not forbidden is mandatory. If you want to forbid some bizarre phenomenon, you have to kill it by showing that a law of physics prevents it."

As discussed earlier, we could always learn to utilize Zero Point Energy to move freely and quickly about the Grid. Once we manage to extract this energy, the sky, and all the skies above and below our own, is the limit. We would just need to build the ships that could take us there. Of course, to do all of this, we are assuming the existence of parallel universes and alternate dimensions we can travel to.

Most theoretical and quantum physicists posit the existence of universes that exist alongside our own, perhaps infinite in number, and that one day, advanced civilizations may find the means by which we can travel in spaceships to these other worlds. String Theory requires alternate dimensions in addition to the four we live with every day, and newer theories such as M-Theory, F-Theory, and the braneworld scenario also demand more than three spatial dimensions to work in a mathematical sense.

Though no one as of yet has proof that these theories are fact, we might look to the experiments in Cern, Switzerland, with the Large Hadron Collider (LCH), which might prove the existence of a string, thus adding credence to String Theory. According to the U.S. Website of the LHC, "LHC will be the world's most powerful particle accelerator. Scientists predict that its very-high-energy proton collisions will yield extraordinary discoveries about the nature of the physical universe. Beyond revealing a new world of unknown particles, the LHC experiments could explain why those particles exist and behave as they do. The LHC experiments could reveal the origins of mass, shed light on dark matter, uncover hidden symmetries of the universe, and possibly find extra dimensions of space." Perhaps we might even open up a portal to another universe, create a little black hole, or prove any other number of cutting-edge theories that drive physics today.

MIT professor and cosmologist Max Tegmark stated in a 2003 issue of *Scientific American* magazine that we may be looking at the existence of infinite worlds, each with a copy of ourselves that is identical in all ways except for one minor choice that splits off into another universe. For example, Marie exists in Universe A with brown hair, but in Universe B she dies it blond, and in Universe C she shaves her head in honor of Yul Brenner. And so on and so on. Each universe features a replica of Marie, but with one minor tweak, and each time Marie makes a new choice, another bunch of universes spring into existence in which she makes *every other available choice...or no choice at all.* This does not mean Marie can access any of these other universes at will, but as we will expound upon in the next chapter, perhaps she can do so through dreams, trance states, altered consciousness, meditation, and other means of "travel." Still, she would love to transport herself into a universe where she had Stephen King's career and Oprah Winfrey's money.

Infinite universes, one branching into the next instantaneously each time a decision is made, a choice committed to. And this happens with each and every living thing on earth, every second of every day.

Mind-boggling, to be sure. But if there are indeed all these other places out there, real places with physical laws and features and life, then who is to say we are not already accessing them? And who is to say we are not already welcoming some visitors from those worlds into our own, and on a regular basis? Might this not help to explain the abundance of reports of ghosts, aliens, cryptoids, and creatures that should not exist? Regardless, reports of the unknown don't seem to go away no matter how much science wants to deny them, or skeptics defy them.

Michio Kaku suggests that if we were to see something appear from another universe or dimension, it might look like "magic" to us. There may be parallel universes hovering over our heads, but because they exist in another dimension, our access to them is thought to be impossible. These other dimensions could be so tiny and curled up we could never get inside one, or massively huge in size.

M-Theory posits that our universe is a three-dimensional membrane that is one of many other membranes floating in an even bigger universal structure, perhaps even a higher dimension of space-time. The Big Bang might have been a collision of two branes, forming the birth of our known universe. These braneworlds might be of varying sizes and dimensions, some two, some three, and might also explain some of the stranger properties of gravity, as well as the existence of that elusive dark matter. Gravity might even be a weak signal that leaks out of one of these parallel universes, or branes, into our own. And to those who believe in the paranormal, gravity may not be the only thing leaking out of those other worlds.

What these and other cutting-edge theories suggest, then, is that there is a multi-layered infrastructure in which our little neck of the woods is simply one point in space-time. The entirety of the infrastructure may have form, but no boundaries, no beginning or end, yet can contain actual "levels" or realms in which the laws of math and physics and nature are just a little bit different, if not quite a bit different, from our own. If Tegmark is right, there is a universe next door where each of us has two heads, three legs, and 10 eyes. And one where we each win the lottery. And one where we each win

American Idol…. It sounds silly, but that is basically what he is saying. *Every potentiality creates another level of reality in which that potentiality is fulfilled.*

And now, the quest is on in the halls of science and academia to find out not just if these other realms exist, but how we can get to them.

Yet, as science always tends to do, we focus only on accessing these other realms through physical means, such as spaceships, machines, and technology. What if the machines we needed were not outside of us, but within us? For even as we seek proof of these shortcuts and travel routes through space and time, universe and dimension, we might want to instead begin to turn our attention inward.

Maybe we already hold the key to traveling the Grid. Come to think of it, maybe "they" do, too. Ghosts…aliens…angels…and spirits.

10

GHOSTS IN THE GRID

An idea, like a ghost, must be spoken to a little before it will explain itself.
—Charles Dickens

If form, matter, and energy move from floor to floor of the building we call our reality, those things we call paranormal may likewise move in similar fashion, finding shortcuts and routes to change the frequency of their vibratory nature until it is in phase, or in synch with our own. Through resonance, a ghost might finally lock into just the right frequency to show itself to a room full of terrified tourists. Or perhaps resonance is the key to a UFO appearing out of nowhere over an urban sky, only to blink back into the nothingness from which it came.

As we explored in Chapter 8, there may be a paraconsciousness that allows us to perceive these paranormal beings. And as we examined in Chapter 4, a particular frequency range may be associated with their ability to show up in our reality. Maybe the things we deem paranormal don't actually show up in our reality, but instead *we* show up in *their* subjective realties. Are we the ghosts or the UFOs? It all has to come from somewhere, and the Zero

Point Grid, if indeed it is the infrastructure of reality, which includes the entire landscape of time, is most likely that somewhere.

Take ghosts for example. Theories abound regarding the likely possibilities. Most of us assume they are imprinted memories of the dead, or the leftover energy of a dead person who didn't have Jennifer Love Hewitt to help them cross over to the other side, once the physical body has returned to dust. Either way, it has been posited by many that a ghost is nothing but energy, albeit in a different form from our own, and perhaps operating on a different vibratory level. It comes from somewhere, and goes back there. Why is this? Well, according to traditional physics, the law of conservation of energy is in force. Within this universal construct, the first and second laws of thermodynamics are in effect. The first law of thermodynamics simply states that energy can be neither created nor destroyed (conservation of energy). Thus, power generation, as well as any existing energy sources, actually involves the conversion of energy from one form to another, rather than the creation of energy from nothing.

Condensed to its most basic tenet, this law posits that the energy of the universe is a constant. In other words, the energy existing in the universe is all that there is, was, and ever will be. Moving on to the second law of thermodynamics, we find quite a bit more complexity. The second law basically dictates the way in which energy flows. According to the law, energy has an absolute, unfailing tendency to move from more concentrated (higher potential) to less concentrated (lower potential). Throughout this process, energy will continue to keep flowing from higher concentration to lower concentration until the concentrations are in a state of equilibrium.

If the Grid is the repository of past, present, and future thought, action, and event, it is here that we can look for the place where we all must go when we die. The return to equilibrium. Back to the Source, so to speak.

Using resonance, a ghost operating on a particular vibratory frequency might synch up with a particular frequency of our own brain, our consciousness, or perhaps even our environment, and manage to slip through the thin veil between worlds. Interestingly enough, ghostly apparitions are rarely consistent and are often described as "erratic" and "fuzzy," to name a few of the vague terms oft associated with such fleeting visions. Some ghosts appear almost as three-dimensional projections, suggesting the holographic nature of reality, and furthering the idea that the visual image is somehow being projected onto our reality from an alternate dimension.

We can look to the ancients and their ability to access paranormal and psychical states while experiencing Samadhi, or a rapturous state. In the Vedic traditions, meditation is used to access this field of unity for benefits of health and peace of mind. The levels of consciousness associated with psychic events often involve higher awareness, even an ecstatic state, such as those obtained via chanting, meditation, and trances (not to mention hallucinogens!). Shamans have traditionally utilized rituals involving drumming, dancing, and chanting to "allow the mind to transcend the mundane," where they can "see with the eyes of an eagle and discover the approach of an enemy." So too do Sufi dervishes who whirl and twirl in a strange trance-inducing dance. This sounds very much like what remote viewers do, albeit without the whirling and dancing, looking outward from "within" to locate target objects at a distance. But not everyone has to be high on life to experience a paranormal event. Ghosts, UFOs, and psi abilities often occur to people who are not expecting them to, even people who claim they never believed in them before.

Non-locality, an accepted fact of quantum physics, allows for the exchange of information within all points of the Grid. Particle communicates with particle, allowing for information to be spread across the landscape of time. This may help to explain precognition, psychic abilities, and mind reading, and might even assist in the understanding of déjà vu. Haven't we had this conversation before? Sure, in another parallel universe just last week....

In the final part of the 20th century, the idea of non-local information stopped sounding so much like magic and more like reality. If the Grid is there, or the Field if you wish, then non-local quantum effects could verify how common or shared experiences happen as information flows in and out of the Grid. These experiences include psi abilities, remote viewing, past-life regression, and the collective consciousness.

The Grid is filled with everything that ever happened and will happen, on every level of reality. Although we would never be able to focus enough to survive if we had access to everything in the Grid (we've all heard the phrase

"TMI—Too Much Information!"), there is no reason to believe we cannot ever access anything in the Grid. We probably do more so than we imagine, but pass it off to intuition, a hunch, or a trick of the eye.

Andrija Puharich, a medical doctor, inventor, and author, with an intense interest in parapsychological research, explains psychokinesis, the ability to move objects with the mind, with his theory of resonant effects and extra-low electromagnetic frequencies that operate in "tachyon" dimensions, or dimensions that are faster than the velocity of light. In these realms, the harmonic vibrations succeed light speed and operate at a higher principle of the laws of vibration. If you happen to be a Star Trek fan, you are undoubtedly familiar with the concept of the tachyon as is relied upon quite heavily for both light-speed transport and the core technology behind the Romulan cloaking device. Although tachyons are generally still considered theoretical in nature, they are gaining acceptance within the scientific community. This tachyon field is similar to the ZP Grid in that it allows for laws that go beyond our normally accepted physical and mathematical laws. The association of other realms or dimensions, even other types of base or ground energy (think orgone, chi, or quintessence) are an integral part of various theories that might explain how supernatural events such as mental psi abilities may be possible.

Puharich believed the mind lived in the tachyonic realm, and with the help of harmonic resonance, operated on the lower physical plane. He went on to patent a number of biomedical devices while utilizing his background in science to study the neurophysiology of psi abilities. Puharich even introduced the infamous Uri Geller to the United States in the 1970s and arranged for special testing to be conducted by the military think tanks operating at the time. Puharich also set up tests with supposed telepaths using a Faraday cage, which is an enclosure designed to block out specific external EM frequencies via conductive shielding. Using this device, he was able to determine that psychic abilities did not use conventional EM frequencies as carrier waves from one person to another.

It's a longstanding fallacy that scientists have not been involved in the study of paranormal phenomena. Many physicists, psychologists, neurophysiologists, and other learned men and women of science have engaged in research into the connections between the known laws of nature and the unknown realms of the supernatural. Although the term *paranormal* is generally associated with ghosts, this is not necessarily the true and correct meaning. According to *The American Heritage Dictionary of the English Language, Fourth Edition,* the term is defined as "Beyond the range of normal experience or scientific explanation." Nowhere does the definition infer or imply that the term pertains strictly to ghosts! Of course, likely based upon the current popularity of paranormal programming on television, the general public instantly associates *paranormal* with ghosts. With that being said, much of the legitimate research conducted by scientists has focused on psychic abilities and remote viewing. Very little formal research has been conducted into the ghost phenomenon. With the cutting-edge discoveries of quantum and theoretical physics, that research has spread to include potential propulsion methods (such as antigravity) and travel routes, for unidentified flying objects that may come from advanced civilizations tooling about our humble universe.

The concept of the Grid opens the door to not only a place from which these unknown anomalies may arise, but how they get to us as well. Physicist Claude Swanson proposes an interesting theory that he has termed the Synchronized Universe Model. This theory states that resonance can be used to explain how paranormal phenomena can move between levels, or layers, of universes and dimensions via coherence and phase synchronization. In his book *The Synchronized Universe: New Science of the Paranormal,* he presents a vast study of the paranormal past and present before finally getting to his own theory, bringing together the worlds of quantum physics, the new science of consciousness, and the world of things that go bump in the night.

Just as theoretical physicists such as Michio Kaku and Brian Greene propose parallel universes, additional dimensions, and braneworlds, Swanson suggests that each universe is like a sheet, upon which other sheets or universes exist. Each sheet follows its known laws of physics and mathematics, and rarely does any energy or matter cross over from one sheet to another. But, when coherence is present and there is a synchronization of matter and energy between sheets, or, as Swanson puts it, when they are locked in phase with each other, this opens the door for energy to cross over from one sheet to another, and possibly in the form of psychic or paranormal phenomena.

Those, like Larry, who regularly investigate paranormal phenomena out in the field using strict scientific methodology and equipment, can attest to the rarity of occurrences. These stubborn ghosts, goblins, and other entities just don't cooperate by following our timescales or show up when we want them to. They are scattered at best, and most often don't make an appearance here on our realm at all. If the movement of energy from one sheet to another arises from such erratic means as the phase synching of the two sheets, then it is easy to see why it's not every day that you see a ghost walking through your living room, no matter how haunted your family insists that living room might be.

Swanson describes his Synchronized Universe Model, or SUM, as a single synchronized universe represented by one sheet of paper in a stack. Each sheet has its own frequency and/or phase, characterizing the synchronized motion of the electrons in that system. Other sheets are "parallel realities" or other "parallel dimensions" that cohabit the same space and time, yet each sheet is unaware of each another.

This model suggests how matter or energy might cross between dimensions, by altering the phase of one "universe" to allow coupling and crossover to another. In our view of the Grid, the stacked sheets are the levels of reality, each independent yet part of the whole. And with the potential of locking individual frequencies in phase with each other, the means arise by which we can move about the levels of the Grid, and allow for other entities to move about as well.

Perhaps this frequency "locking" is similar in function to a PLL or Phase Locked Loop, which, according to circuitsage.com, is "is a closed-loop circuit that compares its output phase with the phase of an incoming reference signal and adjusts itself until both are aligned, i.e., the PLL output's phase is 'locked' to that of the input reference. Once the loop is locked (the phase difference between the output and the input signals is very close to zero), the frequency of the output signal is a multiple (integer or fractional) of the input signal's frequency." This sounds remarkably similar to the natural process of equilibrium and the covalent bonding of energy as we discussed in the second law of thermodynamics. Is it possible that this is an entirely natural, organic process...and maybe even automatic?

The paranormal knows nothing of regularity and consistency, which is what makes it almost impossible to study and reproduce in accordance with the scientific method in a laboratory setting within a tightly controlled environment. UFOs and ghosts never seem to leave enough information behind as to how they show up in our reality, except via subjective witness reports that amount to nothing more than experiential, and quite subjective data. Yet we can look for environmental factors present before, during, and after a paranormal event to help us identify what laws of nature this phenomena may be manipulating or utilizing.

And again, if paranormal phenomena originates in that implicate layer of reality, where we do not see causality, and where we do not see the entirety of connectivity, it will continue to appear irregular and inconsistent to us, no matter how much science you put behind it.

Swanson agrees that quantum physics may hold some of the keys to explain paranormal phenomena, and that resonance plays a major role. Even DNA seems to work with this coherence to create force fields that help get molecules into their proper place for replication and nucleosynthesis. Coherent energy is also used in biomolecules such as enzymes. Once again, our own bodies may provide clues as to how reality works on the larger, cosmic scale.

These coherent, resonant processes that allow the trillions of molecules in the body to communicate and function in resonance, bring up the possibility of the body as a macroscopic quantum system, with a set of coherent quantum states. "If this is the case, then some of the weird phenomena we have called 'paranormal' might really be just quantum mechanics working its strange magic on the large scale of every day life."

Consciousness interacts between these parallel dimensions of the SUM model, and can reduce or affect the quantum noise and even synchronize motions between the parallel realities. Just as in quantum physics, consciousness drives the outcome even in this particular model, with the most paranormal effects expected when the most coherent coupling of motions occur across the parallel realities represented by each stacked sheet. It may be subtle energies moving across these parallel realities, such as the energy of the Zero Point Grid. This synchronous interaction of energy and particles across the realities, and across time and space, is the core of a synchronized universe system.

This system, as well as the Grid, also allows for the possibility of time displacement, physical time travel, and as visibility into the past and future. If the Grid contains the landscape of time, then everything that will happen in the future is accessible at some point, as all of time is really a unified "here and now" with no distinction on a cosmic scale. The future exists as pure potentiality, a superposition of which we then collapse the wave function to create the present moment. Ervin Lazlo proposed that time displacement in the Zero Point Field is possible. His idea focuses on the fact that the field, or Grid, is made of electromagnetic waves and has a substructure, or secondary fields, which are caused by the motion of subatomic particles in the field itself.

These "scalar waves" are directionless and can travel beyond light speed, similar to tachyons, and the scalar waves are encoded with information about space and time, as Lynne McTaggart writes in *The Field*. This "Lazlo model" acts as a sort of ultimate holographic blueprint of the world, past and future. It is this blueprint that we tap into when we see into the past or future? Thus, precognitions, psychic abilities, ESP, remote viewing, and even past-life regression all have a home within the structures of the grid-like field.

Lazlo calls it the common cosmic womb, from which all matter and mind evolved. "The interaction of our mind and consciousness with the quantum vacuum links us with other minds around us, as well as with the biosphere of the planet. It 'opens' our mind to society, nature and the universe." The cosmic womb of the Grid is where those who predict the future look upon events that already exist on one level, yet have not yet happened on ours. The cosmic womb of the Grid is where those who see into remote locations without leaving a room tap into the storehouse of details about a military base halfway around the planet. The cosmic womb of the Grid is where the craft of advanced civilizations fuel up and zip about without the effects of gravity, using the shortcuts of wormholes to traverse the farthest reaches of our universe, and other universes. It is where our spirit and energy goes when we die, and where we get a glimpse of death during a near-death experience.

Dozens of studies into telepathy, consciousness, and mental coherence by the likes of Ervin Lazlo, Dean Radin, William Braud, Roger Smith, Helmut Schmidt, Charles Tart, Russell Targ, and many others show a distinct connectivity between people, even when they are not in the same room.

Random Event Generators, or REGs, have been experimented with for years, indicating distinct influence of collective thought and intention on inanimate machines. Dr. Dean Radin, author of *Entangled Minds*, has been involved with his colleagues for years utilizing these small black boxes to see if there truly is something called the collective power of intention. These devices, the PEAR portable REG, the Mindsong Mircoreg, and the Orion RNG, are used in lab experiments using "quantum-indeterminate electronic noise." The devices provide random sequences that are functionally equivalent. The major REG studies at PEAR, the Princeton Engineering Anomalies Research lab, involve using the REG and RNG machines to detect quantum level phenomenon that produce "a well-behaved broad-spectrum voltage fluctuation," according to the PEAR website. It all begins with white noise, with a cut off at the 1,000 Hz range to eliminate frequencies at or below the data-sampling rate.

These machines are part of a network of more than 60 host sites across the globe, all of which are part of the PEAR experimentation to acquire and assess data. The data comes in the form of tangible fluctuations of the REG readouts during high-stress events such as the O.J. Simpson trial, the September 11th terrorist attacks, and Princess Di's death, among many others. By examining the fluctuations that occur during these times of collective distress, researchers can better understand the role of consciousness and intention upon physical systems, devices, and processes, as well as the more metaphysical implications that we are all connected and we all respond to events as one, within a unified field. These experiments are part of a broader organization called the International Consciousness Research Laboratories, made up of more than 75 members in the fields of scientific and consciousness studies. Their goal is to "expand the boundaries of scientific understanding, and to strengthen the foundation of science by reclaiming its spiritual heritage."

The REG experiments, which indeed showed that collective thought leaves its mark on the black box readouts, posits very strongly the existence of a grid in which we all move and have our being. These REGs recorded fluctuations for both planned events, such as Y2K, and for totally unplanned events, such as the terrorist attacks. Either way, the grand human reaction was the same, and it was provable. Radin even suggests that the REG fluctuations, ESP, and telepathy are types of quantum entanglement, connecting everything in all of time, and allowing for a sort of "when I poke, the other one flinches" reaction between the entangled parties...and we are all entangled parties. This entanglement can happen between two people, or between two million. It doesn't matter; the law works the same either way.

Our emotions and thoughts have energy, and, according to traditional scientific tenets, that energy is recordable and transferable. We have more power than we thought we did, and the Grid is what connects us all, and opens the doorways to shared experience. Shared experience can be anything from the global excitement felt during the Olympic games, to the mass hysteria of the Dark Ages, or even to a wave of UFO sightings that grip an entire city.

UFO sightings often occur in families and groups. Likewise, people who are together on ghost hunts tend to experience the same things, the same noises and apparitions. As children, this kind of suggestiveness is rampant. We don't want to be left out, and so we go along to get along. Perhaps this has a purely behavioral basis, but perhaps it is rooted in the fact that we are all tapped in to the Grid, and when one person has an experience, a few others in his or her vicinity are bound to experience it, too.

Charles Tart's early experiments showed empathy between people who can feel each other's pain when one is administered an electrical shock. William Braud's research points to proof that people respond to remote communication and attention, and that ordinary humans could remotely influence others mentally and physically. Some of the most successful experiments involved the Ganzfeld protocol, which eliminates all sensory input. It's not as though there aren't any real scientific studies out there to back up the concepts presented in this and many other books. There are, and they continue in both the halls of science and the halls of paranormal research alike.

Additional studies done in Mexico suggested that the brainwaves of two people in separate rooms would synchronize when asked to sense each other's presence. EEGs measured the increased synchronization, which often occurs during deep meditation. According to Lynne McTaggart in *The Field*, these experiments showed that when the ordinary boundary of "separateness" is crossed and coherence achieved, "The brain of each member of the pair becomes less highly tuned to their own separate information and more receptive to that of the other. In effect, they pick up someone else's information from the Zero Point Field as if it was their own."

If that isn't a description of ESP, remote viewing, or clairvoyance, what is?

This idea of two people having a synchronized bandwidth led to Lazlo's idea that "expanded bandwidth would account for a number of puzzling and highly detailed reports of people who undergo regression therapy or claim to remember past lives...." Again, the resonance of brainwaves to other brainwaves, or the resonance of brainwaves to that of the higher dimensional Grid allow the access of information from the past and the future, as well as the present. And the amount of information is infinite, but we, or perhaps we could say our consciousness, chooses which information it needs to access on a daily basis, usually for purposes of survival and need.

But that abundance of "other" information is out there...

Have you ever had the suspicion that your pet may know what you are thinking? Larry often feels that with Dodo (whom you might remember from my acknowledgements in our previous book *11:11—The Time Prompt Phenomenon: The Meaning Behind Mysterious Signs, Sequences, and Synchronicities*). I was quite relieved to find that my pet's seemingly psychic sense experiences were not isolated. In his research, Rupert Sheldrake, author of *Dogs That Know When Their Owners Are Coming Home*, determined that there are actually three categories that these psychic pets may fall under:

1. Telepathy—a connection that some pets may establish with their owners, which is most often manifested in their pet's ability to "know" when their owners are on their way home.

2. The Sense of Direction—this extraordinary ability accounts for the incredible journeys that some animals undertake to be with, or follow their owners.

3. Premonitions—may help to explain why some animals seem to know when geological events such as earthquakes, tsunamis, and volcanic eruptions are about to occur.

Sheldrake's research into psychic pets led him to develop his theory of morphic fields and morphic resonance (as we discussed in a previous chapter), as the means by which information moves in these fields. "These morphic fields connect things together in the present and are sustained by their memory of the past." Using psychic pets as an example, he stated that there are fields of social groups, and that dogs adopt the field of their owner.

Morphic fields also contain attractors, which draw organisms toward future states. The idea behind psychic pets suggests that as people are going home, the home is the attractor in their field. Getting home is their goal, their intention, and the dog somehow picks up this change in the field and knows their owner is on the way. Remember the experiments described previously, where the brainwaves of two people synched up even when they were not in the same room? This may have been an example of human morphic fields, and the synching of their brainwaves on the EEGs acting as the morphic resonance that allowed them to "feel" each other's presence. These fields link people through sensory experience, feeling, and energy.

Again, we cannot see these fields or prove their existence, but we do see the results of them when we sense something beyond our usual five senses, or when we have an experience that does not seem to follow the usual laws of physics. We can almost bet, and win, that these experiences have happened to everyone at some point in their lives, though most will pass them off as "just one of those things!" Until the brain is entrained to accept a new idea or perception, we just won't accept one!

The problem with paranormal activity is its inconsistency, and its often erratic, if not downright exotic nature by which it manifests, as well as the potential for much of what we call paranormal to be as influenced by human consciousness as it may be by actual outside physical manifestations…indeed, perhaps both. As a paranormal investigator in the field, Larry can personally attest to the hundreds of locations his team has spent countless hours in, with absolutely no results to speak of. If a ghost doesn't want to show up, it won't. And when it does, we have little if any advance warning. This is truly spooky physics!

If a paranormal event cannot be reproduced at will, science generally discards it, yet it obviously exists and is being reproduced in the form of experiences by thousands, if not millions of people all over the world. Just because there may not be empirical proof of ghosts, aliens, and spirits, that certainly does not invalidate the visions and interactions of the masses who, throughout the course of human history, have continued to insist that they are real. The question remains—how much of this is physical and how much of this is the construct of our own consciousness and imagination? But regardless, this stuff is real, and it is coming from somewhere. Until we can identify the laws by which these phenomena operate, we struggle to fit a square peg into a round hole.

The laws of the Grid may mirror our own universal laws to some extent, but we can't forget that the Grid would also contain all the laws of every other dimension, realm, and universe within its infinite "boundaries." In addition, we must keep in mind that those laws may not behave as we expect them to. We might not even be able to imagine the physical laws that operate in another parallel universe. Maybe they have laws so bizarre we would only recognize them as pure magic. Maybe they follow our laws, but have learned ways of manipulating them to allow for energy to transfer and move among levels of reality. Their worlds, and their modus operandi, might be totally alien to us—no pun intended.

Only when coherence is achieved, when synchronization occurs, when frequencies are locked in phase and resonate, does that doorway squeak open for just a short, short time, and then, and only then, does our brain make the neural connections and we see the ghost in the Grid before us.

11

WALKING THE GRID: VIBRATION, CONSCIOUSNESS, AND THE ZERO POINT GRID

Because the rules of quantum theory are supposed to apply to all matter, not just subatomic matter, by extension of this uniquitous, interconnected "resonance,' the suggestion is that all nature is in some sense wavelike, fieldlike, and mindlike in a way that isn't fully understood.

—Edgar Mitchell, *The Way of the Explorer*

*It don't mean a thing
if it ain't got that swing….*

—Duke Ellington

Wave. Mind. Field. Leave it to a brilliant man like Edgar Mitchell to, in one quote, sum up the entirety of this book. Wave. Mind. Field. Vibration. Consciousness. The Grid. This is nature. And within nature, it is resonance that holds the key to unlock the door, linking the three "natures" of nature into one cohesive whole, a whole that forms all of reality, including every level of the onion from the first thin coating to the firm and pungent core.

Imagine a shiny new car and you are the proud new owner. (With the current state of the economy, and oil prices being artificially inflated, it would be politically incorrect if we were to imagine anything but a hyper-efficient, gas-saving hybrid.) Now, imagine that this cute little people-transporter represents our body, our vibratory being. What good is having a car if we don't go anyplace? Well, to do so we need fuel. The fuel that powers that car is our consciousness, and it is responsible for driving us in a particular direction. Now that we have a fully gassed-up vehicle (or charged-up if we are in hybrid mode), we are almost ready to embark on our journey. Next we must decide where to go…and how to get there. The roads we travel upon are the Grid, and they can take us anywhere if we have enough fuel, we know where we want to go, and the car is kept in top working order. All of the parts of the car must be in superb, humming condition to get us to our destination…just as our own vibratory frequency must be in synch with our consciousness, and therefore in synch with the open road that calls to us.

During the writing of this book, coauthor Marie was deeply engrossed in Stephen King's *Wolves of the Calla*, the fifth installment of the Dark Tower series. For anyone who has read this epic tale that spans seven books, each one fatter than the next, you can recall the links between vibration, consciousness, and what could be described as the Zero Point Grid. Recall the mysterious chimes that send Roland and his tet into parallel worlds? Every time those beautiful, awful chimes sounded, resonating through the gunslingers' minds and bodies, they would go "todash" and enter a parallel world in a different temporal dimension. They referred to this as the "where" and the "when." The chimes were the resonant vibration that allowed them to change consciousness and move between different levels of reality along the Grid.

Yes, this is a piece of fiction, and an amazing and horrific one at that, but how easy it is for us to accept these concepts in a novel or a movie, when all the while both cutting-edge science and the paranormal are telling us that maybe, just maybe, they are real. In fact, we can often look to the fictional writers of fantasy and science fiction of yesteryear to predict what one day will become science fact. Just think of the tales of H.G. Wells and Jules Verne…not to mention Mary Shelley, the queen of bionics!

Science has long known about these things, but rarely has chosen to look at the less tangible evidence of resonance at work. When Larry and Marie, your illustrious authors, first made e-mail contact, we somehow knew that we needed to work together. Despite the fact that we lived in separate states 1,700 miles apart, we resonated. We were on the same page from the start. Now, neither of us could be taken into a lab and hooked up to a machine, and prove the existence of that resonance between us as coauthors and partners. But we know it, and this book is proof of and testament to it.

We must, at some point, look beyond what our five senses alone tell us is real, and take notice of the more subtle truths that point to the power of resonance to create what we experience as "our lives." Just look at human language, which often holds great truths tucked away in phrases and sayings that sometimes do more to "tell it like it is" than the most stringent scientific test. "I resonated with her." "That place gave me bad vibes." "We are on the same frequency." "Get off my wavelength!" And our favorite, "Great minds think alike." These simple sayings speak of the inherent understanding that we, as human beings, vibrate, and that everything around us does as well. And often, what we cannot verbalize quite yet in mathematics, physics, and science, we do so in our language.

To understand what it is like to walk in the Grid, we can often look to our own lives. Experiences of this are all around us. Those who have walked before us led the charge, but even today we each walk the Grid in our own ways.

■ ■ ■ ■ ■ ■ ■ ■ ■ ■ ■

Marie's story:

"Many, many years ago, while living in Burbank, California, I attended a special three-day intensive Shamanic training course with Michael Harner, author of The Way of the Shaman, and one of his colleagues. I had always been interested in native belief systems, and in the shamanic use of sound to journey to other levels of reality. I thought it far safer than smoking or imbibing some strange hallucinogenic drug! Having never even smoked pot, I just wasn't one to be in any situation in which I was not in control.... Little did I know what was to come throughout the course of those three days.

I, being the child of a scientist, often am skeptical first, and open-minded second, and I went into the training with a lot of attitude. I had tried meditation before this, with little results, and had resigned myself to the fact that my analytical monkey-mind had become way too dominant. But I was open. My momma had taught me that much!

As the first day progressed, we ended with our first "journey" to the sound of rattles we had brought with us, and drums provided by the staff. Michael chanted, and we all learned a song: "I circle around, I circle around, I circle around the boundaries of the earth...." Those are the only lyrics I can remember, but the idea was to feel like a hawk, to take on the eyes of a hawk, to fly as if I was a hawk. I did what I was told, moving around the circle, rattling and singing, feeling a little stupid and silly, until something happened.

I began to feel as though I was soaring, high above a landscape that was foreign, yet beautiful. The sensation was great, and lasted throughout the exercise. I remember going home that night singing that song and feeling "high." I had left my own level of reality, and though I could never "prove" it to anyone, it did happen.

The next two days were devoted to finding our totem animals, helping others to find theirs, and making contact with them. I was told not to reveal my totem at the time (although I can now say it was a bear), but suffice it to say, I rebelled when I was given it by my journeying partner. I had always thought of myself as a wolf, but that was not the totem I was given. Again, my skepticism and judgment kicked in, and I spent the second day feeling pissy...until my journeying partner and I had to do a soul-retrieval for one another. I don't remember my partner's name (although "Ben" comes to mind), but we did our thing to the sound of rattles and drums, moving through dark tunnels to the other worlds of Shamanic wisdom (there are three: upper, middle, and lower), and the exercise proved to be very interesting. Once my partner breathed the spirit into me at the end of the exercise, I suddenly felt...like a bear.

That night, we did the chanting and drumming circle again, and were told to take on the qualities of our totem. I watched at first as others stalked, flew, and pounced around the circle, and again felt like an idiot, but as the rattling and drumming and chanting grew louder, I'll be damned if I didn't rise up on my two strong legs and start roaring like a frikkin' black bear! Again, with the sound to accompany me, I was transported out of my current state of awareness to another world, where I was bear, not human, and the feeling was incredibly powerful. I stomped and pounced around that circle, growling and roaring and swiping at enemies, and I was really not in my body anymore. At least, not in my human body. I went home again singing the circle song, and growling good-naturedly at everything I saw.

The final day and night was made up of more journeying, and by this time I was truly convinced of the power of sound, especially rhythmic sound, to create a vibration within the body and outside of it, conducive to altering consciousness. I still love wolves, but to this day, when I am feeling scared or weak, I remember. I still have my rattle, and it reminds me...

I am bear. Great, mighty, fierce, strong.

■ ■ ■ ■ ■ ■ ■ ■ ■ ■ ■

The use of sound and other means, such as light, to raise vibratory frequencies has been proven to change body, mind, and spirit. In fact, as I, Larry, and writing this particular section, I am being bathed in the soft blue glow from my trusty GoLite M2 Blue Spectrum Light Therapy Device. This little gadget has been a lifesaver in helping me deal with the symptoms of SAD (Seasonal Affective Disorder) brought on by the dark, cold, icy Arkansas winter days (Marie lives in Southern California and scoffs at this!). In addition, it instantly boosts my mood, energy levels, and stamina—all from a mere 15 minutes of shining light! Beyond personal, anecdotal experiences regarding sound and light, we explored the foundation behind the "why" in previous chapters. Regardless, until someone experiences walking the Grid, and moving within wave, mind, and field, it is nothing but a vague concept. Those who pray and meditate regularly walk the Grid by using chanting, drumming, words, or even focusing intended thought in order to lift the mind into a consciousness of reverence, stillness, and receptivity.

Whether we use mind-altering drugs, machines, or drums and rattles to lead us into these other realms of experience, we all have the means to access them. Within the Grid, just as there may be different levels of reality and manifestation, there are different levels of consciousness as well. Once we have reached equilibrium, or have "phase-locked" our own consciousness and vibratory rates to those of the level we wish to access, we manage to "slip between the veil of worlds" and have a mystical, metaphysical, or paranormal experience.

If you want to experience walking the Grid, an easy way to do so is to find a labyrinth in your area. These are elaborate, maze-like structures that offer a single path to the center (unicursal maze) and are much easier to navigate than most mazes. Labyrinths date back to Greek mythology, built by Daedelus for King Minos of Crete in Kossos, where a huge Bronze Age labyrinth has been discovered. The labyrinth was designed to pen in the ferocious Minotaur, a half-man, half-bull creature. This original labyrinth was designed to hold in something negative, but today, people walk labyrinths all over the world to achieve a positive result, often a sense of incredible inner calm and stillness. Most labyrinths people see today are circular, but some are square in shape.

The circle labyrinths are most often associated with the metaphysical movement of today, and even many churches in the New Thought movement have them in their basements for attendees to walk before and after services. Yet they are far older, and the classical labyrinth shapes that we see most often today have their roots in medieval times.

■■■■■■■■■■■

Marie's story:

I walked my first labyrinth in Burbank, California, in the basement of the Church of Religious Science. It was drawn onto the floor, in a quiet room with candles and soft music. Just looking at the labyrinth invokes a sense of spiritual presence, and even holiness. I did not know what to expect when I slowly took my first step, and tried not to make eye contact with the other three people at different points in the labyrinth. I was afraid at first their presence would disrupt my experience, and vice versa. I had nothing to fear.

Once you begin to walk along the path, slowly and with focus, you change. Suddenly, there is no one in the room but you. Your mind goes quiet. Chatter ceases. Thoughts dissipate. And, by the time you reach the center, you have entered a completely different place, a higher state of awareness, yet also a profound inner sense of serenity. I stood in the center for a few minutes, absorbing the experience, then, to accommodate others waiting to walk, started the path outward.

On the way out, as you move further and further away from that "holy center," you feel yourself returning to "normalcy," and the regular state of day-to-day awareness. And once you exit the labyrinth, you feel refreshed. This indeed is a walking meditation.

I walked another labyrinth just a few months ago, on the top of a mountain at the Questhaven Retreat, a Christian mystic retreat hidden away in the woods here in San Marcos, northern San Diego County's rural area. This was an outdoor labyrinth, made of small white pebbles, and the effect of the crunching pebbles under your feet, coupled with the stunning mountaintop view, truly made for a mystical experience. This time, in the center, I felt an expansiveness some might call "rapturous," and again, as I moved back to the beginning point, I felt my brainwaves shift, and my consciousness move lower into the state of normal activity. I strongly suggest walking one. It is a wonderful way to experience different levels of reality and consciousness without ever leaving the ground. After all, the ground beneath our feet is sacred.

■■■■■■■■■■■

Figure 11-1. White pebble labyrinth on Questhaven Mountain, San Marcos, California, right. Image courtesy of Marie D. Jones.

Perhaps it helps to look at the Grid in a more metaphysical sense, for without this spiritual connection, the idea of the Grid remains somewhat foreign and distant to us.

The Grid is like the Matrix of reality within which we live and move and have our being, as other beings are doing the same in their part of the Matrix. We experience only one layer of that proverbial onion at a time, sometimes getting a glimpse of others, but rarely do we spend any length of time there. Still, we know that those other levels exist. Our souls tell us. So too does our consciousness, which, as it grows and expands in awareness, allows for even greater inter-grid experiences.

If reality, and thus, the Grid itself (for it encompasses all of reality) is about the evolution of consciousness, then, by proxy, reality must be a never-ending process of change, growth, and expansion. There is no fixed truth. All is fluid, and dynamically changing. Quantum physics suggests that we, through the act of conscious observation, change the outcome of a physical experiment.

Several possible interpretations of this idea have been proposed, with the fundamental basics (that of the spectator modifying the outcome merely by observing it) being inherently similar among them. One such hypothesis was conceived by George Sudarshan and Baidyanaith Misra of the University of Texas, and popularly referred to as the Quantum Zeno effect. The Quantum Zeno affect basically states that if an unstable particle is observed, it will never decay. In his 2007 book, *Mindful Universe,* Henry Stapp, professor of quantum physics at UC Berkeley, claims that the Quantum Zeno effect is the main method by which the mind holds a superposition of the state of the brain in the attention. He advances that this phenomenon is the principal method by which the conscious will effects change, a possible solution to the mind-body dichotomy. Remember the old saying, "a watched pot never boils"? This idea of observation is behind the growing movement of resonance in the self-help and empowerment field.

Ultimately, if a concept has no value to us as human beings having a human experience, we have little use for it. It may be a concept that runs the very laws of science, or drives the creative forces of evolution or of the universe. But if we can't use it, we tend to lose it. Resonance, it seems, has incredible value in doing much to shape and direct our individual realities. This is not science, but a new psychology based upon using vibration to lift consciousness to match that which we seek to attract from the substance of life—the Grid.

Are you starting to get the impression that most of what we not only perceive, but what we ultimately may manifest, may be a construct of our internal state? If you haven't read *The Secret,* you've obviously been living under a rock for the past year or so. The new wave of books, movies, and television shows, not to mention lecture series, Websites, and whatever other media you can imagine, are all devoted to the "law of attraction." At the very core of this law is the foundational use of resonance to align thought with intent. The goal of focused intention is to shape reality into being, to manifest goals and make things happen. And it is a wave that is taking the world by storm.

By the time this book hits the shelves, no doubt there will be a plethora of additional items out there pushing the use of the "attractor factor" in daily life. This is not a new idea by any means, having long been a part of religious traditions that posited, "you shall receive what you believe." In more recent popular culture, in books such as Napoleon Hill's *Think And Grow Rich* and Rhonda Byrne's aforementioned mega-seller, *The Secret*, people have been putting their focus on the use of resonance, vibration, and consciousness to obtain what they want to experience in life. The release of the popular sleeper movie and subsequent book, *What The Bleep Do We Know!?* led the new and revitalized charge toward understanding that our thoughts have power to create.

If the Zero Point Grid is the repository of all matter, form, thought, and action, then that is where we must go to find the stuff of life: Ideas that become objects. Inspirations that become inventions. Anything physical starts with a thought—even life itself. You have to first think about having sex to make a baby! The law of attraction in quantum physics is based upon entanglement, that when two particles "meet" they stay in instantaneous contact with each other, no matter how far apart they may be. But it also comes from the wave/particle duality that states all is in a state of superposition until we collapse the wave function through an act of observation, and make something "real" and fixed.

Because everything is in this superposition state, we might suggest that our consciousness is what collapses the wave function. Our thought is what drives it to do so in a particular way, depending on the vibratory nature of our intention. If we have powerful, positive intention to find our car keys, the resonance of that intention causes us to collapse the wave function and look down on the floor and see them peeking out from under the couch. Well...ok, this is rather simplistic, but think about this from William Tiller, PhD: "We are running the holodeck. It has such flexibility, but anything you can imagine it will create for you. Your intention causes this thing to materialize once you're conscious enough and you learn how to use your intentionality. You learn to control intentions."

Or this from Amit Goswami, PhD: "In the new view, yes, mathematics can give us something; it gives us the possibilities that all this movement can assume. But it cannot give us the actual experience that I'll be having in my consciousness. I choose that experience and therefore, literally, I create my own reality."

In fact, let's take a look at the viewpoints of a variety of people on the subject of using resonance to focus thought, change vibratory rate, and create the manifestation of intent. It's interesting to note that many of them are from scientific fields.

- ▶ "What most people don't understand is that thought has a frequency. We can measure a thought." —John Assaraf, *The Secret*.

- ▶ "There is a thinking stuff from which all things are made, and which, in its original state, permeates, penetrates, and fills the interspaces of the universe." —W.D. Wattles.

- ▶ "The vibrations of mental forces are the finest and consequently the most powerful in existence." —Charles Haanel, author of *The Master Key*.

- ▶ "Quantum physics really begins to point to this discovery. It says that you can't have a Universe without mind entering into it, and that the mind is actually shaping the very thing that is being perceived." —Dr. Fred Alan Wolf, PhD, quantum physicist and author.

- ▶ "Every person is surrounded by a thought atmosphere.... Through this power we are either attracting or repelling. Like attracts like and...we attract just what we are in mind." —Ernest Holmes, creator of *Science of Mind*.

- ▶ "The world is a looking-glass, and gives back to every man the reflection of his own face." —William Makepeace Thackeray.

▶ "Quantum mechanics confirms it. Quantum cosmology confirms it. That the Universe essentially emerges from thought and all of this matter around us is just precipitated thought…" —Dr. John Hagelin.

▶ "Man is all mind. He is one with Universal Intelligence. He is expressing himself on the material plane. He builds his own dwelling place and thought is the bodybuilder." —E.H. Anderson, *A Mental Scientist.*

▶ "I have no doubt that reality is in a very large part a construct of the imagination. I am not speaking as a particle physicist or even as someone who is totally aware of what is going on in the frontier of that discipline, but I think we have the capacity to change the world around us in quite fundamental ways." —biologist Lyall Watson, *Supernature.*

▶ "Matter is the mother, the receptive principle (the yin), form is the father, the active principle (the yang). But all these principles are expressions of the differentiating consciousness, which itself is beyond differentiation." —Father Bede Griffiths, Benedictine monk.

▶ "The universe was a vast, dynamic cobweb of energy exchange, with a basic substructure containing all possible versions of all possible forms of matter. Nature was not blind and mechanistic, but open-ended, intelligent, and purposeful, making use of a cohesive learning feedback process of information being fed back and forth between organisms and their environment. Its unifying mechanism was not a fortunate mistake, but information which had been encoded and transmitted everywhere at once." —Lynne McTaggart, *The Field: The Quest for the Secret Force of the Universe.*

And finally…

▶ "A man may be the greatest philosopher in the world but a child in RELIGION. When a man has developed a high state of spirituality he can understand that the kingdom of heaven is within him." —Swami Vivekananda.

▶ "Man has to learn to seek first the kingdom of heaven, the place of stillness and quiet at the highest level of which he is capable, and then the heavenly influences can pour into him, re-create him and use him for the salvation of mankind." —White Eagle

▶ "And I will give to you the keys of the kingdom of heaven: and whatever you shall bind on earth shall be bound in heaven: and whatever you shall loose on earth shall be loosed in heaven." —Matthew 16:19, *King James Bible.*

▶ "The laws of nature are the laws of our own nature. If I were not Sun-like, I could not perceive the Sun." —Roland Fischer.

Every single one of these quotes, from such diverse sources, points to a reality that is based upon thought, vibration, consciousness, and the interaction within a field or "kingdom" that is generative and creative. Whether using the mind to align vibrations with an intended physical object, or acting as the observer to collapse the wave function, all three elements must be present for reality to come into existence. Vibration is the resonant frequency of creative power, consciousness the modus operandi by which that power creates, and the Zero Point Grid as the pool of potentiality from which all is created.

Even Carl Jung, the father of analytical psychology, believed in a cosmogony that, based upon Gnostic creation myths, had at its source a ground state from which all of reality was born. The Pleroma was both the nothingness and the fullness of everything; eternal and infinite in that it had no qualities, yet had all qualities. Similar to the Zero Point Grid, the Pleroma was empty, yet not empty at all, teeming with this formless state of substance in which universes were enfolded and the world of order, the Creatura, sprung forth. Jung's theory of the universe is mind and matter, and includes an animating power of the world that arises within the realm of dualities. In the Pleroma, which is both empty and full, there are no distinctions. It is all and nothing at all. The entirety of all, yet empty of entirety. Dualities of light and dark, empty and full, good and evil, the one and the many, appear in the Creatura, or the explicate realm of surface, manifest reality, where they rise from the simple act of perception.

"As above, so below" speaks about more than just an ancient cosmic worldview whereby the microcosmic and the macrocosmic are mirror images of one another. What happens on a grand scale is mirrored in the subatomic world, and even within our own consciousness. As if we are but cells in the body of some infinite deity, or individual parts in a mighty machine, the Grid interconnects us all, and we all have access to the potentiality that exists within it. But first, we must realize the importance of aligning vibration and consciousness to the frequency of the Grid. And we can do so for means of destruction just as easily as for means of creation. The choice, via free will, has been given to us alone. Without that choice, we are lost in a sea of discord and chaos, and nothing makes sense. Nothing seems to "click."

Maybe when Jesus Christ admonished his followers to "Do Unto Others," he was thinking of resonance, and how we have personal energy that is broadcast to others, and thus sent broadcast back to us in return. We get what we give. In her book *Quantum Success: The Astounding Science of Wealth and Happiness*, author and counselor Sandra Ann Taylor talks about the resonant power of energy we as humans send and receive: "The Universe is alive with energy; nothing exists without it. Everything that you see—and most of what you don't—is full of waves and vibrations. No matter where you go or what you do, you're constantly sending and receiving energy, and you live in a confluence of unseen frequencies all the time."

The idea is to broadcast only the kind of energy, at the kind of frequencies that brings back to us what we truly wish to experience. The last thing we want is to focus on negatives, because that is what we ship off to the Universal Warehouse, which then ships up more negative stuff to send back to us, usually via overnight mail! You can never get enough of what you don't want, unless you change your vibration, change your thoughts, and shift your own frequency to that which you do want. This is at the core of all the greatest teachings in the personal power and self-growth movements.

We are constantly broadcasting the resonant energy that then draws back to us what we are sending out. Our lives, it can be said, are the exact culmination of what we have been broadcasting from the moment we were born…maybe even before then. We then become the generators of our own destiny, and the links between vibration, our own, and our consciousness create exactly what we desire to manifest from the Grid: Beliefs. Ideas. Actual physical objects. What we send out is what comes back to us in return. Remember the old playground song "I'm rubber, you're glue, whatever you say bounces off of me and sticks back on you"? Even as kids we understood.

Resonance is matched vibration, synched frequency, and the coming together of attracting forces, to allow or create or manifest that which did not exist before. Whether it is a different state of awareness, a ghost or entity appearing out of nowhere, or a spark of clairvoyant insight about a future event, that which did not exist before did exist…in the Grid. Resonance is the key to locating it, and making it real.

Language has power. Words, and sound, have a creative force, a frequency of their own. When things are "in synch," life rocks. When there is chaos, decoherence, discord, and "white noise," we are not happy campers. Every single one of us has experienced times, which we usually blame on Mercury going retrograde, when nothing in life seems to flow, despite the fact that Mercury is nothing more than a poor little planet we like to blame everything on now that Pluto has been demoted. In contrast, we have all had those days when things life just flowed perfectly, we succeeded at everything we tried, and everything seemed to "fall into place." We felt like King Midas, and that everything we touched turned to gold. We were experiencing what the Beach Boys once sang about:

I'm pickin up good vibrations
She's giving me excitations
I'm pickin up good vibrations
(oom bop bop good vibrations)
She's giving me excitations

Just one problem, though. Unless the particular Beach Boy singing that song was resonating on that same vibratory level, that little beach bunny was bound to take off and go vibrate to someone else's frequency!

Resonance works in nature and science, in mechanics and music, and in electronics and medicine. But until we come to understand how it also works in our everyday lives, it remains a vague concept. Yet it just might be the most important concept there is when it comes to why we are not living the life of our dreams. It all begins with the thoughts we have, which in turn form the actions we take, which in turn radiate outward into the world of energy and brings back to us the very same thoughts and actions in return, albeit at the hands of other people. Victimhood can be said to be the belief that we have nothing to do with reality: Things happen *to* us. We are reactive, not proactive. We have no part in the happiness, or the suffering, we experience.

We are reacting only to what the world hands us, as if we had no choice in the cards we were dealt, or how to play them. Resonance tells us that not only can we choose our own hand (heck, even in poker you can draw a new card), but we can also choose how to play that hand. It all comes down to the level of our energy—conscious, physical, emotional, spiritual... If we don't like the radio station we are broadcasting, we can completely change the format. If we are not broadcasting loud enough, we can change the frequency. We are not victims. We are Station Owners who control the content of our broadcasts. We are the Master Programmers who get to choose whether we want to put out country music, oldies, or techno-pop.

We are made of energy. Excitations of energy. So is everything around us. And it is all vibrating to its own frequency, seeking out that which matches it to create new frequencies and new experiences. And we choose the good or the bad. It's the structure, and the nature, of the ultimate reality of everything that walks within the Grid. What excites us makes us happier and more alive. What does not, depresses us and makes us tired and out of synch.

The Aboriginal cultures and traditions believe that their ancestors sang the world into being. The power of song, of sound, is creative, and every rock, tree, plant, star, animal, and person was sung into manifest form as the natives wandered the land, giving to each thing they saw a name based upon sound and harmony. They intuitively understood that the energy of their song was responsible in some implicate way for the world that sprung up around them.

In a sense, we sing our own world into creation, with our vibration, with our consciousness, and with the stuff in the Grid from which it is all formed. And the notes are the resonance that glues it all together. Those who came before us understood. The wisdom of Lao Tzu in the *Tao Te Ching* speaks of the Way as a force of all life energy that permeates empty space.

The Way is empty,
yet never refills with use;
bottomless it is,
like the forefather of the myriad creatures.
It files away sharp points,
Unravels tangles,
Diffuses light,
Mingles with the dust.
Submerged it lies,
Seeming barely to subsist.
I know not whose child it is,
Only that it resembles the predecessor of God.

In the Kabbalah of mystical Jewish tradition, we read: "We cannot identify the abundant vitality within all living beings; from the smallest to the largest, nor the hidden vitality enfolded within inanimate creation. Everything constantly flows, vibrates, and aspires. Nor can we estimate our own inner abundance. Our inner world is sealed and concealed, linked to a hidden something, a world that is not our world, not yet perceived or probed. Everything teems with richness, everything aspires to ascend and be purified. Everything sings, celebrates, serves, develops, evolves, uplifts, aspires to be arranged in oneness."

Again, that understanding of what uplifts us, what brings up our vibratory rate of being, aligns us with the essence of the universe itself, is present throughout the wisdom of the ancients. The power to turn water into wine, to move mountains with faith, to raise the dead and heal the sick, to feed the poor masses with five loaves of bread, all of these elements of religious mythology point to the conclusion that we are capable of the miraculous once we understand the mechanisms of the miraculous. There is a "science" behind the ability to make possible the impossible, yet we are only now beginning to rediscover that science and acknowledge those mechanisms.

The classic wisdom of the Egyptian sage Hermes Trismegistus, which means "thrice great," was written around 3000 BCE. Known as the Hermetica, this collection of divinely inspired knowledge speaks as well of the links between Atum, the One-God, our minds, our consciousness, and the Grid of Oneness we all are immersed in:

Atum is everywhere.

Mind cannot be enclosed,

Because everything exists within Mind.

Nothing is so quick and powerful.

Just look at your own experience.

Imagine yourself in any foreign land,

And quick as your intention

You will be there!

Think of the ocean—and there you are.

You have not moved as things move,

But you have traveled, nevertheless.

Fly up into the heavens—

You won't need wings!

Nothing can obstruct you—

Not the burning heat of the sun,

Or the swirling planets.

Pass on to the limits of creation.

Do you want to break out

Beyond the boundaries of the Cosmos?

For your mind, even that is possible.

Can you sense what power you possess?

If you can do all this,

Then what about your Creator?

Try and understand that Atum is Mind.

This is how he contains the Cosmos.

All things are thoughts

Which the Creator thinks.

—*From* The Hermetica: The Lost Wisdom of the Pharaohs *by Timothy Freke and Peter Gandy*

And from the Bhagavad-Gita, the sacred text of Hindu culture, written in the first century AD:

The whole universe is pervaded
by my unmanifest form;
all creatures exist in me;
but I do not exist in them.

The field contains the great elements,
individuality, understanding,
unmanifest nature, the eleven senses,
and the five sense realms.

Beyond this unmanifest nature
is another unmanifest existence,
a timeless being that does not perish
when all creatures perish.

These ancients did not have telescopes or computers with which to discern the inner workings, let alone the outer workings, of the cosmos. They did not have the kinds of machines that could peer into the subatomic world, or shoot particles for miles and watch what happened when they collided in a vast, underground tube. Yet they knew that something existed beneath, beyond, and between all things that they could see and perceive, and that whatever that something was, it was capable of everything. Indeed, they may have understood truth and reality far more than we, with all our technology and progress, ever could.

Sometimes, the greatest journeys and most amazing discoveries come from deep within, and not millions of miles away in distant galaxies.

Coauthor Marie has always hated magic tricks. Not because the magicians who performed them usually looked like Vegas lounge lizards, but because, try as she might, she could never step past the veil of illusion to see *exactly how the damn trick worked.* We all tend to turn away from things we cannot fully understand, even as we buy into the illusion. Yet magic tricks look real, as if someone is being cut in two and living to tell about it, or a rock can indeed move between a plate of glass. Despite being tricks to the unsuspecting eye, we buy it lock, stock, and barrel, and walk away feeling like idiots because we couldn't see how they did it to us.

Yet there is a science to doing magic tricks. If there wasn't, they would never work, and David Blaine and Chris Angel would both be out of a TV show. Thus, we can look to our reality as the result of a science we cannot yet figure out, but has the capacity to oftentimes look like magic to us. If those magicians can fool us, why can't the universe? Reality may be the Master Magician, hiding behind the veil of illusion except to those who find a new way of looking at "what they are seeing."

If only we were all given a guide to seeing behind the illusion. Maybe we all would look upon the paranormal, the unknown, and the mysterious as nothing out of the ordinary (of course, that would take so much of the fun out of life!).

Reality is mind, thought, intention, and energy cast upon the Grid, creating all form and matter and manifestation—The normal and the not-so-normal. We see what we expect to see, yet every now and then, when we resonate just right, we see what we never thought we would, and a new expectation is born. This would explain progress, new ideas, new inventions, and new paradigms. If reality were fixed, we would never create anything new in our lives. If perception was complete, we would never see anything in a new light, or change our minds, or suddenly come up with a brilliant eureka realization. It would all be said and done.

Yet we know on a deeper, intuitive level that nothing is fixed. Life changes, and ebbs and flows, often mirroring the ebb and flow of our beliefs, our thoughts, and our desires.

And it all happens because we, through our consciousness, vibrate in resonance with that which we hope, or expect, to create. This isn't new. This is ancient wisdom, with new ways of describing it, new words to define it. We vibrate. We consciously perceive. We walk the Grid. And the coolest thing of all is that at anytime, we can change our thoughts, change our consciousness, boost up our resonance, and walk a whole new part of the Grid.

Does that resonate?

BIBLIOGRAPHY

Abraham, Ralph, Terence McKenna, and Rupert Sheldrake. *The Evolutionary Mind: Conversations on Science, Imagination and Spirit.* Rhinebeck, New York: Monkfish Press, 2005.

Alexjander, S., and D. Deamer. "The Infrared Frequencies of DNA Bases: Science and Art." *Engineering in Medicine and Biology Magazine* 18 (1999): 74–79.

Arntz, William, Betsy Chasse, and Mark Vicente. *What the Bleep Do We Know?!* Deerfield Beach, Fla.: Health Communications, Inc., 2005.

Fuller, John G. *The Ghost of 29 Megacycles.* London: Grafton Books, 1987.

Gooch, Stan. *The Origins of Psychic Phenomena.* Rochester, Vt.: Inner Traditions, 2007.

Gregor, M. Darren. "The Reconnection: Exploring the Next Level of Healing for Humanity." *New Dawn* magazine, May-June 2009.

Griffiths, Huw. "Exploring the Power of Spiritual Intention and Distant Healing." *New Dawn* magazine. May–June 2009.

Hancock, Graham. *Supernatural: Meetings with the Ancient Teachers of Mankind.* New York: The Disinformation Company, 2007.

Hawkins, David R. *Power Vs. Force: The Hidden Determinants of Human Behavior.* Carlsbad, Calif.: Hay House, 2002.

Hayes, Michael. *The Hermetic Code in DNA: The Sacred Principles in the Ordering of the Universe.* Rochester, Vt.: Inner Traditions, 2008.

Heath, Richard. *Matrix of Creation: Sacred Geometry in the Realm of the Planets.* Rochester, Vt.: Inner Traditions, 2008.

Heath, Richard. *Sacred Number and the Origins of Civilization.* Rochester, Vt.: Inner Traditions, 2007.

Jeffrey, Jason. "Earthquakes: Natural or Man Made?" *New Dawn* magazine, March–April 2005.

Jung, Carl. *Synchronicity.* New York: Bollingen Foundation, 1960.

Kenyon, J. Douglas, editor. *Forbidden Science: From Ancient Technologies to Free Energy.* Rochester, Vt.: Bear & Co., 2008.

———. *Forbidden Religion: Suppressed Heresies of the West.* Rochester, Vt.: Bear & Co., 2006.

———. *Forbidden History: Prehistoric Technologies, Extraterrestrial Intervention and the Suppressed Origins of Civilization.* Rochester, Vt.: Bear & Co., 2005.

Lee, Ilchi. *Brain Wave Vibration.* Sedona, Ariz.: Best Life, 2008.

Lipton, Bruce. "Mind Power." *New Dawn* magazine, January–February, 2008.

McTaggart, Lynne. *The Field: The Quest for the Secret Force in the Universe.* New York: HarperCollins, 2002.

Mitchell, Dr. Edgar. *The Way of the Explorer: An Apollo Astronaut's Journey Through the Material and Mystical World.* Franklin Lakes, N.J.: New Page Books, 2008.

Michell, John. *The Dimensions of Paradise: Sacred Geometry, Ancient Science and the Heavenly Order on Earth.* Rochester, Vt.: Inner Traditions, 2008.

Michell, John and Christine Rhone. *Twelve Tribe Nations: Sacred Number and the Golden Age.* Rochester, Vt.: Bear & Co., 2008.

Peat, F. David. *Synchronicity: The Bridge Between Mind and Matter.* New York: Bantam Books, 1987.

Randles, Jenny. *Time Storms: The Fact Behind the Fiction.* New York: Berkley Books, 2001.

Seifer, Marc. *Transcending the Speed of Light: Consciousness, Quantum Physics and the Fifth Dimension.* Rochester, Vt.: Inner Traditions, 2008.

Swanson, Claude. *The Synchronized Universe: New Science of the Paranormal.* Tuscon, Ariz.: Poseidia Press, 2003.

Talbot, Michael. *The Holographic Universe.* New York: HarperPerennial, 1991.

Taylor, Jill Bolte. *My Stroke of Insight: A Brain Scientist's Personal Journey.* New York: Viking, 2006.

Taylor, Sandra Anne. *Quantum Success: The Astounding Science of Wealth and Happiness.* Carlsbad, Calif.: Hay House, 2006.

Valone, Thomas. "Tesla's Wireless Electricity." *Nexus* magazine, May–June, 2005.

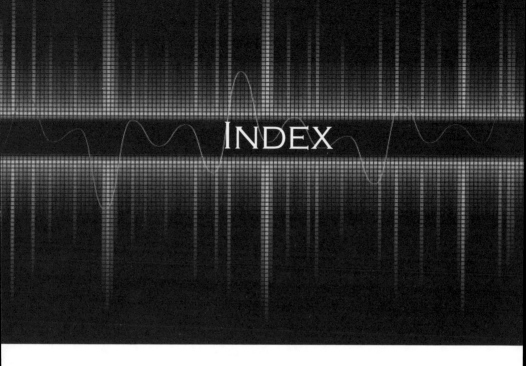

INDEX

About the Authors

Marie D. Jones has been involved with science, metaphysics, and the paranormal in one way or another for most of her life, which led to a fascination with quantum physics and the writing of her popular and highly regarded book, *PSIence: How New Discoveries in Quantum Physics and New Science May Explain the Existence of Paranormal Phenomena*. Marie is also author of *2013: End of Days or a New Beginning?*, which features essays from some of today's leading thinkers and cutting-edge researchers. She coauthored with her father, geophysicist Dr. John Savino, *Supervolcano: The Catastrophic Event That Changed the Course of Human History*. She is coauthor of *11:11— The Time Prompt Phenomenon* with Larry Flaxman, her partner in ParaExplorers.com.

She has an extensive background in paranormal, science, and metaphysical studies. She worked as a field investigator for MUFON (Mutual UFO Network) in Los Angeles and San Diego in the 1980s and 1990s, and cofounded MUFON North County, and currently serves as director of special projects for ARPAST, the Arkansas Paranormal and Anomalous Studies Team.

Marie began her extensive writing career as a teenager writing movie and video reviews for a variety of national magazines, as well as short stories, including award-winning science fiction and speculative fiction for small press genre and literary magazines. She is now a widely published author with hundreds of credits to her name.

Her first nonfiction book, *Looking for God in All the Wrong Places*, was chosen as the "Best Spiritual/Religious Book of 2003" by the popular book review Website, RebeccasReads.com, and the book made the "Top Ten of 2003" list at MyShelf.com. Marie has also coauthored more than three dozen inspirational books for Publications International/New Seasons, including *100 Most Fascinating People in the Bible*, *Life Changing Prayers*, and *God's Answers to Tough Questions*, and her essays, articles, and stories have appeared in *Chicken Soup for the Working Woman's Soul*, *Chicken Soup to Inspire a Woman*, *If Women Ruled the World*, *God Allows U-Turns*, *UFO Magazine*, *The Book of Thoth*, *Paranormal Magazine*, *Light Connection Magazine*, *Alternate Realities*, *Unity Magazine*, *Whole Life Times*, *Science of Mind Magazine*, and many others. She is also a popular book reviewer for such Websites as BookIdeas.com and CurledUp.com.

Her background also includes more than 15 years in the entertainment industry, as a promotions assistant for Warner Bros. Records, and experience as a film production assistant and script reader for a variety of film and cable TV companies. She has also been an optioned screenwriter, and has produced several nationally distributed direct-to-video projects, including an award-winning children's storybook video.

In her capacity as an author and researcher, Marie has appeared at several major conferences, including CPAK and the Queen Mary Ghost Hunting Weekend. She has been interviewed on more than 100 radio talk shows, including "Coast To Coast with George Noory," NPR, KPBS Radio, "Dreamland" (of which she now is a co-host), and the "Shirley MacLaine Show," and has been featured in dozens of newspapers, magazines, and online publications all over the world. She lives in San Marcos, California, with her son, Max.

Larry Flaxman has been actively involved in paranormal research and hands-on field investigation for more than 12 years, and melds his technical, scientific, and investigative backgrounds together for no-nonsense, scientifically objective explanations regarding a variety of anomalous phenomena. He is the president and senior researcher of ARPAST, the Arkansas Paranormal and Anomalous Studies Team, which he founded in February of 2007. Under his leadership, ARPAST has become one of the nation's largest and most active paranormal research organizations, with more than 150 members worldwide dedicated to conducting research into the paranormal using the most stringent scientific methodology. ARPAST is also now a proud member of the TAPS family (The Atlantic Paranormal Society). Larry supervises a staff of fully trained researchers and more than $250,000 worth of top-of-the-line equipment. Widely respected for his expertise on the proper use of equipment and techniques for conducting a solid investigation, Larry also serves as technical advisor to several paranormal research groups throughout the country.

Larry has appeared in numerous print interviews, including features in local and regional newspapers, magazines, and online publications such as *The Anomalist, Times Herald News, Jacksonville Patriot, ParaWeb, Current Affairs Herald, Unexplained Magazine,* and *The Pine Bluff Commercial.* He has been interviewed for several local and regional news television outlets such as "Ozarks First," as well as national cable television, most recently appearing in a two-part special on ARPAST for MudTruck TV, and he has been interviewed on dozens of radio programs, including "Coast to Coast with George Noory," "The Jeff Rense Show," "X-Zone, Radio," "The Kevin Smith Show," "Ghostly Talk," "Eerie Radio," "Crossroads Paranormal," "Binall of America," "Encounters Radio," "BBS Radio," "World of the Unexplained," and "Haunted Voices."

Larry has authored several published articles regarding science and the paranormal, and was a regular columnist for The Paranormal Awareness Society Newsletter. He is also co-creator (with Marie D. Jones) of

ParaExplorers.com, devoted to the exploration of ancient and modern unknown mysteries, and is developing a line of related books and products. In addition, Larry is co-creator of the popular new ParaTracker software program for documenting data from paranormal investigations. His own ARPAST online research database system, SOCIUS, is considered one of the most comprehensive in the field. His enthusiasm for education and training in the paranormal field has also garnered many requests for special events and seminars, including popular charity investigations at haunted locations across the South, lectures on paranormal awareness for the Breckenridge Movie Theatre chain, and Teen Technology Night at the Nixon Library.

Larry is co-author of *11:11—The Time Prompt Phenomenon: The Meaning Behind Mysterious Signs, Sequences, and Synchronicities* with Marie D. Jones.

Larry also currently works in law enforcement/information technology. He is married, and lives in Little Rock, Arkansas.